BEYOND
ETHNOCENTRISM

Recent Titles in
Contributions in Sociology

Invisible Victims: White Males and the Crisis of Affirmative Action
Frederick R. Lynch

Theories of Ethnicity: A Critical Appraisal
Richard H. Thompson

Population and Community in Rural America
Lorraine Garkovich

Divided We Stand: Class Structure in Israel from 1948 to the 1980s
Amir Ben-Porat

A Fragile Movement: The Struggle for Neighborhood Stabilization
Juliet Saltman

The Sociology of Agriculture
Frederick H. Buttel, Olaf F. Larson, and Gilbert W. Gillespie, Jr.

The Urban Housing Crisis: Economic, Social, and Legal Issues and Proposals
Arlene Zarembka

Time, Memory, and Society
Franco Ferrarotti

Homelessness in the United States. Volume II: Data and Issues
Jamshid A. Momeni, editor

Promises in the Promised Land: Mobility and Inequality in Israel
Vered Kraus and Robert W. Hodge

Switzerland in Perspective
Janet Eve Hilowitz, editor

Rethinking Today's Minorities
Vincent N. Parrillo, editor

—————————BEYOND ETHNOCENTRISM

A Reconstruction of Marx's Concept of Science

CHARLES McKELVEY

Contributions in Sociology, Number 94

GREENWOOD PRESS—————————
New York • Westport, Connecticut • London

Library of Congress Cataloging-in-Publication Data

McKelvey, Charles.
    Beyond ethnocentrism : a reconstruction of Marx's concept of
science / Charles McKelvey.
      p. cm.— (Contributions in sociology, ISSN 0084–9278 : no.
94)
    Includes bibliographical references and index.
    ISBN 0–313–27420–7 (alk. paper)
    1. Sociology—Methodology. 2. Sociology—Philosophy. 3. Marxian
school of sociology. I. Title. II. Series.
HM24.M365   1991
301'.072—dc20   90–45602

British Library Cataloguing in Publication Data is available.

Library of Congress Catalog Card Number: 90–45602
ISBN: 0–313–27420–7
ISSN: 0084–9278

First published in 1991

Greenwood Press, 88 Post Road West, Westport, CT 06881
An imprint of Greenwood Publishing Group, Inc.

Printed in the United States of America

The paper used in this book complies with the
Permanent Paper Standard issued by the National
Information Standards Organization (Z39.48—1984).

10 9 8 7 6 5 4 3 2 1

Copyright Acknowledgments

Grateful acknowledgment is given for permission to reprint excerpts from the following items:

"Althusser's Marxism: An Account and Assessment" by Norman Geras, originally published in *New Left Review* 78 (1972). Used by permission.

Capital, vol. 1, by Karl Marx. Published by International Publishers, 1967. Used by permission.

The German Ideology, part I (1970), and *Collected Works*, vol. III (1975), vol. IV (1975), vol. XII (1979), by Karl Marx and Friedrich Engels. Published by International Publishers. Used by permission.

Insight by Bernard Lonergan. Published by Philosophical Library Publishers, 1958. Used by permission of the publisher and the Longman Group UK.

Karl Marx: Early Writings edited by T. B. Bottomore. Published by McGraw-Hill, 1964. Used by permission.

Late Marx and the Russian Road edited by Teodor Shanin. Copyright © 1983 by Teodor Shanin. Reprinted by permission of Monthly Review Press and Routledge.

Marx Before Marxism by David McLellan. Published by Macmillan Publishers, 1970. Used by permission.

Marx's Theory of Ideology by Bhikhu Parekh. Published by Johns Hopkins University Press, 1982. Used by permission.

Theories of Surplus Value, vols. 1 & 2, by Karl Marx. Published by Lawrence & Wishart Ltd., 1967. Reprinted by permission of the publisher.

"The Working Class and the Birth of Marxism" by Goran Therborn, originally published in *New Left Review* 79 (1973). Used by permission.

To the memory of my parents,

to Jan,

and to Edie, Casey, and Gina

CONTENTS

PREFACE

This book is the result of nearly twenty years of study and reflection. In many respects, this quest began when I was an undergraduate student at the Pennsylvania State University in the late 1960s. In the context of the turmoil of that time, I found my socially grounded assumptions challenged by the struggles of people of color in such diverse places as Alabama, Watts, and Vietnam. This experience led me, in the early 1970s, to the Center for Inner City Studies in Chicago, where I was privileged to learn an analysis of modern history and society from an African-American and African nationalist point of view. As a result of my study at the Center for Inner City Studies, I became aware of the fact that black scholars and white social scientists often have fundamentally different assumptions about history and society. This brought me to the question, Is there any objective understanding of society, or do understandings of society necessarily reflect social position? Is there an objective social science, or is there simply a black social science and a white social science, the legitimacy of which is ultimately not a matter of truth but of power? When I completed my studies, I believed the latter option to be the case. My interest in such questions took me to Fordham University, where I had an opportunity to study both sociological theory and philosophy, including the cognitional theory of the Catholic philosopher Bernard Lonergan as well as the understandings of objectivity of mainstream sociological thinkers. Lonergan's penetrating analysis of the process of knowing in all its forms convinced me of the possibility of obtaining an understanding independent of social position through encounter with persons of diverse social positions. I concluded that the problem with the social science of our time was that it had not taken seriously the writings of the intellectuals and theoreticians of the African nationalist and African-American nationalist movement.

In the late 1970s and early 1980s, I turned to a study of neo-Marxist social theorists such as Immanuel Wallerstein, André Gunder Frank, Max Horkheimer, Herbert Marcuse, and Jürgen Habermas. The analyses of all these thinkers struck me as important and insightful, particularly Wallerstein's world-systems perspective, which I saw as having an affinity with the formulations of African and African-American nationalism. In the mid–1980s, I undertook a study of Karl Marx, focusing particularly on Marx's concept of science, and this study brought me to a culmination in my investigation. Marx, I found, had a far more penetrating understanding of epistemological issues than any other sociologist. I came to the realization that it would be possible to formulate an understanding of objectivity by reconstructing Marx's concept of science in light of Lonergan's cognitional theory and in light of Third World national liberation movements in the twentieth century. This book is the product of that effort.

I hope that this book will help social scientists and philosophers of science to develop a greater understanding of the process through which social scientists can attain a greater understanding of society. In the last fifteen years, the world-systems perspective has emerged in sociology as the predominant perspective for understanding issues of Third World underdevelopment, and sociologists who address such issues have organized themselves in the Political Economy of the World-System section of the American Sociological Association. I take this development to be significant in social science as a socially organized enterprise. This book elucidates the epistemological and methodological implications of this social fact and demonstrates that the social sciences are in the process of redefining the philosophical assumptions that constitute the foundation of social scientific analysis.

This book is going into print in the aftermath of significant developments in Eastern Europe. Some might be inclined to interpret these events as signaling an end to the relevance of the work of Karl Marx. I hope to demonstrate that Marx was the archetypal social scientist and that his scholarship continues to have vitality and relevance for important issues of the day.

I would like to thank all who have contributed to the development of my ideas, especially my teachers at the Center for Inner City Studies, Jacob Carruthers, Anderson Thompson, Elkin Sithole, and Gerald McIntosh; and my teachers at Fordham University, Joseph Fitzpatrick, S. J., James R. Kelly, and Gerald McCool, S. J. I also would like to thank those who took the time and effort to offer constructive critical feeback on the manuscript at various stages in its formulation, especially Bertell Ollman, Jack Bloom, Larry Reynolds, Alan Schafer, and Anthony L. Hayer, reviewer for Greenwood Press. None of these scholars should be held accountable for the book's limitations, for which I alone am responsible.

In addition, I would like to thank my wife, Janis McKelvey; our children, Edie, Casey and Gina; and my friends and colleagues in the Association for Humanist Sociology for their constant support.

1

THE PROBLEM OF
KNOWLEDGE

CYNICISM AND THE ECLIPSE OF REASON

In 1967, Jürgen Habermas was so struck by the significance of student protests
in the Federal Republic of Germany that he wrote an essay re-examining the
political role of students in industrial societies as well as an essay examining
the functions of the university in industrial societies (Habermas, 1970). However,
in the 1990s, as we in the academy reflect on higher education in the 1980s, we
find a very different mood. In the 1980s, what was striking about university
students was not their activism but their cynicism. And it was their cynicism
rather than their conservativism that was significant. To be sure, elements of the
student mood reflected conservativism: the career orientation, materialism, pa-
triotism, unquestioning acceptance of the expectations of authority. But behind
this conservative appearance was a fundamental cynicism that expressed itself
in a lack of faith in the institutions of the social order. Students in the 1980s
did not believe in the capacity of their government to protect their basic rights
and interests. They did not believe in the honesty and integrity of the political
leadership. They did not believe that their economic system provides equal
opportunity for all. They accepted inequality in the world, not because they
believed that it was justified, but because they believed that it was inevitable.
They did not believe that the educational system was teaching them anything
significant for their personal development.

At the same time, this lack of faith in the institutions of the established order
was not accompanied by a corresponding faith in the possibility of social reform.
Students did not have faith in reason as an arbiter of truth, and therefore they
did not believe in a collective capacity to discern truth from distortion and to
discern the basic elements of a just social order. Accordingly, they did not

believe in the capacity of social movements to promote the interests of subjected groups in the name of reason and justice and thereby create a more just society. They were unaware of the many social movements of the twentieth century, and therefore, they were disconnected from recent human history. They lived only in the irrational present, seeking to provide for their own status, comfort, and security within an irrational system. They found meaning in the private realm.

The cynicism of Western youth in the 1980s is paralleled by a similar tendency in Western scholarship to express cynicism in regard to reason and to deny the possibility of an objective knowledge that discerns truth above and beyond particular interests. For Hans Barth, this cynicism is rooted in the notion of ideology. Barth maintains that people are always accusing others' ideas of being ideologies.

The person using it always tries to devalue his opponent's intellectual or political position by proving that it is only a perspective conditioned by interest and point of view. At the same time he attempts, before the court of reason, to legitimize his own view and attitudes as universally valid. (1976:xv)

But the opponent can muster the same countercharge.

When opponents thus mutually reproach each other with holding ideologically tainted positions, the need arises for an objective judgment to resolve the conflict. But clearly no such judgment can be forthcoming. For if the accusation be true that the human mind produces only ideologies, there is no court of appeal with criteria for arriving at objective judgment. (1976:xv)

Thus, the notion of ideology has in the course of time undermined faith in reason and in the possibility of an objective knowledge that does not promote particular interests.

Barth maintains that the theorists who articulated the notion of ideology (Antoine Destutt de Tracy, Francis Bacon, Claude-Adrien Helvétius, Paul Henri Holbach, Karl Marx, and Arthur Schopenhauer) all had faith in reason, for, although they identified the obstacles to social knowledge, they all had strategies to overcome these obstacles. However, the effect of their analyses was to "cast doubt on the quality and structure of the mind" (1976:194). In the wake of this development, Friedrich Nietzsche radically revised Western thought, for in his view "the question of truth becomes a question of power" (1976:144; see 144–76, 181). Hence, philosophical historicism emerged: "Truth became relativized: every epoch, every unified social group, every nation or culture was said to have its own truth" (1976:181). The result was anarchy of thought (1976:182). A disintegration of the Christian world view accompanied this loss of faith in reason, with the result that no meaning could be discerned in human history either through reason or through a divinely revealed plan. Hence, "modern historicism renounced the idea of a cosmic reason" (1976:184).

The tendency in Western scholarship to deny the efficacy of reason also has been analyzed by Horkheimer, who refers to this phenomenon as the "eclipse of reason" (1974). Horkheimer believes that the problem is rooted in the Enlightenment. Ironically, the Enlightenment affirmed reason and reason alone, as against revelation, as the arbiter of truth. However, there was an element of Enlightenment philosophy that would ultimately lead to the eclipse of reason, namely, the notion that truth is based on empirical observation. On the basis of this notion Enlightenment philosophers rejected religion. However, the notion that truth is based on empirical observation can be applied against the Enlightenment philosophy itself. It can be asked: What is the empirical basis of such notions as democracy, equality, and liberty? On what empirical grounds are they more valid than their negations? As a consequence, reason came to be increasingly defined in a narrow and empirical sense. Reason came to refer only to its technical dimensions: classification, inference, deduction, logic. The formulation of ends or goals was increasingly dropped from the meaning of reason. Reason lost its capacity to define the good life; it could only provide the means for getting to the good life once its definition was decided. As for decisions in regard to the good life, they belonged to the realm of opinion. Goals and ends, like philosophy and ethics, thus became matters of personal choice. Reason could no longer resolve which choices are more valid.

THE SOCIOLOGICAL TRADITION

The emergence of the eclipse of reason in modern Western scholarship can be seen in the development of the discipline of sociology. The earliest sociological theorists were products of the Enlightenment, and they sought to base the validity of the new science of society in empirical observation of the social world. In varying degrees, they were aware of the problem of distortions of understanding rooted in social position. For the most part, they sought to overcome the problem by limiting the scope of sociology to what was empirically observable and by asserting the possibility of a separation of subject and object. Accordingly, they believed that sociologists could discern truth by basing their judgments on empirical observation and by bracketing value judgments and interests that are rooted in their own particular societies and social positions. However, as sociological theory developed, this doctrine of value freedom became increasingly problematic. Sociologists were becoming increasingly aware of the influence of social position on the understandings of sociologists and of the unavoidable interaction between the sociologist and society. The increasingly cynical implications of this awareness culminated in the assertion that knowledge of society is ultimately a question of power. This development from value freedom to cynicism in regard to the efficacy of reason can be seen in the works of Auguste Comte, Herbert Spencer, Emile Durkheim, Max Weber, Georg Simmel, Karl Mannheim, Talcott Parsons, Alvin Gouldner, and C. Wright Mills.

Auguste Comte

Auguste Comte, "the first to use the term *sociology*" (Ritzer, 1988:15), published a six-volume work outlining its principles in 1842. Comte believed that human progress and development is fundamentally progress in the realm of ideas. In examining the history of ideas, he discerned three stages: the theological, the metaphysical, and the positive. In the theological stage, natural phenomena are interpreted as having supernatural causes. The metaphysical stage is a transition between the theological and the positive. In this stage, rather than invoking supernatural explanations, efforts are made to discover laws that govern natural events. However, these efforts are not successful, because they are based upon philosophical assumptions. Only in the positive stage, when philosophical assumptions are discarded and understanding is based on observation and experiment, are the laws that govern nature discovered. Hence, Comte believed that humanity stood at the dawn of a new scientific age, characterized by a new and advanced method of knowing. And this scientific method, Comte believed, would make possible new scientific knowledge not only in regard to nature but also in regard to society. He coined the term sociology to refer to this new science of society. In sociology, demonstrated faith replaces the revealed faith of the theological and metaphysical stages. Not everyone accepts the propositions of revealed faith because they are based on revelation. But the propositions of demonstrated faith can be understood and accepted by all who are in a position to see and hear the evidence, because these propositions are based on empirical observation and as such are verifiable. The propositions of sociology, therefore, are verifiable propositions based on empirical observation. In order to formulate such propositions, sociologists must observe in a particular way. In the first place, they must be disinterested, in that they must not allow political beliefs or interests to influence the direction of their thought. In the second place, they must be detached, in that they must separate themselves from what they are observing (Levy-Bruhl, 1973:23–25, 35–38, 43–45, 61, 83, 90, 232–34, 239–40).

In such epistemological claims, Comte formulated principles that were to become widely accepted in sociology in the twentieth century, especially that society is governed by social laws, and these laws can be grasped through detached and disinterested observation. Moreover, the sociological knowledge attained in this way has a higher degree of validity than theological and philosophical propositions. In this formulation, we see evidence of the Enlightenment rejection of revelation and the Enlightenment exaltation of a form of reason based on empirical observation. We also see the assumption of the possibility of detached and disinterested observation, the assumption, in other words, of the possibility of the separation between subject and object, the separation between the sociologist and society. As a result of this assumption, Comte perceived no great difficulty in overcoming the influence of social position on understanding.

However, this assumption was to become increasingly problematic in the development of sociological theory.

Herbert Spencer

Herbert Spencer published *The Study of Sociology* in 1873. Like Comte, Spencer believed in the possibility of the application of the scientific method to the study of society. However, due to characteristics of society as an object of study, characteristics of humans as observers, and the relation between individuals and society, "there arise impediments in the way of Sociology greater than those in the way of any other science" (Spencer, 1961:65). Spencer identified three such impediments. First, unlike the objects of study in the natural sciences and psychology, social phenomena are not directly observable. Second, because of our intellectual and emotional nature, we tend to fall victim to emotions that distort our judgment. We tend to find evidence that supports our thoughts and feelings. Third, there is the influence on understanding rooted in the social position we occupy, particularly those of nation, race, and class. However, the sociologist can overcome these impediments. Unlike ordinary citizens, sociologists are aware of these impediments to knowledge, and being aware of them, sociologists are able to hold them in check and overcome the limitation on understanding that they pose.

Spencer, then, in contrast to Comte, is more fully aware of the problem of the influence of social position on understanding, and he takes more seriously the need to investigate this issue. However, he believes that sociological reflection on the issue makes possible a freedom from the influence of social position on understanding, and therefore he ultimately shares Comte's optimism in regard to the formulation of a sociology detached from society.

Emile Durkheim

Emile Durkheim, like Comte and Spencer, maintained that the scientific method could be applied to the study of social phenomena. As Durkheim understood it, the scientific method involves observing empirical reality without preconceptions, assumptions, or a prioris of any kind and allowing understanding to be shaped by the objects of observation. Accordingly, Durkheim wrote that in scientific observation "all preconceptions must be eradicated" (1964b:31); when observing "objects of knowledge" (1964b:31), sociologists must "assume a certain mental attitude toward them on the principle that when approaching their study we are absolutely ignorant of their nature" (1964b:xliii). In accordance with this approach, the sociologist must learn to ignore common sense beliefs. Common sense beliefs, "having been made without method and criticism, are devoid of scientific value, and must be distinguished from the scientific mentality" (1964b:xliv). The sociologist, therefore, must "repudiate resolutely the use of concepts originating outside of science for totally unscientific needs. He must emancipate himself from the fallacious ideas that dominate the mind of the layman'' (1964b:32). At the same time, the scientific method requires the elimination from the mind of presuppositions and assumptions of a philosophical nature. Although philosophical beliefs, in contrast to common sense, are reflective, they are products of an analysis of ideas rather than an analysis of society. Moreover, whenever philosophers turn to empirical observation, they select from empirical reality only elements that support pre-conceived philosophical ideas and assumptions (1964b:14ff.). Accordingly, in order to adhere to the scientific method, the sociologist must be independent from philosophical doctrines (1964b:141).

Durkheim, therefore, envisioned the possibility of a new science of society. The judgments and observations of this science would be more valid than those of either philosophy or common sense, because they would be based on the method of empirical observation and not based on preconceived ideas. In formulating this conception of sociological method, Durkheim assumed the possibility of sociologists separating themselves from everyday conceptions and philosophical assumptions that are rooted in culture and are deeply ingrained in the socialization process. As sociological theory developed, this assumption of the possibility of consciously separating oneself from social position and culture would be increasingly questioned.

Although Durkheim assumed the possibility of a separation between sociologist and culture in sociological method, he in no sense believed that the new science of society would be characterized by neutral descriptions that would take no stance in regard to social issues. On the contrary, Durkheim envisioned sociology as a science that would contribute to the uplifting of the human condition. His entire work is a testimony of his belief in the efficacy of sociology in regard to social reform. In *The Division of Labor in Society*, first published in 1893, Durkheim focused on the problem of order. He maintained that societies maintain order and cohesion either through mechanical solidarity or organic solidarity. Mechanical solidarity emerges from the fact that there is no occupational specialization beyond that of age and gender. In contrast, in organic solidarity, there is occupational specialization, and unity is based on mutual dependency. Organic solidarity, according to Durkheim, has been evident in agricultural societies since the agricultural revolution. But with the Industrial Revolution, there are indications of the breakdown of organic solidarity. The conflict between capital and labor is one indication of this breakdown. Durkheim's subsequent study on suicide (1951), originally published in 1897, reflected his concern with the breakdown of organic solidarity. He interpreted the increase in the suicide rate in the nineteenth century to be another indication of the breakdown of order in modern society. In his study, he came to the conclusion that the increase in the suicide rate was caused by egoism, which he defined as the insufficient integration of the individual into the social group (1951:209), and by anomie, which he defined as the insufficient regulation of individuals due to the absence of clearly defined norms (1951:258). Near the end of *Suicide*, Durkheim proposes "reconstituted corporations" (1951:380) as a remedy to the problem of egoism and anomie. His hope was that new social group ties and new norms emerging from the workplace could rectify these problems.

However, Durkheim was not satisfied with this solution. In search of a force that could restore order in modern societies, Durkheim turned to a study of religion. In *The Elementary Forms of the Religious Life* (1965), Durkheim documented the importance of religion as a unifying force in pre-modern society. Given the decline of religion in modern society, what was needed was a restoration of religion. Durkheim believed, however, that modern people would not accept the beliefs of a traditional religion, such as Christianity. Therefore, what was needed was a new religion appropriate for modern people, a religion characterized by belief in such modern principles as reason, democracy, progress, and freedom of thought. The inculcation of this modern religion is an important function of educational institutions in modern society, Durkheim believed.

Durkheim's sociology, therefore, was characterized by a humanist theme. On the one hand, Durkheim understood the scientific method to require a separation between the sociologist and society in the quest for understanding and insight. On the other hand, sociologists are in significant ways engaged in society. The engagement occurs in asking questions, as can be seen in the centrality of concern with the breakdown of social order in Durkheim's sociology. Moreover, the engagement occurs in proposals for social reform, as in Durkheim's proposal for reconstituted occupational associations and for the inculcation of a modern religion of reason, democracy, and progress through the educational system. In Durkheim's formulation, sociologists raise questions through engagement in society, but seek answers through detachment from society. They make proposals that reflect an engagement in society, but the proposals reflect an understanding attained through detachment from society. The sociologist both is and is not a part of society.

Max Weber

In Max Weber's epistemological writings, these issues are characterized by greater complexity, for there is, on the one hand, Weber's well-known concept of ethical neutrality, while on the other hand, there is his less well-known concept of value relevance. Weber's concept of ethical neutrality is similar to Comte's notion of detached and disinterested observation and to Durkheim's dictum that the sociologist bracket commonsense beliefs and philosophical assumptions. Weber articulated the concept of ethical neutrality in his 1904 essay, "Objectivity in Social Science and Social Policy" (Weber, 1949:50–112) and the 1917 essay, "The Meaning of Ethical Neutrality in Sociology and Economics (1949:1–41), as well as in a speech at Munich University in 1918, "Science as a Vocation" (1949:129–56). According to Weber's concept of ethical neutrality, empirical science is ethically neutral in the sense that it contains no value judgments, where value judgments are defined as "practical evaluations of the unsatisfactory or satisfactory character of phenomena subject to our influence" (1949:1). Weber articulates three principles that follow from the fact that value judgments do not belong to the realm of science.

(1) Weber maintains that college professors ought not make value judgments in their capacity as teachers. In principle, Weber accepts the notion that it is appropriate for college teachers to assert value judgments in the classroom, if the teacher makes clear to students which assertions are scientific and which are expressions of value judgments (1949:1–2). However, Weber maintains that, in the German universities of his time, some issues, such as the stance of the monarch in international affairs, cannot be discussed freely. Therefore, in view of the fact that the assertion of some value judgments is prohibited, all proclamations of value judgments in the classroom ought to be banned (Weber 1949:8). At the same time, Weber is not opposed to the expression of value judgments by professors in a more appropriate public forum outside the classroom, such as the press, public meetings, associations, and essays.

(2) Weber maintains that there is a distinction between the use of value judgments and the scientific analysis of value judgments. In using value judgments, the individual evaluates what one should or should not do in certain situations and what attitudes are right or wrong. Such evaluation is beyond the scope of science, but this does not mean, for Weber, that science has no interest at all value judgments. To the contrary, analysis of value judgments is an important part of the social scientist's task. In such scientific analysis of value judgments, the scientist discusses the internal consistency of an individual's ethical ideals, the presuppositions of ethical ideals, the consequences of the ethical ideals, and the appropriateness of the means for achieving a desired end. Such analysis is conceptually distinct from suggesting to which value judgments a person should adhere (Weber 1949:20–21, 52–54).

(3) Weber maintains that a system of ethics cannot be derived from empirical science. Here Weber is reacting to that nineteenth-century optimism that believed that science would provide clear solutions to moral and social problems. For Weber, science merely provides the technical means to implement agreed upon goals of social policy. Whenever there is no consensus in regard to social policy goals, such a consensus cannot be forged by social science. "Normative standards of values" (Weber 1949:56) cannot be derived from science.

Although sociology is, in Weber's view, ethically neutral, it is not entirely objective. Weber defines objective knowledge as a knowledge that is "independent of all individual contingencies" (1949:85), that is, as knowledge that is independent of the personality and the personal beliefs of the person who formulates knowledge (1949:52–54). In accordance with this understanding of objectivity, value judgments (*Werturteile*) and values (*Werte*), for Weber, are not objective but are subjective. Weber defines value judgments, as we have seen, as practical evaluations. He uses the term values in two different ways. In some cases, he uses it interchangeably with value judgments as when he refers to the exclusion of "political values" (1949:8) from German universities. In other cases, he uses the term in the sense of cultural values, that is, as referring to conscious and unconscious beliefs and attitudes of an individual that are rooted in cultural milieu and life experiences. Weber believes cultural values unavoidably and necessarily enter sociological analysis, and this is why sociology is not entirely objective.

Why does Weber believe that cultural values are unavoidably present in sociological analysis? Weber views the world as infinite and complex, as presenting itself as "an infinite multiplicity of successively and coexisting emerging and disappearing events" (1949:72). In order to make sense of this infinite and complex reality, the scientist must select a finite portion of reality as an object of scientific analysis. Moreover, because reality is infinitely complex, there is always an infinite number of causes for any event (1949:78). The process of selection, then, in Weber's sense, involves more than selecting an object of study in the sense of a scientist choosing to do a study of juvenile delinquency. Rather, selection involves the process of prescinding some elements from reality and leaving others behind, and it involves the process of prescinding some causes to particular events and leaving others behind. Analysis of the social world, therefore, involves a process of selecting some elements from the social world and organizing these elements into causal relationships.

By what criterion does a scientist select some elements of social or cultural reality? For Weber, the key criterion is significance: the scientist selects from social reality that which has significance. Further, what is significant to the scientist is that which is important in accordance with cultural values:

Only a *part* of concrete reality is interesting and significant to us, because only it is related to the cultural values with which we approach reality. Only certain sides of the infinitely complex concrete phenomenon, namely those to which we attribute a general *cultural significance*—are therefore worthwhile knowing. They alone are objects of causal explanations. (1949:78)

Weber, then sees cultural values as unavoidably constituting a basis for the selection and organization of social reality.

Because of the unavoidable function of cultural values, sociological analysis, for Weber, necessarily reflects a particular point of view. Weber notes that there are obvious examples of analyses that take a particular point of view for heuristic purposes. Examples include "the explanation of everything by economic causes alone" (1949:70) and "the explanation of capitalism by reference to certain shifts in the content of the religious ideas which played a role in the genesis of a capitalistic attitude" (1949:70). But there is nothing unique about these examples. Analyses of social phenomena, for Weber, always involve use of points of view that are grounded in cultural values, whether or not the social scientist is aware of it. As a result, social scientific analysis can never be completely objective. Weber writes: "There is no absolutely 'objective' scientific analysis of culture...independent of special and onesided viewpoints according to which—expressly or tacitly, consciously or unconsciously—they are selected, analyzed, and organized or expository purposes'' (1949:72).

Although Weber maintains that there is no sociological analysis that is completely objective or completely independent of the cultural values of the sociologist, Weber denies that sociological analysis is merely subjective, that is, that it has no objective dimension whatever. Although the sociologist selects and organizes in accordance with a point of view grounded in cultural values, the sociologist must carry out the investigation in accordance with rules of logic (1949:84). Thus sociologists can and must be objective in degree, in that they are bound to commonly accepted rules of thought. However, such objectivity occurs within the context of a point of view that reflects cultural values. Accordingly, sociological conclusions are not absolutely or entirely objective, but objective within the context of a conceptual scheme, which is grounded in culture.

In *The Theory of Social and Economic Organization* (1947), Weber formulates an objective dimension to sociological method beyond and in addition to the dictums to bracket value judgments and follow rules of logic. Central to Weber's methodological approach in this work is the concept of *Verstehen*. The goal of sociology, in Weber's view, is interpretive understanding (*Verstehen*) of action, which involves understanding the action in the context of the meaning system of the actor. In order to understand social action, therefore, sociologists must endeavor to encounter and understand the meaning system of the actor. Such encounter constitutes an objective dimension in sociology, for it places constraints on the culturally grounded conceptual schemes of the sociologist. The values of the sociologist, therefore, are not given free reign, for they are held in check through confrontation with the meaning system of the actor. The conceptual schemes are not entirely products of the values of the sociologist, for they to some extent take into account the meaning system of the actor. However, in Weber's view, the capacity of *Verstehen* to provide an objective dimension to sociological analysis is limited, for sociologists can not in all cases understand the meaning system of the actor. The sociologist can understand this meaning system only in the case of rational action or in those circumstances of emotional action in which the orientation of the sociologist is similar to that of the actor (1947:90–91). Therefore, there are many cases in which the sociologist would not be able to understand the meaning system of the actor.

Weber, therefore, had a more sophisticated understanding of the problem of objectivity than Comte, Spencer, or Durkheim. He clearly saw the issue as more complex than they. Moreover, in contrast to their analyses, Weber saw the strategies for overcoming the obstacles to objectivity as only partially successful. Bracketing value judgments and following rules of logic occurs within the context of culturally grounded points of view. *Verstehen* constitutes an objective check on culturally grounded points of view, but such interpretative understanding can be attained only in some cases. *Verstehen*, for Weber, is not a possibility for most social action involving actors with orientations different from the sociologist. This would suggest that there is no possibility for interpretative understanding of social action when the actors are of social positions or cultures different from the sociologist. With Weber's methodological reflections, the sociological tradition begins to wrestle with the possibility that sociology is unable to attain objective knowledge or knowledge that does not reflect the vantage point of the social position of the sociologist.

Georg Simmel

Georg Simmel was a contemporary of Weber who also wrestled with the problem of objectivity in social science. His most important book on the issue is *The Problem of the Philosophy of History: An Epistemological Essay* (1977). In this work, Simmel rejects historical realism or historical empiricism, which believes that "historical science is simply a mirror image of the event 'as it really happened' " (1977:vii). Historical realism, in other words, is the view that "history is a simple reproduction of the event" (1977:viii) and that knowledge involves a passive reception of what is transmitted by social reality. In opposition to the naive realism of historical empiricism, Simmel asserts that in the process of knowing, a prioris, pre-suppositions, language, and conceptual schemes shape the object of knowledge and represent it in a particular way (1977:23–24, 42–43). Simmel writes: "The a prioris plays a dynamic role in our thought. It is a real function which is precipitated or crystallized in its final, objective results: knowledge.... The significance of the a prioris is determined by its efficacy in producing the world of our knowledge" (1977:46). Like Weber, Simmel sees such assumptions which shape reality as deeply ingrained through socialization, in that he views a prioris as "relatively unconscious" (1977:43). Accordingly, they appear to the individual as self-evident. Moreover, like Weber, Simmel views such partially conscious conceptual schemes as necessary for making sense out of a chaotic empirical world. Simmel writes that without the use of a prioris and assumptions, "the conduct of every other person would remain nothing but a meaningless and incoherent chaos of disconnected impulses" (1977:45). Simmel, however, is not a relativist who sees all knowledge of society as relative to conceptual schemes and assumptions that are grounded in culture and of which individuals are only partially aware. He believes objectivity is attained as a result of a dialectical relation between a prioris and empirical evidence. The dialectical relation between constructed conceptual schemes and empirical evidence leads to the correct interpretation (Simmel, 1977:56–57).

Thus, like Weber, Simmel understands the process to knowledge in social science as a process in which the social scientist gives meaning to a chaotic social world through the application of culturally grounded conceptual schemes, although this process is not usually fully conscious. At the same time, unlike Weber, Simmel does not believe that this creates a problem of objectivity, because through empirical observation the social scientist encounters empirical reality, and through such encounter can develop conceptual schemes that lead to correct interpretations of social reality. Whereas Weber views objective checks on culturally grounded conceptual schemes as only partially successful, Simmel views empirical reality as imposing a check on culturally grounded conceptual schemes such that objective knowledge can be attained.

Karl Mannheim

Karl Mannheim's *Ideology and Utopia*, first published in German in 1929, is the most thorough and systematic attempt to address the issue of the relation of knowledge of society to social position. In *Ideology and Utopia*, Mannheim maintains that knowledge is related to historical period or social context, and hence, there is no such thing as absolute knowledge or knowledge that is true for all social contexts (Mannheim, 1936:84–85). Accordingly, he maintains that social scientific knowledge does not exist "independently of the values and position of the subject and unrelated to social context" (1936:79). Rather, social scientific knowledge is formulated "with reference to the position of the observer" (1936:79). As an illustration of the fact that knowledge is related to social context and is not absolute, Mannheim maintains that a prohibition on usury is appropriate for a medieval social context but inappropriate for a modern social context (1936:95–96). Thus, he observes that "the vain hope of discovering truth in a form which is independent of an historically and socially determined set of meanings will have to be given up" (1936:80).

Although Mannheim maintains that knowledge is not absolute, he does not maintain that there are no standards whatever of truth or falsity or of right or wrong. He rejects relativism and asserts that genuine knowledge does not reflect merely personal viewpoint or social position. Mannheim's view is that there is objective knowledge, but such knowledge is objective in relation to social context. Truth, in this view, is neither absolute nor relative, but relational (1936: 85–86, 78–80). For example, in relation to the modern social context, there is a true and objective answer to the question, What is the relation between theory and practice? There are a number of viewpoints in modern society concerning this question, reflecting the differing occupational and class positions within modern society. For Mannheim, the key to working through this multiplicity of viewpoints grounded in diversity of social position is, at the outset, to recognize that there is some truth in all viewpoints. Every social position provides a particular "standpoint" (1936:149) from which the world is perceived, and each standpoint makes possible a grasping of some aspect of the truth. Once one recognizes that there is some truth in all viewpoints, knowledge can be attained by synthesizing each of the viewpoints, that is, by the "integration of many mutually complementary points of view into a comprehensive whole" (1936:149). Through this process, truth in its relational sense can be attained. In Mannheim's view, the "socially unattached intelligentsia" (1936:155) can achieve this synthesis by virtue of its education and its relatively classless position, for its members do not participate in the process of production (1936: 153–64).

Mannheim's *Ideology and Utopia* marks a significant step forward in sociological reflection on the problem of the relation of knowledge to social position. To a greater extent than even Weber and Simmel, he formulated in a systematic way the influence of social position on understanding and the significance of such influence for social scientific knowledge. Having thoroughly understood the problem, he was in a better position than any of his predecessors to formulate a solution. His formulation of a socially unattached intelligentsia synthesizing complementary viewpoints into a comprehensive whole was a milestone in sociological theory. However, as sociological theory developed, the possibility of Mannheim's achievement constituting a resolution to the problem of knowledge was undermined by two contradictory developments. First, there was the problem that his key insights into the problem were not incorporated into mainstream sociology in the United States. This created a tendency for epistemological reflection in the United States to be less sophisticated in approaching the problem than Mannheim's work. Talcott Parsons illustrates this tendency. Secondly, Mannheim's solution to the problem of knowledge was brought under attack by sociologists who had studied his formulation of the problem. Alvin Gouldner, for example, argued that intellectuals are not socially unattached but constitute a social class. Formulations of intellectuals, therefore, cannot represent comprehensive viewpoints but legitimations of the interests of a particular social class. In debunking Mannheim's solution while accepting this penetrating description of the problem, a tendency was established in the 1960s in the United States toward cynicism in regard to the capacity of sociology to formulate objective knowledge. This tendency can be seen in the work of Gouldner and C. Wright Mills.

Talcott Parsons

The preeminent sociologist in the United States in the 1950s and 1960s was Talcott Parsons. Parsons' understanding of the issue of objectivity in sociology is based on assumptions that are similar to those of Weber and Simmel.[1] Parsons maintains that in social science, as in natural science, the scientist selects from empirical reality in accordance with conceptual schemes. This follows from the fact that there is an infinite number of things that are empirically knowable about a given unit of empirical reality. Since exhaustive explanation of empirical reality is impossible, scientists must develop conceptual schemes that constitute partial explanations of empirical reality. Parsons offers his own theory of action as an example of such a conceptual scheme. The theory of action (1) focuses on the system of relations between the individual actor and other actors, (2) assumes that this system of relations has boundaries and strives to maintain its boundaries, and (3) focuses on the symbols that are central in communication among actors. Through such assumptions and definitions of scope of investigation, conceptual schemes make an infinite and complex social reality comprehensible. Conceptual schemes therefore are necessary and unavoidable. Moreover, more than one conceptual scheme is possible. For example, rather than viewing human behavior from the vantage point of the theory of action, a scientist could view human behavior from a biological frame of reference. From a biological point of view, the actor is viewed not as an element in a symbol system but as a physical-chemical system that has physiological responses to environment.

Unlike Weber and Simmel, however, Parsons views conceptual schemes in social science not as emerging from cultural values and society, but as emerging in a scientific discipline that is in significant ways autonomous from society. Parsons maintains that scientists interact with one another and thereby constitute a sub-system in a society. Through such interaction in a scientific sub-system, norms and values that are unique to science emerge. Such scientific norms and values include the belief that scientific conceptual schemes ought to be general rather than particular, for science aspires to long-range knowledge rather than knowledge of immediate practical use; the belief that concepts ought to be precise and consistent; and the belief that scientists ought to confine themselves to empirically verifiable statements. Parsons maintains that, in the scientific process, conceptual schemes are proposed by individual scientists, and such proposed conceptual schemes are evaluated by scientists on the basis of scientific norms and values. Thus, for Parsons, when conceptual schemes are widely accepted in a scientific discipline, they are accepted not on the basis of cultural values but on the basis of the norms and values of the scientific sub-system. Accordingly, social scientific knowledge possesses an autonomy from sociology. There ought not be, therefore, a German sociology, that is, a sociology which reflects the norms and values of German culture. For sociology at its best reflects the norms and values of science and is autonomous from the values of a particular nation or culture.

Parsons acknowledges that there are important connections between the scientific sub-system and the social system of which it is a part. First, the scientific sub-system must adhere to norms and values of the social system. Experimentation, for example, cannot violate social standards of proper treatment of humans and animals. Second, an autonomous scientific sub-system can emerge only in a social system that values scientific knowledge. Parsons maintains that this has occurred to a considerable degree in the modern West. Third, when a scientific sub-system emerges, the institutionalization of the scientific role occurs. Thus, the scientist is provided a status in a recognized and legitimate institution, such as a professor in a university. Parsons maintains, however, that these connections between a scientific sub-system and the social system of which it is a part do not violate the essential autonomy of science. Natural and social scientific disciplines in the modern West are autonomous, because conceptual schemes are evaluated in light of, and only in light of, scientific norms and values.

Like Weber and Simmel, therefore, Parsons grasped the role of conceptual schemes in the process of knowing. He thus avoided the naive realism of Comte and Durkheim, who assumed that sociologists could observe social reality without interests or preconceptions. Like Spencer and Simmel, he was aware of impediments to an objective knowledge of society, and, like them, he believed that sociology as a science overcame these obstacles. His concept of science as an autonomous sub-system creatively combined what sociologists in the twentieth century had come to understand about social processes with the Enlightenment faith in the efficacy of reason. His formulation for overcoming obstacles to objective knowledge of society was therefore much more developed and credible than the relatively simplistic formulations of Spencer and Simmel. This formulation enabled Parsons, unlike Weber, to formulate a strategy for attaining objective knowledge in spite of the fact that the knowing process necessarily and unavoidably uses conceptual schemes.

Parsons' formulation was in important respects less sophisticated than that of Mannheim. Parsons does not address as thoroughly as Mannheim the issue of several understandings of society rooted in different social positions. Parsons' concept of an autonomous scientific sub-system addresses the issue, but this was an inadequate formulation, given the diversity of views on social policy questions. In his epistemological writings, Parsons seems to not take seriously the questions that Mannheim addresses. Parsons' shortcomings in this regard became especially apparent when he and other modernization theorists were criticized by Third World scholars as ethnocentric.[2] Parsons' limitations in regard to the issue of the influence of social position on understanding were to become an important issue in the writing of Gouldner and Mills.

Alvin Gouldner

Alvin Gouldner rejects what he calls "the myth of a value free sociology" (Gouldner 1962:199), which is the myth that "social science should and could be value-free" (1962:199), the myth that sociologists can and should avoid the expression of value judgments in their roles as sociologists. Writing in the early 1960s, Gouldner maintained that the notion of value-freedom was widely disseminated by prominent sociologists in the United States, including Parsons (1962:199). And he maintained that the prominence of the notion of value-freedom was the result of an over-simplification of Weber's concept of ethical neutrality (1962:200).

In opposition to the concept of value freedom, Gouldner maintains that sociological theory and research proceed in a value context. In his widely read book, *The Coming Crisis of Western Sociology* (1970), Gouldner discusses the importance of what he calls prior assumptions in sociology: "Like it or not, know it or not, sociologists will organize their researches in terms of their prior assumptions; the character of sociology will depend upon them and will change when they change" (1970:28). There are, for Gouldner, two forms of prior assumptions. Postulations are those prior assumptions of which the sociologist is aware and which are explicit. Postulations are distinct from background assumptions, which are inexplicit assumptions of which the sociologist is only partially aware. Gouldner refers to these inexplicit assumptions as background assumptions, because "on the one hand, they provide the background out of which postulations in part emerge and, on the other hand, not being expressly formulated, they remain in the background of the theorist's attention" (1970:29). Background assumptions include assumptions about what is real and what is not, as well as assumptions about human nature and society. Examples of background assumptions include: that human beings are rational and that society is characterized by equilibrium. Gouldner maintains that background assumptions are learned in social interaction as a dimension of learning a particular language and culture. Background assumptions are thus deeply rooted in socio-cultural milieu. Accordingly, background assumptions are distinct from explicitly formulated points of view that are consciously used by the sociologist for heuristic purposes. Gouldner writes:

It is in the essential nature of background assumptions that they are not originally adopted for instrumental reasons, the way, for example, one might select a statistical test of significance or pick a screwdriver out of a tool kit. In short, they are not selected with a calculated view to their utility. This is so because they are often internalized in us long before the intellectual age of consent. They are affectively-laden cognitive tools that are developed early in the course of our socialization into a particular culture and are built deeply into our character structure. (1970:32)

Moreover, background assumptions influence social theory: "from beginning to end, they influence a theory's formulation and the researches to which it leads" (1970:59). Gouldner does not claim, it should be noted, that sociology unavoidably and necessarily is based upon background assumptions. He explicitly leaves this question aside, deferring to philosophers of science. Gouldner's claim here is that, regardless of whether sociology necessarily depends upon background assumptions, sociologists do in fact use them (1970:32).

Given his view that the sociological enterprise emerges from a context of cultural values, Gouldner believed that an objective knowledge of society, a knowledge that does not reflect the social position of the sociologist, is impossible to attain. Accordingly, he sought to redefine objectivity in a way that took into account the fundamental fact that sociology proceeds in a value context. In Gouldner's formulation, objectivity requires that the sociologist possess the quality of "personal authenticity" (1968:114). Objectivity requires the sociologist not merely to adhere to a set of methodological procedures but to become a particular kind of person. Objectivity in this sense of authentic personhood has three dimensions. First, to be objective, the sociologist must be committed to the pursuit of self-awareness or awareness of what one's value premises are. As Gouldner states in his advocacy of a Reflexive Sociology, "The ultimate goal of a Reflexive Sociology is the deepening of the sociologist's own awareness, of who and what he is, in a specific society at any given time, and of how both his social role and personal praxis affect his work as a sociologist'' (1970:494). Gouldner is not proposing here merely that sociologists should state their value premises, as Gunnar Myrdal does in *The American Dilemma* (1944), when he states that his investigation proceeds from the value premises of the American Creed. For Gouldner, sociologists do not necessarily know what their values, assumptions, and premises are. Gouldner illustrates this in his discussion of Becker (Becker, 1966), for Becker thinks he is committed to the side of the underdog, but in Gouldner's view, Becker is committed to the side of the new social reform establishment (Gouldner, 1968). Gouldner is proposing, then, not merely a statement of value premises, but a quest for awareness of what one's values are. This quest for self-knowledge and self-awareness will always be successful in degree if the quest is authentic. But it cannot be completely successful, for there always are values that are deeply ingrained through the process of socialization and that one does not make explicit to oneself. To be objective, therefore, is to be committed to the pursuit of self-awareness.

Second, to be objective in the sense of authentic personhood is to make moral judgments and to be morally committed. Just as a judge in a court of law is considered impartial insofar as the judicial decision is made in accordance with normative standards formulated in law, so sociologists are objective insofar as they make judgments based on explicitly stated standards of justice in society. The most objective sociologists, therefore, are not those who attempt to be aloof from the social processes they observe. Such sociologists who aspire to neutrality in the face of social conflicts are in danger of becoming ''spiritless technicians who will be no less lacking in understanding than they are in passion, and who will be useful only because they can be used'' (1962:212). Objective sociologists undertake moral evaluations of what they observe on the basis of explicitly stated values to which they are committed. Objective sociologists, therefore, are characterized by partisanship and commitment (1968:113). And a sociology that is objective is a moral sociology, a sociology based upon commitment to moral values (1970:491).

Third, to be objective is to admit facts that violate hopes. This ''involves the capacity to acknowledge 'hostile information'—information that is discrepant with our purposes, hopes, wishes, or values'' (1968:114). Thus, the objective sociologist is one who gives the desire for truth priority over other desires, one who believes that ''truth is the vital thing'' (1962:212).

Objectivity as personal authenticity, therefore, involves becoming a particular kind of person. Objectivity involves becoming a self-reflective person, seeking to attain an increased level of self-awareness of value premises and assumptions. It involves commitment to explicitly stated moral standards and moral evaluation based on such standards. And objectivity involves a commitment to truth as the highest goal. And since working toward being such a person is what it means to be objective, all this is inherent in the task of sociology. These are not moral qualities that the sociologist out to possess above and beyond being a sociologist. Rather, these are qualities that are intrinsic to the sociological task itself. As Gouldner asserts:

The historical mission of a Reflexive Sociology, as I conceive it... would be to *transform* the sociologist, to penetrate deeply into his daily life and work, enriching them with new sensitivities, and to raise the sociologist's self-awareness to a new historical level. (1970:489)

Gouldner, then, rejects the concept of value-freedom, which he attributes to Parsons and other prominent sociologists. In fairness to Parsons, it should be noted that his version of value-freedom was considerably more sophisticated than the value-freedom of Comte and Durkheim. According to the naive conception of Comte and Durkheim, objective knowledge can be attained by detached and disinterested observation (Comte) or by observing without pre-suppositions or assumptions (Durkheim). In contrast to these simplistic notions, Parsons recognized that the sociologist selects and organizes elements from empirical reality in accordance with a conceptual scheme, but he believed that scientific conceptual schemes are autonomous from cultural values, because they are accepted by a relatively autonomous scientific sub-system in accordance with scientific norms and values. But even though his understanding is more sophisticated, Parsons, like Comte and Durkheim, ultimately maintains that sociological theory and research are independent of the influence of cultural values. In this respect, Parsons's formulation is in some respects similar to those of Spencer and Simmel. Spencer perceived obstacles to the attainment of objective knowledge, but he believed that awareness of these obstacles enables the sociologist to overcome them. Simmel saw that conceptual schemes ground sociological analyses, but he saw encounter with empirical reality as constituting an objective restraint on conceptual schemes. Parsons, Spencer, and Simmel all identified, in different ways, difficulties in the attainment of objective knowledge, but they all believed that these difficulties can be overcome. They all therefore advocated a version of the concept of value-freedom. Like Comte and Durkheim, although in a more sophisticated way, they came to the conclusion that sociology can and should exclude values. Gouldner, however, saw more clearly than the proponents of value-freedom the penetrating influence of social position on understanding of society as a result of the processes of socialization, from which sociologists are in no sense exempt, however much they might desire to be so.

In his grasping of the influence of social position on understanding, Gouldner was similar to Mannheim, who labored to rescue the social sciences from the relativistic implications of this fact. Mannheim's effort to preserve sociological objectivity stands as an important achievement in the history of sociological theory. His formulation was that knowledge independent of social position within society, but relative to broad social context and historical time period, can be attained by socially unattached intellectuals who formulate a synthesis of complementary viewpoints rooted in different social positions. But in spite of the similarity between Gouldner and Mannheim, Gouldner could not accept Mannheim's solution to the problem of objectivity. The difficulty here was Gouldner's rejection of Mannheim's notion that intellectuals are socially unattached. Against Mannheim, Gouldner argued that intellectuals constitute a class like any other. In *The Future of Intellectuals and the Rise of the New Class*, Gouldner maintains that the intellectuals, along with the technical intelligentsia, comprise a new class which has emerged in the twentieth century (1979:1–5). In terms of status in capitalist society, this class of intellectuals is ranked below the capitalist class in prestige, power, and wealth, but above the workers and the peasants. Like any class, it has particular interests. It has, for example, an interest in state ownership of the means of production (Gouldner, 1985:36). Like any class powerful enough to do so, the intellectual class advances its interests through ideology, which in its case is the ideology of Marxism. Marxism claims to be an analysis of society from the standpoint of the working class. But in fact, Marxism is the ideology of the intellectual class (Gouldner, 1979; 1985).

Given his rejection of Mannheim's solution to the problem of objectivity, Gouldner arrived at a position that was not too different from Weber's concept of value relevance. Weber and Gouldner formulated the problem somewhat differently. For Weber, sociological analysis proceeds in the context of conceptual schemes which are grounded in cultural values, and accordingly, elements from empirical reality are selected and organized according to their cultural significance. For Gouldner, sociological theory and research are influenced from beginning to end by background assumptions that are rooted in sociological processes and often are not explicit to the consciousness of the sociologist. These formulations, however, were similar in that they both described sociological analysis as proceeding in a value context. Given their formulations, neither Weber nor Gouldner could conceive of the possibility of an objective social science, autonomous from cultural values and independent of the social position of the sociologist. Given this impossibility, Weber came to the conclusion that complete objectivity is impossible to attain, but the sociologist should endeavor to be as objective as possible by seeking to understand the point of view of the actor and by conforming to rules of logic. In contrast, Gouldner sought to redefine objectivity altogether, so that objectivity would no longer be understood as independence from social position and cultural values but as the possession of personal and moral qualities.

Gouldner's concept of objectivity as personal authenticity is in many respects a moving formulation of the qualities a scholar ought to possess. It is a call to critical self-examination, to honesty and integrity, and to commitment to truth and to social justice. Nevertheless, Gouldner's concept of objectivity as personal authenticity represents an abandonment of the quest for knowledge that is independent of cultural values and social position. Accordingly, this notion has exceedingly cynical implications in relation to the capacity of human reason to discern the true and the right. These cynical implications were expressed in the work of C. Wright Mills.

C. Wright Mills

Like Gouldner, Mills conceived of sociology as proceeding in a value context. Mills maintains that in sociology values have an important influence on the selection of problems, the understanding and formulation of these problems, and the proposed solutions to these problems (Mills 1959:78). Moreover, this relevance of values to the sociological task is unavoidable: "there is no way in which any social scientist can avoid assuming choices of value and implying them in his work as a whole" (1959:177). Given that sociology unavoidably proceeds in a value context, objectivity, according to Mills, cannot mean bracketing values. Rather, objectivity requires making values and problems explicit (1959:130). Once sociologists make explicit the values and problems that ground theories, concepts, and methods, they have the further obligation to follow these theories, concepts, and methods to their logical conclusion in light of the empirical evidence, and they must not allow bias to influence the results. As Mills writes:

So far as conceptions are concerned, the aim ought to be to use as many "value-neutral" terms as possible and to become aware of and to make explicit the value implications that remain. So far as problems are concerned, the aim ought to be, again, to be clear about the values in terms of which they are selected, and then to avoid as best as one can evaluative bias in their solution, no matter where that solution takes one and no matter what its moral or political implications may be. (1959:78)

Thus, objectivity, for Mills, means the explicit articulation of values and the following of this value-laden theoretical and conceptual system to its logical conclusion, even if this conclusion is not what the sociologist had expected or hoped it would be. Objectivity proceeds, therefore, in a value context.

For Mills, the limited objectivity of sociology means that there are some questions that sociology will be unable to answer. As Mills sees it, sociologists are objective enough to address questions of fact, but they are unable to address questions of value. For example, in a conflict in regard to a social issue, sociologists can resolve conflicts over what the facts are by correcting errors of fact and unclear conceptions. But whenever a conflict in regard to a social issue is rooted in a conflict in values, sociologists are unable to resolve this conflict (1959:77). Thus, given the situation that sociologists themselves possess value-laden conceptual schemes, they are in no better position than anyone else in society to resolve conflicts in value. They must confine themselves, therefore, to questions that are factual and logical in nature.

Mills's understanding of sociological objectivity is quite similar to that of

Weber. Like Weber, he sees sociology as proceeding within a value context, and he believes that a degree of objectivity is possible through adherence to rules of logic. And like Weber, Mills maintains that judgments of value are beyond the scope of sociology. But unlike Weber, Mills faced squarely the most cynical implications of this understanding. Since sociologists are unable to resolve them, the ultimate arbiter which resolves such conflicts becomes political power. In Mills' words:

When there are values so firmly and so consistently held by genuinely conflicting interests that the conflict cannot be resolved by logical analysis and factual investigation, then the role of reason in that human affair seems at an and. We can clarify the meaning and the consequences of values, we can make them consistent with one another and ascertain their actual priorities, we can surround them with fact—but in the end we may be reduced to mere assertion and counter assertion; then we can only plead or persuade. And at the very end, if the end is reached, the final form of power is coercion.

We cannot deduce—Hume's celebrated dictum runs—how we ought to act from what we believe is. Neither can we deduce how anyone else ought to act from how we believe we ought to act. In the end. if the end comes, we just have to beat those who disagree with us over the head; let us hope the end comes seldom. (1959:77)

With this assertion Mills brings the sociological tradition to precisely the position that Horkheimer had described as the eclipse of reason. For Mills here takes the position that sociology must confine itself to logical and factual questions and that sociology is unable to address questions other than logical and factual questions. Such non-factual and extra-logical questions are beyond the scope of sociology and can only be resolved through power. The efficacy of social science and of reason is eclipsed. Truth becomes what those in power say it is.

Mills and Gouldner were contemporaries who both grasped that cultural values ground sociological analysis. They both maintained, as a result, that objectivity, in the sense of independence from social position and cultural values, cannot be attained. They developed different responses to this fact. Gouldner sought to redefine objectivity in such a way as to place hopes in the moral qualities of the sociologist. Mills, reflecting a greater despair, arrived at the conclusion that questions of truth are not ultimately resolved in the domain of science and reason but in the arena of power. According to this understanding, a whole range of questions and issues are beyond the scope of science and of reason. What policies should the United States pursue in regard to the poverty, domination, exploitation, racism, sexism, militarism, and the environment? With Mills' formulation, we arrive at the belief that social science and reason cannot address the most important questions of our time. We have lost faith in the capacity of social science and reason to address questions that really matter. We turn instead to less important, sometimes even trivial questions. However unimportant they are as questions, at least they are questions for which we have confident answers. Our questions are confined to the narrow, the technical, the factual, the logical.

This tendency to narrow and technical questions, Horkheimer had observed, often accompanies the eclipse of reason. And Mills had observed and lamented this tendency in sociology, a tendency which he called "abstracted empiricism" (Mills 1959:50–75).

SOCIOLOGY AS AN ARBITER OF TRUTH

This book seeks to affirm faith in reason by formulating a social scientific method for the attainment of objective knowledge. It is primarily an analysis of Marx, who possessed a far more penetrating understanding of this issue than other sociological theorists. The analysis of Marx proceeds through several stages. First, it notes Marx's belief in science as a form of knowledge that understands the essence, as against the appearances, of capitalism. Second, it describes Marx's belief that science is grounded in the common interest, which is the interest of all in a particular economic system in maximizing human well-being. Third, it discusses Marx's critique of political economy in *Theories of Surplus Value* and in *Capital*. This discussion makes clear Marx's understanding of the interrelationship between social movements and social science. According to Marx's understanding, scientific insight into the essence of a social system is not possible until revolutionary movements emerge. As a result, revolutionary movements constitute new possibilities for social science. Fourth, the analysis turns to a discussion of Marx's view that a scientific understanding of capitalism is attained by taking the proletarian point of view, that is, by taking as given the objective conditions of the proletariat. Grasping such objective conditions, according to Marx, is not possible until the proletariat constitutes itself as a revolutionary class. The book discusses the many difficulties in interpreting Marx's concept of the proletarian point of view and notes that these difficulties indicate the need for a reconstruction of Marx's concept of science. Fifth, the book describes the intellectual and moral conversion that Marx experienced in 1843–1844. This conversion resulted from Marx's encounter in Paris with the working-class struggle and from his study of British political economy. As a result of these experiences, Marx was able to synthesize German philosophy, British political economy, and socialism in order to formulate a critique of political economy that takes as given the objective conditions of the worker.

Although recognizing that Marx's concept of science possesses remarkable insights, the book notes shortcomings in Marx's analysis. Accordingly, the book turns to a discussion the cognitional theory of Bernard Lonergan. Lonergan, like Marx, possessed a strong faith in reason. However, whereas Marx was a product of nineteenth-century faith in science and in its capacity to discern the true and the right, Lonergan, as a product of the twentieth century, had much greater reason to doubt the efficacy of reason. But as a Catholic philosopher and theologian, he was driven by religious faith to find the basis for which reason can discern the true and the right. In his analysis of all forms of human knowing, from mathematics to common sense, Lonergan describes, based on actual cases of human knowing, the process through which knowledge independent of social position is attained, in spite of the fact that knowing occurs in social context. He shows that objective knowledge is attained by discovering relevant questions through encounter with persons of different horizons. Lonergan's theory has limitations, particularly in its failure to address the issue of social power in understanding. However, Lonergan's understanding is helpful in reformulating Marx's concept of science in a manner appropriate for the twentieth century.

Having analyzed Marx's concept of science and reviewed relevant insights from Lonergan's cognitional theory, the book turns to a reconstruction of Marx's theory of knowledge. It formulates the basic elements of such a reconstructed theory of knowledge. First, social scientists can overcome the limitations imposed on understanding by horizon through encounter with social movements constituted by subjected groups. Second, such social movements are created by economic development, and they contain insights into the objective conditions of the subjected group. Third, through encounter with such social movements, social scientists become aware of insights, discover relevant questions, and formulate alternative theoretical understandings that transform science. Such alternative theoretical understandings constitute objective knowledge, that is, a knowledge that transcends particular interests and formulates an understanding that is correct for a particular stage in the development of an economic system. In addition, the book maintains that there have been two important instances of adherence to this method, namely, Marx's formulation of the theory of historical materialism and Immanuel Wallerstein's formulation of the world-systems perspective. Thus the analyses of Marx and Wallerstein represent scientific achievements that illustrate and confirm Marx's reconstructed concept of science.

Finally, the book turns to an analysis of the writings of the so-called "late Marx" in relation to the Third World. In 1870, Marx began a study of Russia, prompted by the emergence of a revolutionary movement there. This study led him to a revision of his earlier views; he began to envision a multilineal development in the world economy and agrarian socialism in Russia. Some view Marx's thought in the 1870s as significant for the Third World today. However, given the relatively undeveloped stage of social movements in the periphery in his time, Marx could not be expected to grasp their full significance. Since Marx wrote prior to the emergence of Third World national liberation movements, his vantage point limits the possibilities for his understanding of the Third World in the twentieth century.

This book, then, seeks to formulate a social scientific method through which social scientists can develop objective knowledge. The method, in short, involves seeking encounter with social movements constituted by subjected social groups. By objective knowledge I mean an understanding that does not reflect the particular interests rooted in the social position of the sociologist who formulates the understanding. It is knowledge that formulates the common interest of all who are bound together in an economic system in a particular stage in its development. I take the terms objective knowledge and scientific knowledge to be synonymous. Scientific knowledge is knowledge that does not reflect particular interests. Scientific knowledge is attained through the scientific method of encounter with social movements constituted by subjected social groups.

Insofar as sociologists have adhered, at least implicitly, to this method of encounter with social movements of subjected social groups, they have formulated understandings that do not reflect particular interests and are objective. However, much of sociological analysis in the twentieth century reflects a vantage point of social position and thus promotes particular interests. To be sure, many sociological analyses, particularly in the areas of social stratification and feminist sociology, have incorporated insights that emerge from the vantage point of subjected groups. But much of sociological analysis continues to reflect the vantage point of the dominant groups and thus function to preserve the established order. The mainstream introductory sociology textbooks in the United States, for example, describe social processes in the United States as though other peoples and cultures of the world were unimportant. Further, these texts treat only superficially, if at all, the relationship between the economic development of the Western world and the underdevelopment of the Third World through European colonial domination. These texts, therefore, have an ethnocentric orientation which leaves unchallenged the commonly accepted notion in the culture of the United States that the technological achievements of the Western world are primarily a consequence of cultural characteristics of the West. This ethnocentrism of sociology in the United States is even found in such areas as social stratification and race relations. For the most part, social stratification texts discuss the United States. They provide insufficient treatment of the global inequality between the developed and the underdeveloped world, which is clearly the most important aspect of inequality in the world today. Moreover, the sociology of race and ethnic relations proceeds within the context of the American Creed and its belief in equality of opportunity. As a result, it treats relations between whites and people of color in the United States in a way that is disconnected from the international context of European colonial domination, and it discusses social movements of people of color in the United States in a way that ignores their actual social and historical connections to national liberation movements in the Third World.

Sociology, therefore, often fails to escape ethnocentrism. It often analyzes social reality from the vantage point of the more privileged social positions to which sociologists for the most part belong. As such, it often promotes the particular interests of the more privileged social groups in the modern world economy. It thus tends to preserve the fundamental economic and social relations of the modern world economy as well as the inequalities that those relations generate and maintain.

This book challenges the ethnocentrism of modern social science. It offers social scientists a fundamental method for arriving at understandings that do not promote particular interests but are grounded in the common interest of all who are bound together by the modern world economy. It rejects the cynicism of the age and argues that the attainment of an objective knowledge that does not reflect the vantage point of privilege is possible if social scientists incorporate insights that emerge from social movements constituted by subjected social groups. It rejects the notion that truth cannot be known and that truth, consequently, is what those in power say it is. It insists upon reason as both a possibility and a responsibility for social science.

This book, therefore, is written by a sociologist to other social scientists and to scholars interested in the philosophy of social science. As such, the author occupies a relatively privileged position in the world economy and writes to others who are relatively privileged. It addresses the question of how scholars who occupy a relatively privileged position in the world economy can overcome the limitations on understanding imposed by that social position. In addressing this question, it takes as a model the life and work of Marx. Marx was a middle-class German educated in the tradition of German philosophy who overcame the limitations imposed on understanding by that social position through encounter with the working-class movement of Western Europe. This process of relatively privileged persons seeking truth through encounter with social movements constituted by subjected social groups represents one path to truth. Another pattern in the quest for truth is expressed by Antonio Gramsci's notion of the "organic intellectual" (1971:3). Organic intellectuals are members of particular classes who endeavor to formulate the ideas and aspirations of their class. In the case of the working-class struggle, organic intellectuals are members of the working class. In the Third World in the twentieth century, there are important thinkers who, as members of subjected social groups, illustrate the pattern of the organic intellectual. Frantz Fanon, Kwame Nkrumah, and Gustavo Gutiérrez immediately come to mind as the most profound scholars of this type. A description of this pattern, in which members of subjected groups articulate new knowledge from the vantage point of the subjected group, is beyond the scope of this book. This book addresses the question of how persons of higher status can learn from the insights of "organic intellectuals" and arrive at an understanding that does not reflect the vantage point of their higher status. The book is thus addressed to persons of higher status in the modern world economy. It is a mandate to listen to the insights of organic intellectuals in order to overcome the limitations on understanding which are imposed by privilege.

NOTES

1. The following account of Parsons' understanding of sociological objectivity is drawn primarily from Parsons (1951; 1961; 1967).

2. This issue is discussed in Chapter 7.

2

CRITICAL MARXISM

POSITIVIST MARXISM

The central thesis of this book, that social scientists can attain scientific and objective knowledge through encounter with social movements constituted by subjected groups, stands in the tradition of critical Marxism. Accordingly, the book rejects the claims of positivist Marxism, such as the claims that science formulates eternal laws and that science is value-free. The positivist tendency has been important in the history of Marxism. It is found in the writings of Karl Kautsky (Kolakowski, 1978:319), Nikolay Bukharin (Kolakowski, 1978:57–58), and Vladimir Lenin (Kolakowski, 1978:321); in the epistemological assumptions common in the Second International (Korsch, 1970:30–38, 54–59); and in the codifications of Stalinism (Kolakowski, 1978:91–104). Let us look at the form that this positivist tendency takes in the case of Lenin.

Lenin maintains that there is an objective truth that is a mirror image of objective reality. Truth is objective in the sense that it is "independent of the subject" (Lenin, 1962:123), and likewise, objective reality is "independent of man" (1962:129). Objective truth consists in sensations that have objective reality as their source. Such sensations are "a true copy of this objective reality" (1962:129). They "are images of the sole and ultimate objective reality" (1962:129). They are "images of the external world" (1962:130). Objective reality, accordingly, "is copied, photographed, and reflected by our sensations, while existing independently of them" (1962:130). Moreover, truth is eternal. With reference to Friedrich Engel's example that "Napoleon died on May 5, 1821" (1962:132), Lenin observes that "if you do not assert that it may be refuted in the future, you acknowledge this truth to be eternal" (1962:132). Lenin further writes:

The example given by Engels is elementary, and anybody without the slightest difficulty can think of scores of similar *truths* that are eternal and absolute and that only insane people can doubt (as Engels says, citing another example: "Paris is in France"). (1962:132–33)

However, for Lenin, although knowledge is objective and eternal, our discovery of this knowledge is conditioned by social and historical factors. There is an objective truth that formulates a picture of an objective reality, but as a result of social and historical limitations, we do not always have an accurate image of objective reality. Human progress involves moving toward an understanding of objective reality (1962:132–37).

In this book, I argue that there is an objective truth independent of social position. However, in taking this position, I do not mean to imply acceptance of the notion that objective truth consists of an image that copies objective reality. I find compelling Lonergan's argument that even natural scientific knowledge does not formulate a picture of objective reality. Lonergan notes that the physicist, for example, in observing empirical reality, anticipates finding a differential equation (Lonergan, 1958:35–46). Accordingly, in the process of abstraction, the physicist selects those elements from empirical reality that are significant and relevant to formulating a differential equation. In the process, elements of empirical reality are ignored (Lonergan, 1958:30–31, 90, 110). As a result, there is no one-to-one correspondence between scientific formulations and empirical reality (Lonergan, 1958:135–37). In opposition to the notion that objective truth is a copy of empirical reality, I will argue, following Lonergan, that we arrive at objective truth when we have asked all relevant questions.

Moreover, I will reject the idea that truth is eternal. I will argue, following Marx and in the tradition of critical Marxism, that truth is relative to historical time period. When we affirm something as true, we affirm it as true independent of social position and therefore to a particular historical time period and therefore as objective, but as true only for and with reference to that particular historical time period. In regard to such assertions as "Paris is in France" and "Napoleon died on May 5, 1821," Lonergan has again formulated useful and relevant concepts. Although these statements are true with certainty and are eternally true, they fall into a category that Lonergan calls concrete judgments of fact (Lonergan, 1958:281). Most scientific judgments, however, are more complex than the concrete judgment of fact. Scientific judgments are never made with certainty, because the scientist can never be certain that there are not more relevant questions to be asked. Moreover, scientific judgments are not eternal, because new relevant questions, which could not previously have been known, can be discovered in the future (Lonergan, 1958:283–87, 299–304, 375–79). Thus, for Lonergan, scientific judgments and concrete judgments of fact are fundamentally different types of knowing. The concrete judgment of fact represents an elementary type of knowing, which involves simply looking or in some way sensing what is out there in the empirical world. But the scientific judgment represents a much more complex form of knowledge, which involves not simply sense experience of data but also selecting elements from empirical reality in accordance with what is significant from a point of view, formulating an understanding, and affirming, modifying, or rejecting the understanding by raising relevant questions. To develop a philosophy of science on the basis of the elementary type of knowledge is a fundamental error that has contributed, Lonergan maintains, to much confusion in the history of philosophy (1958:44, 76, 130–31, 135, 251–53, 257, 320, 406, 411–13, 424–25, 537–38, 646; 1972:76, 238).

This book, then, rejects the claims of positivist Marxism that science is value-free and formulates eternal laws. It stands in the tradition of critical Marxism represented by Antonio Gramsci, Georg Lukács, Karl Korsch, Max Horkheimer, Herbert Marcuse, and Jürgen Habermas. Critical Marxism rejected the notions that science is value-free and that scientific laws are eternal. Against these positivist notions, critical Marxism formulated the ideas that social scientific insights emerge in relation to historical time period and develop in dialectical relation with social movements.

THE CRITICAL MARXISM OF THE 1920s

We begin our discussion of critical Marxism with the work of Antonio Gramsci. Gramsci maintains that Marxism is a critique of common sense and philosophy formulated by intellectuals who are organically connected to the masses. For Gramsci, all intellectuals are organically connected to a social class, and they unify and formulate the interests of the social class to which they are organically connected (Gramsci, 1971:3–7). However, intellectuals traditionally have denied their connection to a particular social class. Traditional intellectuals are organically connected to the dominant class, but they believe that they are "autonomous and independent of the dominant social groups" (Gramsci, 1971:7). Marxism, in contrast, is formulated by intellectuals who emerge from and are organically connected to the masses (1971:334, 340). They formulate a critique of common sense, defined as the uncritical and commonly accepted ideas of an epoch (1971:322–23, 348, 419–24). They also formulate a critique of the philosophy of the traditional intellectuals. This philosophy of the traditional intellectuals is more reflective than common sense, but it is a conception of the world from the vantage point of the more dominant social groups. The philosophy of the intellectuals in actuality is the common sense of the educated strata (1971:322–23, 330–31).

For Gramsci, Marxism seeks to understand objective reality, that is, reality that exists in and of itself, independent of human conceptions of it. However, since the pursuit of knowledge is a human activity, in which the world is understood on the basis of practical and scientific interests, this objective reality cannot be grasped in the present social and technical conditions (1971:368). Objective reality can only be grasped when divisions within society no longer exist, because

these divisions generate different interests as well as ideologies that distort un
derstanding in order to promote particular interests. Thus, knowledge of objective
reality can be attained only when humanity has become "unified in a single
unitary cultural system" (1971:445). The struggle for truth is therefore interrelated with the struggle for social change and social justice: "There exists
therefore a struggle for objectivity (to free oneself from partial and fallacious
ideologies) and this struggle is the same as the struggle for the cultural unification
of the human race" (1971:445).

This book is written from a vantage point different from that of Gramsci's
analysis. Whereas Gramsci describes the quest for truth from the vantage point
of the organic intellectual, I seek to describe the process through which a scholar
who is not a member of a subjected social group can understand social reality.
However, I concur with Gramsci on three specific points. First, like Gramsci,
I will argue that the process of formulating insights requires a connection with
the subjected class, for I will argue for the necessity of encounter with social
movements constituted by subjected social groups. Such encounter makes possible the discovery of relevant questions which can be known from the vantage
point of the subjected class. Second, I share with Gramsci a recognition of the
limits of understanding as a result of the fact that knowing is a human activity.
I will designate precisely what these limits are, and accordingly, I will argue
that the attainment of an understanding that is true beyond historical context is
not possible. At the same time, I will seek to describe the possibilities for
understanding within those limits. Accordingly, I shall argue that an objective
understanding that transcends differences in social position and culture within a
historical time period is a possibility that has in some cases been attained in
social science. I will describe the process through which such objective knowledge can be attained. Third, I share with Gramsci the notion that the struggle
for truth and the struggle for social justice are intertwined, for if the social
scientist attains understanding through encounter with the social movements of
subjected social groups, then such social movements constitute the necessary
pre-conditions for the discovery of further relevant questions and the advancement of knowledge. Without such social movements, not only would the struggle
for social justice not proceed, but the struggle for truth also would not proceed.

A second important example in the history of critical Marxism is the work of
Georg Lukács, particularly his classic work, *History and Class Consciousness*.
Originally published in 1923, "today it is regarded as one of the most important
theoretical documents in the history of Marxism" (Kolakowski, 1978:260). In
History and Class Consciousness, Lukács maintains that both British political
economy and German philosophy in the nineteenth century defended the *status
quo*, and therefore, they both presented the social order as immutable. Accordingly, they believed in eternal laws of nature. Marx, however, exposed this belief
as an illusion through critical philosophy and the method of historical criticism,
which reveals the historical origins of all social institutions (Lukács, 1971:47–48).
But in debunking the notion of eternal laws, Marx, according to Lukács, did not

eliminate laws and objectivity altogether. Rather, he made clear that laws and objectivity are relevant only for a particular historical stage of social development (1971:49). At the same time, although it is valid to affirm truth as relative as against absolute or eternal, it is wrong, according to Lukács, to counter absolutism with mere subjectivism. Accordingly, Lukács writes that the absolute should not so much be denied "as endowed with its concrete historical shape and treated as an aspect of the process itself" (1971:188). In this view, it is valid to speak of a truth "within a unique, concretised historical process" (1971:187).

The bourgeoisie, according to Lukács, is unable to discern such truth, for the bourgeoisie observes from the standpoint of its own interest in control of society. Accordingly, the bourgeoisie must deceive itself "in order to be able to support with a good conscience an economic system that serves only [its] own interests" (1971:66). Given the necessity of having to obscure to itself and to other social classes the essence of capitalism, as capitalism develops, it becomes more and more difficult to grasp the essence of capitalism from a bourgeois standpoint. This trend culminates in an ideological crisis of capitalism (1971:61–67).

However, a scientific understanding of capitalism, for Lukács, can be attained by taking the standpoint of the proletariat. Unlike the bourgeoisie, the proletariat has a vested interest in discerning the truth about capitalism. Therefore, only the proletariat is in a position to grasp the essence of capitalism (Lukács, 1971:54, 59, 68–69, 159–60, 163–64). As an exploited worker who is reduced to a tool, the worker is driven beyond the immediacy of the present situation (1971:163–68, 171–72, 180–81) and is driven to a quest for truth and for "authentic objectivity" (1971:164). In contrast, the bourgeoisie is not exploited, and the bourgeoisie is not driven by exploitation beyond the immediacy of the social situation but is imprisoned within immediacy (1971:164).

In this book, I develop further Lukács' argument that truth is neither eternal nor merely subjective but is true within a concrete historical process. I formulate an understanding of the process through which is attained an objective knowledge that transcends differences in social position and cultural tradition within a historical time period. As I discuss the process through which such objective knowledge can be attained, I analyze the difficulties in Lukács' concept of taking the proletarian point of view. Here I argue that Lukács distorts Marx's concept of the proletarian point of view. Marx did not maintain that the proletariat has a greater understanding of capitalism than the bourgeoisie. Rather, Marx maintained that the scientist, once the proletarian movement emerges, will be able to formulate new understandings through analyses that take as given the objective conditions of the proletariat. These new understandings will render outdated the previous scientific knowledge attained by taking as given the objective conditions of the bourgeoisie. Having clarified what Marx claimed, I then argue that Marx's own formulation needs to be reconstructed in light of Marx's scientific praxis and in light of the cognitional theory of Bernard Lonergan. Accordingly, I formulate an understanding of science, according to which objective knowledge is attained through discovering relevant questions through encounter with social movements constituted by subjected social groups. But in spite of the difficulties in relation to Lukács' interpretation of the concept of the proletarian point of view, I share with Lukács a general orientation that the emergence of the proletarian class and the proletarian class struggle created new possibilities for social science, possibilities that social science cannot seize insofar as it remains wedded to assumptions that wittingly and unwittingly promote the interests of more privileged social groups.

A scholar whose stature is equal to that of Lukács in the history of theoretical Marxism is Kark Korsch. Korsch and Lukács were both important in formulating critiques of major tendencies in Marxism in the immediate aftermath of World War I, tendencies that included, on the one hand, Kautsky, the social democrats, and the Second International, and on the other hand, Lenin, communism, and the Third International (Korsch, 1970:12–18, 104–22; Kolakowski, 1978:308). Korsch's most important work was *Marxism and Philosophy* (1970), originally published in German in 1923 (Kolakowski, 1978:309). *Marxism and Philosophy* was greeted with hostility by both social democrats and communists. The Comintern at the Fifth World Congress attacked Korsch and Lukács as too idealistic. Unlike Lukács, however, Korsch did not engage in self-criticism as a political tactic to remain in the communist movement (Korsch, 1970:14–15), and Korsch was expelled from the Communist party in 1926 (Kolakowski, 1978:308; Korsch, 1970:18).

In *Marxism and Philosophy*, Korsch attempts a critique of philosophy and a critique of Marxism. Korsch's criticism of philosophy is that it describes the history of philosophy in an undialectical way as the history of ideas unrelated to economic and social development. Philosophers write of the decline of Hegel in the 1830s and the re-emergence of interest in Immanuel Kant in the 1860s, but they cannot connect these developments in philosophy "to the concrete historical development of bourgeois society as a whole" (Korsch, 1970:38). Philosophers cannot grasp this connection, because to do so would require "abandoning the *bourgeois class standpoint* which constitutes the most essential *a priori* of their entire historical and philosophical science" (Korsch, 1970:37). Philosophers, therefore, reflect a bourgeois viewpoint, and Korsch refers to their philosophy as bourgeois philosophy.

Unlike bourgeois philosophers, Georg Hegel grasped the dialectical relation between philosophy and society and hence understood that a revolution in thought is "an objective component of the total social process of a real revolution" (Korsch, 1970:39) in society. But bourgeois philosophy has lost this insight because the bourgeois class has ceased to be revolutionary (Korsch, 1970:40). Bourgeois historians of philosophy thus erroneously think that idealism and metaphysical speculation did not occur in the 1840s. But what actually happened, according to Korsch, was that the idealist dialectics of Hegel expressed itself in the materialist dialectics of Marx. Hence German philosophy developed into a new science, namely, scientific socialism (Korsch, 1970:41). This connection between Marxism and German philosophy is central to understanding Marxism.

For Marxism is not the rejection of philosophy but, more precisely, the realization of philosophy that makes possible the abolition of philosophy in its old form (Korsch, 1970:83–85).

In his critique of Marxism, Korsch designates three stages in the development of Marxist theory. The first stage (1843–1848) is the original formulation by Marx. During this stage, Marxist theory views society as a totality, and "at this stage there is no question whatever of dividing the economic, political, and intellectual moments of this totality into separate branches of knowledge" (Korsch, 1970:52). Later formulations by Marx and Engels developed the theory further, but these later developments did not alter this essential characteristic.

During the second stage, from 1848 to 1900, Marxism became fragmented into separate specialized sciences, distinct disciplines that described the economic system or the state or educational institutions or religion in capitalist societies. This undialectical form of Marxism searched for laws and causal connections and conceived of itself as objective and value-free (Korsch, 1970:54–57). This revisionist theoretical Marxism emerged as a result of the fact that the working-class struggle had become reformist. Theoretical Marxism was connected to practice, and as the working-class struggle ceased to be revolutionary and became reformist, so theoretical Marxism ceased to be revolutionary and became revisionist (Korsch, 1970:58). During this period, in reaction to revisionist theoretical Marxism, an orthodox theoretical Marxism reasserts itself and attacks revisionism. This orthodox theoretical Marxism became the official Marxism of the Second International. However, orthodox Marxism is nothing but a vulgar Marxism, because it is disconnected from the working-class struggle (Korsch, 1970:58–59).

During the third stage, which began in 1900, the workers' struggle again becomes revolutionary. As a result, the evolutionary doctrines of the revisionists are no longer seen as legitimate. At the same time, as revolutionary issues are given a practical priority by the revolutionary working-class struggle, the orthodox theoretical Marxism of the second stage is exposed as useless abstractions disconnected from the struggle. Hence, the re-emergence of a revolutionary struggle leads to the revitalization of Marxism as a revolutionary theory (Korsch, 1970:60–61).

In 1930 Korsch wrote a postscript to *Philosophy and Marxism*, which was originally published in 1922. Here Korsch maintains that there has emerged a new dogmatic theoretical orthodoxy in Marxism, namely, the Communist, Russian, or Leninist orthodoxy of the Third International. Korsch does not offer a social analysis of this phenomenon. That is to say, he does not attempt to explain why revolutionary developments in Russia led to a dogmatic theoretical Marxism that is in some respects similar to the dogmatic theoretical orthodoxy of the non-revolutionary second stage in Marxism. Nevertheless, Korsch does cast his own work in opposition to the dogmatism of both the Second and Third Internationals. Thus, Korsch sees a conflict in Marxism between the old social democratic orthodoxy and the new communist orthodoxy on the one hand, and anti-dogmatic, historical, and critical Marxism on the other. In spite of his disagreements with Lukács in regard to tactics for dealing with the communist movement, he believes that both he and Lukács are on the side of critical Marxism in this conflict (Korsch, 1970:90–92).

Korsch, then, in his critique of bourgeois philosophy and Marxism, formulates an understanding of knowledge that grasps the relation between insight and social movements. In his analysis, bourgeois philosophy cannot understand philosophy once the bourgeoisie ceases to be revolutionary, any more than theoretical Marxism can understand Marxism once the working-class struggle becomes reformist. As we shall see, Korsch's formulation here is entirely consistent with Marx. In his critique of political economy, found in *Theories of Surplus Value* and in *Capital*, Marx documents the relations between economic developments and class formation, on the one hand, and insights in the science of political economy, on the other. He demonstrates that the scientific achievements of the greatest political economists, Adam Smith and David Ricardo, were made possible by economic development, and that the shortcomings in their analyses were unavoidable given the level of economic development and class formation at the time in which they wrote. Moreover, he notes that the emergence of the proletarian revolution makes possible new scientific insights which can take the science of political economy beyond the stage represented by Smith and Ricardo. He considers all analyses which take the bourgeois standpoint after the emergence of the proletarian revolution to be not science but vulgar political economy. In like manner, Korsch, in his analysis of bourgeois philosophy and Marxism, sees a relation between insight and social movement. Korsch, in effect, applies a Marxist perspective on the development of knowledge to the development of Marxism itself.

Just as Korsch attempted to describe the relation between knowledge and social movements in the development of Marxism from 1843 to 1922, I assess the significance for social science of social movements in the twentieth century. Writing in the early 1920s, Korsch was struck by the re-emergence of a revolutionary working-class struggle after World War I, and he could see the impact of this social movement on theoretical Marxism. In our time, however, important social movements have occurred outside a European context. Beginning in the 1920s, nationalist movements in opposition to colonial rule emerged in the colonized regions of the world, driven by the emerging petty bourgeois class created by the colonial process. In the post-World War II era, the nationalist movements were able to enlist the support of the colonized of all classes and to force de-colonization on a political plane. This dramatic story, in which many colonies became politically independent during the 1950s and 1960s, is only now reaching its final chapter in South Africa, the last bastion of formal colonialism. The European colonial powers, of course, were able to concede political independence while preserving the economic structures that are the essence of colonial domination. Nevertheless, Third World national liberation movements constituted a significant challenge to the European powers. At the political level, formal political independence gives formerly colonized nations some latitude of movement, thus making control by European powers less certain and less absolute. At the cultural level, national liberation movements have been able to challenge European descriptions of social reality and European moral conceptions. In the aftermath of the impact of national liberation movements in the social world of our time, the question emerges: What insights in social science have these social movements made possible? In addressing this question, we see the emergence of new perspectives in social science, such as the world-systems perspective, which take into account questions that can be discerned from a vantage point defined by the objective condition of the colonized. These perspectives see social reality in ways not possible prior to the emergence of Third World national liberation movements. Hence, one is able to see once again the relation between social movements and social scientific insight, originally formulated by Marx in his critique of political economy and applied by Korsch in his critique of bourgeois philosophy and Marxism. In this book, I explore these issues more fully. I examine Marx's analysis of the relation between science and social movements in the development of the science of political economy. And as I endeavor to reconstruct Marx's concept of science, I will turn to the relation between Third World national liberation movements and the world-systems perspective for purposes of illustration.

THE CRITICAL MARXISM OF THE FRANKFURT SCHOOL

The critical Marxism of Gramsci, Lukács, and Korsch was formulated in the social context of the revolutionary fervor of 1918–1920 and in opposition to positivist and dogmatic tendencies in Marxism. Formulated at a time of intense revolutionary activity, their analyses were grounded in a hope for new possibilities for Marxist theory and practice. However, as the twentieth century unfolded, it became clear that these hopeful possibilities were not to be realized. In opposition to revolutionary expectations, fascism and nazism emerged as the dominant political force. When right-wing totalitarianism was ultimately discredited, capitalism was able to develop the capacity to contain the working-class struggle and to legitimate itself in the eyes of the masses in the developed part of the world. In the aftermath of the victory of Western industrial capitalism, the social democratic tendency of Marxism reasserted itself, and reformist rather than revolutionary Marxism became the dominant form of Marxism in the West. As a result of the failure of the proletarian revolution in the West, the proletarian state in the Soviet Union never had the complementary economic relations with the developed West that Marx believed to be necessary for the ultimate success of a proletarian revolution in Russia.[1] As a result, the professional strata in the Soviet Union were able to assert their interests at the expense of the interests of workers and peasants, culminating in Stalinism. Thus, a dogmatic, undialectical, unhistorical, and uncritical form of Marxism emerged in Eastern Europe as the ideological instrument of totalitarian states, and it could assert itself as a secondary form of Marxism in the West. Accordingly, the critical Marxism of the mid-twentieth century was formulated in a context decidedly different from that of 1918–1920.

The major thinkers in the tradition of critical Marxism in the mid-twentieth century were associated with the Institute for Social Research.[2] The Institute for Social Research was established at the University of Frankfurt in 1924 by Felix Weil, Frederick Pollock, and Max Horkheimer. All three were born in the 1890s and were the sons of successful German businessmen. They sought to develop a Marxist scholarship that was independent from mainstream tendencies in the academy as well as from the tendencies of Marxist political parties. To this end, the institute was funded initially by an endowment provided by Weil's father, and it was affiliated with, but independent of, the University of Frankfurt. Of the three, Horkheimer was to become the most prominent. His work became well known, and he served as director of the institute from 1930 until his retirement. In its first decade, Weil, Pollock, and Horkheimer were joined by other scholars whose work would contribute to the growing prestige of the Institute for Social Research, including Theodor Adorno and Herbert Marcuse. In 1933 the institute was closed by the Nazi government, and it relocated to Paris during that year and to New York City in 1934, affiliating with Columbia University. The institute returned to Frankfurt in 1949. Marcuse, however, stayed in the United States for the rest of his life and did not return to Frankfurt with Horkheimer and Adorno. In the post–World War II period, a second generation of scholars affiliated with the institute emerged, the most prominent being Jürgen Habermas. The work of Horkheimer, Adorno, Marcuse, and Habermas formulated a critique of positivism, including its manifestations in mainstream scholarship as well as Marxism, and a critique of advanced capitalist society. Their work redefined critical Marxism in the social context of the mid-twentieth century.

In "Traditional and Critical Theory," written in 1937 (Kolakowski, 1978: 345), Horkheimer maintains that critical theory affirms the "unity of theory and practice" (Horkheimer, 1972:231) and asserts that there is a "relation between time and thought" (1972:239–40). Thus, truth is not permanent but develops through time, and this evolution of truth occurs because society develops through time. For example, the entrepreneur has different characteristics in advanced capitalism from those of the entrepreneur in early capitalism. Therefore, the concept of entrepreneur will develop in a manner that corresponds with the development of the entrepreneur in society. "The representation of the entrepreneur, like the entrepreneur himself, passes through an evolution" (1972:238–39). Critical theory thus rejects "the idea of an absolute suprahistorical subject" (1972: 240) removed from the "historical moment" (1972: 240). Critical theory is "incompatible with the idealist belief that any theory is independent of men" (1972:240).

Horkheimer developed these themes further in *Eclipse of Reason*, which was originally published in 1947 and was based on public lectures presented at Columbia University in 1944 (Horkheimer, 1974:vi). According to Horkheimer, the ancient Greeks viewed reason as determining what human ends and goals ought to be. Horkheimer calls this "objective reason." Objective reason asks such questions as, What is the greatest good? and What is the human destiny? Objective reason believes that there are eternal answers to such questions, and thus there is eternal truth. Thus, in the understanding of reason as objective, philosophy is the quest for eternal truth in regard to questions concerning what human ends ought to be (Horkheimer, 1974:4–5, 10–11, 31–38, 123–25).

In Horkheimer's view, Christianity appropriated the Greek understanding of reason to formulate a notion of eternal and objective truth that is attained through reason and revelation. The Enlightenment challenged the religious claims of Christianity and argued that eternal truth could be attained through reason alone. This Enlightenment critique of Christianity retained the Greek conception of reason as capable of formulating eternal truths in response to "ought" questions. However, the Enlightenment critique of religion, according to Horkheimer, planted the seeds for the destruction of objective reason. The Enlightenment critique maintained that religious claims could not be verified through empirical observation, but this critique of religion could be applied to objective reason, to philosophy, itself. Thus, there emerged the idea that human ends and goals cannot be reasonably determined. According to this idea, ends and goals are irrational, and reason is merely finding means to ends. Thus, an understanding of reason as subjective emerged. According to this understanding, reason cannot determine what goals are desirable. In this conception, our goals are determined by forces outside of reason, such as politics and power. With such a conception, the power of reason to formulate human goals is eclipsed (Horkheimer, 1973:3–4, 14–24).

Fascism, according to Horkheimer, is the culmination of the eclipse of reason. With the emergence of the concept of reason as subjective, Enlightenment ideals such as freedom and democracy cannot be verified through empirical observation. Thus, the question of their truth or falsity is placed beyond the scope of reason. Accordingly, there is no way to demonstrate that democracy is in any sense more reasonable than its negation. Correspondingly, there is no way to demonstrate that fascism is unreasonable. At a superficial level, fascism is an aberration from Enlightenment ideals, because it negates the Enlightenment ideal of democracy. However, at a more fundamental level, fascism is the culmination of the Enlightenment, because the inability to negate fascism is rooted in Enlightenment epistemological assumptions (Horkheimer, 1974:20–24, 31).

Positivism also emerges, according to Horkheimer, as a consequence of the eclipse of reason. Positivists assume that knowledge cannot be attained through intuition or revelation and that there are no self-evident truths (Horkheimer, 1974:60). Thus, positivism rejects reason in its objective sense as the basis for knowledge. For positivists, knowledge is based on empirical observation and is attained through scientific procedures (Horkheimer, 1974:74, 78–79). Scientific research, the experiment, and local deduction constitute the foundation of knowledge. According to this conception, science, and only science, is the arbiter of truth. Science, and only science, therefore, is the basis for human progress (Horkheimer, 1974:59). "Science is the sole power by which humanity can be saved" (Horkheimer, 1974:75). Horkheimer, however, rejects the epistemology of positivism. Positivism, he argues, rests on epistemological assumptions, which it takes to be self-evident. But self-evident principles, positivism has argued, are not valid. Hence, positivism is rendered invalid by its own epistemological assumptions (Horkheimer, 1974:72, 76).

In opposition to the epistemological assumptions of positivism, Horkheimer calls for a reconciliation of objective and subjective reason. "The task of philosophy is not stubbornly to play the one against the other, but to foster a mutual critique and thus, if possible, to prepare in the intellectual realm the reconciliation of the two in reality" (Horkheimer, 1974:174). Because of the predominance of subjective reason, such a reconciliation must focus on objective reason. Objective reason promotes respect for the rights of the individual and restrains the human urge for excessive instrumentalism in regard to nature and other human beings (Horkheimer, 1974:174–77).

Horkheimer and Adorno pursued some of these themes further in *Dialectic of Enlightenment* (Horkheimer & Adorno, 1972), which was written when Horkheimer and Adorno were in the United States and which was originally published in German (by the Social Studies Association in New York) in 1944. Horkheimer and Adorno argue that nazism was a manifestation of progressive ideas that are rooted in the Enlightenment. This occurred because the Enlightenment sought a form of knowledge that would enable human domination of nature. Kolakowski states Horkheimer and Adorno's understanding:

Enlightenment, seeking to liberate men from the oppressive sense of mystery in the world, simply declared that what was mysterious did not exist. It aspired to a form of knowledge that would enable man to rule over nature, and it therefore deprived knowledge of significance, jettisoning such notions as substance, quality, and causality and preserving only what might serve the purpose of manipulating things. It aimed to give unit to the whole of knowledge and culture and to reduce all qualities to a common measure; thus it was responsible for the imposition of mathematical standards on science and for creating an economy based on exchange-value. (Kolakowski, 1978:373)

Hence, the "Dialectic of Enlightenment" refers to the dynamic through which the Enlightenment quest for human liberation culminates in the subjugation of human beings by commodities. As Kolakowski writes:

The "dialectic" consisted in the fact that the movement which aimed to conquer nature and emancipate reason from the shackles of mythology had, by its own inner logic, turned into its opposite. It had created a positivist, pragmatist, utilitarian ideology and, by reducing the world to its purely quantitative aspects, had annihilated meaning, barbarized the arts and sciences, and increasingly subjected mankind to "commodity fetishism." (Kolakowski, 1978:373)

In this book, I address the problem of the eclipse of reason as formulated by Horkheimer. I formulate an understanding of knowledge that rejects the positivist view that reason is unable to address questions concerning what our collective goals ought to be and that reason must focus on the means to attain non-rational goals. The positivist view of reason assumes that issues of fact and issues of value are fundamentally different. In opposition to this assumption, I follow Lonergan in arguing that the knowing process is similar in regard to both issues of fact and issues of value; that this process involves raising questions, marshaling evidence, discovering more relevant questions, and moving to judgment when all relevant questions have been asked; that truth, in issues of both fact and value, is attained when all relevant questions have been asked; that error, in both issues of fact and issues of value, results when relevant questions have been overlooked due to the limitations of social position; and that these limitations, in issues of both fact and value, are overcome through encounter with social movements constituted by subjected social groups. The truth that is attained through this process, moreover, is not eternal truth but a truth that transcends social position within a historical time period. Accordingly, my formulation will further develop Horkheimer's notion of the relation between time and thought.

The modern Western drive to dominate nature, analyzed by Horkheimer and Adorno in *Dialectic of Enlightenment*, is analyzed further by Herbert Marcuse in *One-Dimensional Man*, which was written in English and published in 1964. Modern industrial society, Marcuse maintains, is characterized by the creation of false needs. False needs are distinct from true needs, which are those needs, including food, clothing, and shelter, that are necessary for the full and free development of the personality. False needs, including the need to consume and to have fun, "are superimposed upon the individual by particular social interests" (Marcuse, 1964:5). In imposing false needs on individuals, the private space and inner freedom of the individual are "invaded and whittled down by technological reality. Mass production and mass distribution claim the *entire* individual" (1964:10). The dimension of inner freedom that is destroyed by the technological reality of advanced industrial society is the realm of "the critical power of Reason" (1964:11) and "negative thinking" (1964:11), the inner dimension of reflection that has the capacity to challenge critically the assumptions of the status quo and the interests of the dominant class.

For Marcuse, therefore, advanced industrial society is a one-dimensional society that destroys the inner dimension of freedom and critical thinking. This one-dimensionality of advanced industrial society is seen in its art. Throughout history, art (including the novel, the poem, the short story, the concert, opera, theater, painting, and sculpture) expressed a reflective capacity and a capacity to critique the established order. Accordingly, a gap developed between the arts and the established order of the day. However, in advanced industrial society, the critical dimension of art is transformed, and art becomes a commodity, to be bought and sold like any other commodity. In traditional society, art celebrates its alienation from society, but advanced industrial society turns into a celebrity the artist who successfully sells his or her work as a commodity (Marcuse, 1964:61–64).

For Marcuse, advanced industrial society eliminates dialectical thinking. Dialectical thinking, illustrated by the thought of Plato, grasps the essence as well as the appearance of social reality. The appearance of social reality refers to the actual conditions of social existence, whereas the essence of social reality refers to the potential for human development given the actual conditions. To see the appearance is to see the present human condition. To grasp the essence is to imagine human conditions that are better than existing conditions, and, therefore, to be critical of existing social conditions. Thus, the apparent human condition is toil, which is unfreedom, but the essence of the human condition is freedom. However, the predominant mode of thinking in advanced industrial society is scientific thought, a mode of thinking that does not seek to discern the essence of social reality. Scientific thought observes only that aspect of social reality that appears to the senses, and it attempts to describe this empirical reality using a rational, systematic, and consistent theoretical system. By perceiving social reality as rational and harmonious, it eliminates the contradictions and ambiguities in social reality, including the contradiction between essence and appearance. Scientific thinking eliminates all contradictions in reality because it seeks an understanding that is useful for the domination of nature (Marcuse, 1964:132–34).

But alongside the human desire for domination, there is also the human desire for liberation and emancipation. Accordingly, in advanced industrial society, in opposition to scientific thought, there emerges critical theory, which is a dialectical form of thinking grounded in the human desire for liberation. Marcuse formulated the elements of critical theory in "Philosophy and Critical Theory," an essay written in German in 1937 (Marcuse, 1968:134–58). Critical theory, Marcuse maintains, believes in the possibility of the transformation of society, which establishes the social conditions for human happiness. Critical theory, he writes, is characterized by a "concern with human happiness, and the conviction that it can be attained through a transformation of the material conditions of existence" (Marcuse, 1968:135). Accordingly, critical theory requires "phantasy" (1968:154) or "imagination" (1968:154), which is a capacity to envision new possibilities that can emerge from the present social situation. But critical theory is not utopian, for it "does not envision an endless horizon of possibilities" (1968:154). Accordingly, the imagination of a future society must be constrained by existing technical and social conditions. There are limits to phantasy, and these limits "are prescribed by the level of technological development" (1968:154). Thus, critical theory is concerned with human potentialities, but these potentialities, more precisely, "are exclusively potentialities of the concrete social situation" (1968:142).

As it imagines human potentiality, critical theory advocates collective courses of action (Marcuse, 1968: 135). Yet critical theory does not prescribe a blueprint for the creation of a free society: "the subsequent construction of the new society cannot be the object of theory, for it is to occur as the free creation of the liberated individuals'' (1968:135). Accordingly, critical theory develops in dialectical relation with the emerging society, and critical theory attains its culmination when the human potentiality of a free society has been realized.

Critical theory, therefore, represents a new understanding of reason, an understanding that has emerged as a result of the culmination of the bourgeois revolution. The bourgeois revolution had established the principle of the autonomous individual, the principle that individuals could be free through the use of reason to shape their lives. This was a conception of the individual as possessing freedom of thought and will. However, by the twentieth century, a new social situation, in which human freedom requires collective action, has emerged. As Marcuse writes:

A social situation has come about in which the realization of reason no longer needs to be restricted to pure thought and will. If reason means shaping life according to men's free decision on the basis of their knowledge, then the demand for reason henceforth means the creation of a social organization in which individuals can collectively regulate their lives in accordance with their needs. (1968:141–42)

Thus, the realization of human freedom is possible not through the individual exercising freedom of thought and will but through the creation of a free society that provides for the needs of all. When the struggle for such a society emerges, philosophy, understood as reflection in the realm of pure thought divorced from the human struggle to create a free society, is rendered outdated. It is replaced by critical social theory, which reflects upon human potentiality and seeks the real attainment of that potentiality.

The interest of philosophy, concern with man, had found its new form in the interest of critical social theory. There is no philosophy alongside and outside this theory. For the philosophical construction of reason is replaced by the creation of a rational society. The philosophical ideas of a better world and of true Being are incorporated into the practical aim of struggling mankind, where they take on a human form. (Marcuse, 1968:142)

To what extent is critical theory characterized by objectivity? Marcuse addresses this question in *One-Dimensional Man*. Critical theory, for Marcuse, is objective insofar as it is consistent with real possibilities, given existing technical and social conditions, and insofar as its attainment would facilitate the full development of human potentiality. Every society develops an ideology that is rooted in its structure and organizes social reality and makes it comprehensible. Marcuse refers to this socially accepted way of viewing the world as the established historical project. The established historical project has demonstrated that it is objective or true, in that it has successfully organized the production and distribution of goods. As Marcuse writes:

The established society has already demonstrated its truth value as historical project. It has succeeded in organizing man's struggle with man and with nature; it reproduces and protects (more or less adequately) the human existence (always with the exception of the existence of those who are the declared outcasts, enemy-aliens, and other victims of the system). (1964:219)

However, as the society develops, new possibilities for human potentiality emerge, and these new possibilities render outdated the established historical project. As Marcuse writes, "the established rationality becomes irrational when, in the course of its *internal* development, the potentialities of the system have outgrown its institutions" (1964:221). As this occurs, new historical projects are proposed. These new historical projects, which Marcuse calls "transcendent historical projects" (1964:220), challenge the established historical projects and have the potential to transform existing social institutions. Such transcendent historical projects are objective insofar as (1) they are consistent with real possibilities, given existing technical and social conditions; (2) they offer "the prospect of preserving and improving the productive achievements of civilization" (1964:220); and (3) they facilitate "the free development of human needs and faculties" (1964:220). The task of critical theory, for Marcuse, is to formulate such objective transcendent historical projects.

In this book I build upon and develop further Marcuse's understanding. I concur with Marcuse on several points. First, social theory formulates a tension between "is" and "ought" in social reality, a tension between existing social conditions and the potentialities for social justice contained in social conditions. Second, social theory is formulated in dialectical relation with struggles for social justice. Third, social theory is an imaginative enterprise that envisions the possibilities for the transformation of society in light of existing social and technical conditions. In this book, I expand upon this notion by demonstrating the connection between insight and social movements constituted by subjected social groups. I argue that social movements establish the possibilities for imaginative insights by providing a new vantage point for analysis of existing social conditions and for imagining new human potentialities.

Marcuse has drawn a distinction between critical social theory and scientific thinking. For Marcuse, scientific thinking eliminates contradictions in reality and formulates a body of knowledge useful for the domination of nature. In contrast, social theory grasps the tension between existence and human potentiality and is useful for human liberation. In essence, I concur with this distinction. However, in this book, I argue that critical social theory is a scientific enterprise, for the scientific method involves a process of discovering relevant questions through encounter and formulating insights that emerge through this process. Accordingly, the mere description of social reality in its existing conditions, the scope of much of empirical sociology, represents only one dimension of the scientific enterprise. And insofar as such descriptions overlook relevant questions that emerge from social movements, they are inconsistent with the scientific enterprise. Therefore, I concur with the point that Marcuse is making, but I formulate an understanding of science that conceives critical social theory as a scientific enterprise.

Marcuse has grasped the relation between social scientific formulations and social development. For example, he notes that the bourgeois revolution established the autonomous individual made free through philosophical reflection, but that twentieth-century social conditions make necessary the transformation of society as a pre-condition for human freedom. Accordingly, he sees that social developments have rendered philosophy outdated and have established social theory as a necessary dimension of the struggle for social justice. In addition, Marcuse has seen that, as social development occurs, established historical projects become outdated and new historical projects emerge to challenge predominant ways of thinking and existing social institutions. I expand on Marcuse's formulation here. I argue that as social development occurs, new social movements constituted by subjected social groups emerge. Through encounter with such social movements, social scientists can formulate new insights that challenge the predominant scientific conceptions and the existing social institutions. Hence, I formulate more fully the relation between social scientific understandings and social development.

Marcuse has maintained that critical social theory is objective insofar as it is consistent with real possibilities and it facilitates human freedom. I concur with Marcuse in rejecting the idea that social science is objective insofar as it merely describes and avoids any formulation of social goals. At the same time, in this book I formulate criteria for objectivity different from those of Marcuse. Marcuse's criteria for objectivity focus on the content of the proposed social theory. For Marcuse, social theories are objective insofar as they facilitate the full development of human freedom in light of existing conditions. Therefore, in order to assess the objectivity of a social theory, one must evaluate the content of the theory. In contrast, my criteria for objectivity focus on the process through which a theory is formulated. In particular, I argue that social theories are objective insofar as they are formulated through a process of seeking relevant questions through encounter with social movements constituted by subjected social groups. An analysis of a theory's content is also necessary, particularly with reference to the interests of various social groups, but such analysis is secondary to the analysis of the process through which the theory is formulated, for science is defined essentially as a process and a method.

The first generation of scholars of the Frankfurt School, then, formulated a critique of positivism and advanced industrial capitalism. In their analysis, advanced industrial society is characterized by the unrestrained production and consumption of things, even to the point of the production of frivolous and dangerous things. Such a society is one-dimensional, a society that eliminates the capacity for critical self-reflection and therefore obscures the human potentiality for genuine freedom. In such a society, characterized as it is by a quest for the domination of nature, the form of knowledge that is most highly valued is that which contributes to the domination of nature and enhances productive capacity. But alongside the desire for domination, there is the human desire for liberation. This desire expresses itself in critical social theory, which grasps the possibilities for human freedom. Thus, in advanced industrial society there exist two forms of knowledge in opposition to one another. On the one hand, there is scientific knowledge, which is the dominant form of knowledge and which is grounded in the desire to dominate nature. On the other hand, there is critical social theory, which is a critique of the dominant tendency and which is grounded in the desire for emancipation.

These ideas of the Frankfurt School were subsequently expanded and formulated in a more systematic manner by Jürgen Habermas. Habermas maintains that in the human condition there are three "anthropologically deep-seated interests, which direct our knowledge and which have a quasi-transcendental status" (1973:8). They are quasi-transcendental in the sense that they "arise from actual structures of human life" (1971:194), yet they are invariant. Although Habermas refers to these interests as cognitive interests, they are cognitive in the sense that they establish the possibilities for cognition. They are non-cognitive in the sense that they "are not regulators of cognition" (1973:9). And although Habermas variously refers to them as "viewpoints" (1973:9), "frameworks" (1971:135), and "perspectives" (1971:135), they are not conceptual schemes in the usual sense. They are frameworks of action, not frameworks of knowledge. They are knowledge constitutive in that they give rise to cognitive conceptual schemes. Thus, the cognitive interests are pre-cognitive orientations or frameworks of action that establish the conditions for cognitive conceptual schemes or knowledge. These interests are universal and invariant in the human experience.

For Habermas, there are three human interests: the technical, the practical, and the emancipatory interests. The technical interest is "the interest of possible technical control over natural resources" (1971:35). It is the orientation of human beings in all societies to transform nature into products, a necessary pre-condition for human survival. This orientation is expressed in human labor (1971:194, 196), whether that labor be in the form of the pre-agricultural hunting and gathering or the complex technology of automated industry. Habermas refers to the activity of human labor as instrumental action. Hence, instrumental action is oriented to the control of nature (1971:126), and it establishes necessary conditions for knowledge of nature (1971:133, 211).

The practical interest is the interest of mutual understanding. The practical interest aims at agreement and consensus within the context of a cultural tradition. This interest is invariant and universal in human societies, for consensus is the pre-condition and foundation for practical everyday life. Only within the context of a basic agreement can societies develop standards of human thought and conduct. Mutual understanding is, therefore, a necessary prerequisite for human societies. The practical interest is the universal orientation to reach such understanding. This orientation is expressed in the human activity of symbolic interaction. Such activity is referred to by Habermas as communicative action (1971:191, 211).

The emancipatory interest is the "interest of reason" (1971:198), which "aims at the pursuit of reflection" (1971:198). For Habermas, reason and freedom are one, for the essence of unfreedom is the state of unreflection (1971:310). Through genuine insight and understanding, one becomes liberated from "dogmatic dependence" (1971:287). Through reason, there is freedom from the ideologies and false consciousness that are rooted in the injustices of the age. There is, therefore, a universal and invariant orientation to be free, which is at one with a desire to know what is true and right. The emancipatory interest is the most fundamental of the three interests, for the emancipatory interest gives meaning and purpose to the technical and practical interests. Without an interest in freedom, there is no possibility for an invariant interest in controlling nature and understanding, for the technical and practical interests are particular manifestations of the universal human desire to be free (1971:211).

Human interests, therefore, establish the necessary conditions for human knowledge. Knowledge is grounded in human interests, for knowledge is shaped by the unfolding of the human desires for control of nature, mutual understanding, and liberation. And since there are three human interests, it follows that there are three forms of human knowledge. Accordingly, for Habermas, the technical interest grounds natural science, the practical interest grounds cultural science, and the emancipatory interest grounds self-reflection and critical social science.

In accordance with this view, natural science is the logical and systematic extension of the quest for control of nature. "The natural sciences merely extend in methodical form the technically exploitable knowledge that has accumulated prescientifically within the transcendental framework of instrumental action" (1971:61). Accordingly, in both pre-scientific technical knowledge and scientific knowledge, there is instrumental activity that grounds a "cumulative learning process" (1971:124), which makes possible greater control over nature. Scientific knowledge differs from pre-scientific technical knowledge in that the former is more precise and systematic. Moreover, scientific inquiry "isolates the learning process from the life process" (1971:124), a dimension that appears in its clearest form in the experiment (1971:308). Natural scientific knowledge, therefore, is a particular form of the unfolding of the technical interest. Scientific knowledge thus emerges from the technical interest and reflects its orientation to control nature.

The cultural sciences, in contrast, are grounded in the practical interest, and as such they are a dimension of the unfolding of the universal desire for mutual understanding and communication. They represent, therefore, the scientific extension of communicative action (1971:175, 191). They seek to understand, within the context of a cultural tradition, the meaning of human action and of spoken and written words (1971:310). They receive their clearest expression in the hermeneutic sciences, that is, in the interpretation of texts and literary criticism.

In Habermas's formulation, therefore, there are clear contrasts between the natural and cultural sciences. The natural sciences are grounded in the technical interest and instrumental action, whereas the cultural sciences are grounded in the practical interest and communicative action (1971:140–41, 175, 191). In the natural sciences, isolated observation is central, whereas the understanding of meaning is fundamental in the cultural sciences. The natural sciences seek nomological formulation, whereas the cultural sciences seek interpretations (1971:309). These two contrasting forms of knowledge exist in human knowledge because they emerge from contrasting interests and contrasting forms of action.

Distinct from the natural and cultural sciences, self-reflection and critical reflection about society constitute the reflective forms of knowledge that emerge from the emancipatory interest. Self-reflection is most clearly represented in psychoanalysis. Through psychoanalysis, one is able to overcome self-deceptions (1971:218) that arise from repression (1971:224) and censorship (1971:225). Central to psychoanalysis is the interpretation of dreams, for in sleep censorship functions less powerfully and suppressed motives find expression (1971:224). The path to self-knowledge, therefore, involves understanding and interpretation of one's dreams. Such interpretation, however, goes beyond hermeneutics, for one must understand not only the dream, but the meaning of the dream (1971:220). Such self-reflection requires that one be driven by a desire to understand oneself, to look beyond self-deceptions and enter what Freud called the "internal foreign territory" (quoted in Habermas 1971:218). Self-reflection represents, therefore, the dynamic unfolding of the universal interest of reason.

Analogous to self-reflection is critical reflection about society. Just as there is self-deception at the level of the individual, at the level of society there is ideology. Just as the interest in reason drives one beyond deception to self-knowledge, so the interest in reason drives one beyond ideological rationalizations of injustice to a consciousness of the true and the right (1971:288). The interest of reason therefore grounds a critical analysis of society that has as its goal emancipation from ideology.

Both forms of reflective knowledge constitute the basis of human freedom, for self-knowledge consists in freedom from self-deception, and critical knowledge of society consists in freedom from ideology. Both forms of reflective knowledge are necessary for the full and free development of human potentiality. The orientation to truth is therefore at one with a desire to be free. The interest of reason is an emancipatory interest.

Habermas's understanding of the relation of knowledge to human interests constitutes the basis for his understanding of the particular discipline of sociology. To some extent, sociology, in Harbermas's view, attempts to formulate general principles of social interaction that are applicable to all social groups. The assertions that religion in all societies functions to provide meaning for individuals or that political institutions function to maintain order are examples of such efforts to "grasp invariant regularities of social action" (1971:310). Insofar as sociology produces such "nomological knowledge" (1971:310), it employs the empirical-analytic procedures of the natural sciences (1971:185). Accordingly, sociology to some extent reflects the dynamic unfolding of the technical interest.

But the goal of sociology is not merely to formulate lawlike generalizations.

Sociology often seeks to understand the social world of actors in a particular social group. Weber, for example, maintained that sociology to some extent has the goal of subjective understanding (*Verstehen*), which involves the understanding of action in the context of the meaning system of the actor (Weber 1947:94–97). William F. Whyte's *Street Corner Society* (1955) and Herbert J. Gans' *The Urban Villagers* (1965) are classic attempts to formulate such subjective understanding using the method of participant observation. For Habermas, when sociologists seek such subjective understanding, they do not use the empirical-analytic procedures of the natural sciences but the method of hermeneutic dialogue and the procedures of the cultural-hermeneutic sciences (Habermas, 1973:10–13). In such cases, sociology reflects the dynamic unfolding of the practical interest (Habermas, 1971:175–76).

However, sociology, for Habermas, does not confine itself to lawlike generalizations and subjective understandings. It builds upon these in its quest of its fundamental goal of critique of ideology. Accordingly, it goes beyond producing general statements and seeks "to determine when theoretical statements grasp invariant regularities of social action as such and when they express ideologically foreign relations of dependence that can in principle be transformed" (1971:310). Similarly, sociology goes beyond understanding the social consensus of cultural tradition:

Critical of ideology, it asks what lies behind the consensus, presented as a fact, that supports the dominant tradition of the time, and does so with a view to the relations of power surreptitiously incorporated in the symbolic structures of the systems of speech and action. (1973:11–12)

Sociology, then, seeks freedom from the social deception of ideology. It is a form of reflective knowledge, and as such, it represents the dynamic unfolding of the emancipatory interest (1973:253–56). This desire for freedom grounds the desire for nomological knowledge and hermeneutic understanding, for these types of knowledge are useful for a theory of society only as a dimension of the quest for a critique of ideology. The fundamental goal of sociology is critique. Sociology is essentially a critical science.

As critique, sociology does not confine itself to the realm of a theory of society. It goes beyond theory and enters the realm of political action. As such, it seeks not only the freedom from ideology that knowledge brings. It also seeks transformations of those unjust social structures that ideology defends and legitimates. A theory of society therefore contains "a political praxis which consciously aims at overthrowing the existing system of institutions" (1973:2).

Since critical sociology enters the realm of political action, it enters the realm of value. It goes beyond the realm of describing what is and attempts to formulate what ought to be, in relation to existing social and technical conditions, and to bring this "ought" into being through political action. This presupposes that a science of society is capable of distinguishing valid from invalid claims in the realm of value, and indeed Habermas maintains that valid claims in the realm of value can be ascertained. In doing so, he rejects the epistemological assumptions of decisionism. Decisionism maintains that logical analysis and empirical observation are the basis for testing validity claims in the realm of fact, but that there is no such reliable method for testing validity claims in the realm of value. According to decisionism, judgments of value ultimately reflect personal preference and personal decision (Habermas, 1975:105–6).

In opposition to decisionism, Habermas attempts to designate the conditions in which validity claims in the realm of value can be tested adequately. In this context, he formulates the concept of the "communication community" (1975:105). The communication community consists of individuals who represent a variety of particular interests. The participants in the communication community engage in a "cooperative search for truth" as their paramount goal in an environment that is free of coercion (1975:108). The goal of such a community of discourse, in which argument is the only acceptable means of conversion, is consensus. Such consensus is distinct from a "pseudo-compromise" (1975:112), in which parties of unequal power agree to a settlement that is inconsistent with the common good, as typically occurs in the political processes of advanced industrial societies. The consensus reflects a common understanding arrived at by participants in an atmosphere where coercion is unacceptable. Since the participants represent a variety of particular interests, the communication community, when consensus is reached, has gone beyond grasping what is right from the point of view of particular interests and has arrived at an understanding of what is right from the point of view of the common interest. Such an understanding, therefore, has validity.

Insofar as the norms and values of a society do not reflect a consensus arrived at by persons of diverse interests through reasoned discourse free of coercion, the norms and values are based on inequalities of power and are imposed through force (1975:111). Ideologies emerge to give legitimacy to these norms and values that are based on coercion rather than reason. In such a social context, the task of critical sociology is to expose the coercion that constitutes the foundation of social norms and values and to debunk the ideologies that legitimate such norms and values. Moreover, the task of critical sociology is to attempt to formulate the reasoned consensus that would emerge in such a society if there were the reasoned discourse, which is the essence of a communication community (1975:113–14).

Habermas, then, has endeavored to expand and further develop the formulation of the first generation of scholars of the Frankfurt School. In many respects, Habermas's analysis represents a more systematic formulation of ideas originally presented in less systematic form by Horkheimer, Adorno, and Marcuse. But there are important differences. For example, Horkheimer, Adorno, and Marcuse focus on the negative and repressive aspects of the domination of nature, as the implications of a society characterized by an unrestrained domination of nature had become manifest by the middle of the twentieth century. Habermas, however, takes a more balanced approach to this issue. He views the orientation to dominate nature as universal, and he therefore views this orientation, along with the empirical-analytic procedures that emerge from it, as having legitimacy. For Habermas, the error of positivism is to view such knowledge as the only legitimate form of knowledge. Habermas views empirical-analytic science as one form of knowledge having a legitimate place, but as only one form of knowledge. Cultural science, critical self-reflection, and critical social theory are equally legitimate forms of knowledge, each having their place in the human quest for knowledge and freedom. Habermas' more restrained critique of positivism enables him to formulate a critique of sociology which recognizes the legitimacy of empirical-analytic and hermeneutic methods in sociology, but which sees these procedures as having legitimacy only within the context of a discipline which is fundamentally critical and therefore oriented to human freedom.

In relation to Habermas' critique of sociology, his concept of the communication community is important. The communication community is, of course, an idealization, for the communication community does not exist and cannot exist in the real political world. But the concept of the communication community formulates the process by which knowledge that transcends particular interests ideally can be attained. For Habermas, the task of sociology, given the absence of communication community in the real world, is to endeavor to formulate that knowledge that would result if such a reasoned discourse did in fact exist. In this book, I formulate the reasons why the concept of the communication community is valid. In the first place, a community of discourse in which participants representing diverse particular interests engaged in dialogue free of coercion would lead to knowledge that transcends particular interests because, when consensus is attained, such consensus could only emerge when all relevant questions that can be known at that point in time have been addressed. Since awareness of relevant questions is conditioned by vantage points grounded in particular interests, and if all particular interests are represented, then the dialogue, if free of coercion, would lead to awareness by the community of discourse of all relevant questions, at least all relevant questions that are capable of being known in that particular historical time period. If such a community of discourse arrives at consensus, that consensus would take into account all relevant questions and would have arrived at an understanding that transcends particular interests. These ideas will be formulated in Chapters 6 and 7.

But since the communication community cannot exist in the real political world, the task of sociology, for Habermas, is to endeavor to formulate the understanding that would result from such reasoned discourse. In this book, I formulate the process through which the sociologist can fulfill this mandate. In particular, I argue that the sociologist can arrive at an understanding that transcends particular interests by discovering relevant questions through encounter with social movements constituted by subjected social groups. This, of course, requires that the sociologist possess the personal qualities of openness to others and a commitment to truth as the highest ideal. Although a communication community cannot exist in the real political world, I argue that scholars who possess these qualities and who have formulated understandings that transcend particular interests have existed in fact. I argue that the lives and works of Karl Marx and Immanuel Wallerstein constitute such examples.

This book, then, further develops some important insights of the Frankfurt School. At the same time, the Frankfurt School has important limitations that should be recognized. The insights of the Frankfurt School reflect the vantage point of the new proletariat, or the increasingly proletarianized middle class, of the advanced capitalism of the mid-twentieth century. As I shall attempt to demonstrate in this book, Marx viewed the most progressive advances in science as emerging from the vantage point of a revolutionary class. In developing this view further, I argue that the most advanced formulation emerges from social scientists who are organically connected to a social movement constituted by a subjected social group. In writing from the vantage point of the increasingly proletarianized middle class in the developed sector of the world economy, the Frankfurt School did not analyze the capitalist world economy from the most progressively possible vantage point. Reflecting on some repressive dimensions for the new proletariat of advanced industrial capitalism, they could formulate important insights. Their analysis, however, was disconnected from the national liberation movements of the Third World, and their critique of the capitalist world economy reflected Western assumptions.

This book, then, stands in the tradition of critical Marxism. It seeks to expand and develop further the epistemological arguments of critical Marxism. And it seeks to push critical Marxism to a new horizon which recognizes the significance for theory and praxis of Third World national liberation movements and the world-systems perspective.

NOTES

1. For a discussion of Marx's analysis of the possibilities for agrarian socialism in Russia, formulated during the last years of his life, see Chapter 8.

2. The following summary of the Institute for Social Research is drawn from Jay (1973).

3

SCIENCE AND ECONOMIC DEVELOPMENT

FAITH IN REASON AND SCIENCE

Some scholars have thought that Marx believed that all knowledge reflects social position and that a knowledge of society which reflects no particular interests is impossible to attain. For example, Isaiah Berlin argues that Marx rejects the notion that there are interests common to all people, which transcend class affiliation (1963:150–51, 155–56). This is not at all true. In fact, Marx viewed himself as a scientist, as an heir to Adam Smith and David Ricardo, whom he respected as scientists. He believed that his work was pushing the science of political economy to a new level of understanding and that this work was analogous to Charles Darwin's transformation of the science of biology. In this conception of himself as a scientist and his work as scientific, Marx was in no sense a relativist. He believed that science, as applied to human history and to its unfolding in the present, was above all a quest for truth and an attempt to present the social world accurately and intelligently. He believed that scientific knowledge that reflected no particular class interests is possible and that his own work represented the attainment of such scientific knowledge.

In his faith in science, Marx was very much a product of the Enlightenment ideas that were central to his intellectual and social environment. As David McLellan has noted, fundamental to the Enlightenment was a "limitless faith in the power of reason to explain and improve the world" (1970:15). This faith in reason as an arbiter of truth was a driving force in Marx's life. It is clearly evident in his earliest writings. For example, in 1842, he writes in defense of philosophy, that philosophy "appeals to reason" (Marx & Engels, 1975a: 197) and "promises nothing but the truth"(1975a:197). It tests its claims and studies before it speaks. And even though the truths of philosophy do not flatter the world, the public still recognizes the value of philosophy, because the public rightly "loves truth and knowledge for their own sakes" (1975a:197). In 1843, the youthful Marx would move to Paris and there would meet workers, revolutionary activists, and socialists. As we shall see, these experiences made possible an entirely new and creative development in his thinking, and the theoretical system that made him famous began to be formulated at this time. But even after this horizon shift, Marx remained influenced at a fundamental level by the Enlightenment conceptions of reason and science. In the "Introduction to a Critique of Hegel's Philosophy of Right," which was the essay in which Marx first proclaims the proletariat as an agent of revolutionary change, Marx continues to see truth as the goal of critical thinking. He maintains that the task of philosophy, now that religious "other-worldly" claims have been debunked as illusions, is to discern the truth on the level of this world and in the realm of politics and real human history. "Thus it is the task of history, once the other-worldly truth has disappeared, to establish the truth of this world" (quoted in McLellan, 1970:145). In *The Holy Family*, written in 1844, Marx views socialism and natural science as progressive ways of thinking that are legacies of the French Enlightenment (Marx & Engels, 1975d:124–31). Marx's commitment to truth, science, and reason continued to be evident in his writing throughout his life. In *Theories of Surplus Value*, written in 1862–1863, it is clear that Marx's analysis of theories of political economy is premised on a belief in science as an arbiter of truth. Indeed, as we shall see, Marx's understanding of science emerges in these critiques of the theories of the political economists. Finally, Marx's commitment to science can be seen in his critical reflections on his own work in his study of Russia in the last years of his life. Here Marx modifies aspects of his theoretical system in response to the emergence of a revolutionary struggle in Russia. These ideas of the "late Marx" also will be discussed further. For the moment let us simply note that Marx's writing in the last ten years of his life further illustrates his commitment and self-sacrifice to science, to truth, and to the principles of the Enlightenment.

Marx must be understood at the outset, then, as a product of the Enlightenment and of the Enlightenment faith in reason and science. As Barth observes, "Marx's anthropology was heir to the Western notion of humanity and to the declaration of human rights by the French Revolution" (1976:180). Marx was "a descendant of the Enlightenment" (1976:179–80) who "remained representative of Western rationalism [and] expected history to realize the realm of reason" (1976:180). This was in sharp contrast, Barth notes, to Nietzsche, who wanted to revise Western thought radically and to reduce knowledge to power (1976:144–76, 180). As a dimension of this faith in reason and science, Marx did believe that there is such a thing as a truth that transcends particular interests. He believed in science as a form of knowledge that grasps the essential dynamics of social reality and sees beyond what appears to be true from the vantage point of particular interests. It is true that Marx advocated taking the proletarian point of view. But Marx advocated taking the proletarian point of view in order to grasp those truths that transcend class interests. And exactly what Marx meant by taking the proletarian point of view will have to be carefully examined. The purpose of this book is to work through such complexities in Marx's concept of science.

SCIENCE GRASPS THE ESSENCE OF SOCIAL REALITY

Marx believed that the task of the science of political economy is to grasp the essence of capitalism, and this requires seeing beyond mere appearances. The difficulty of seeing beyond mere appearances is evident in the history of political economy, particularly in regard to the question of the source of surplus value. For Marx, labor power is the source of value, and unpaid labor in the source of surplus value. This is the basis of Marx's distinction between necessary labor time and surplus labor time. Necessary labor time refers to that labor time that is needed to produce commodities that have a value equivalent to the value of those commodities, such as food, clothing, and so on, which are necessary for the subsistence of the worker. Surplus labor time refers to the labor time above and beyond necessary labor time. The capitalist must pay for necessary labor time in order for labor to reproduce itself as a commodity available for use in production. But the capitalist does not pay for surplus labor, and this unpaid labor is the source of surplus value.

During the second period of the labour process, that in which his labour is no longer necessary labour, the workman, it is true, labours, expends labour power; but his labour, being no longer necessary labour, . . . creates no value for himself. He creates surplus value which, for the capitalist, has all the charms of a creation out of nothing. (1967:217)[1]

However, the true source of surplus value in unpaid surplus labor is difficult to grasp. It appears that the worker has been paid for the whole working day. Thus the payment of money for labor conceals the fact of unpaid labor (Barbalet, 1983:27). Political economists have tried to solve the riddle of surplus value, but they have by and large failed to grasp the fact that unpaid labor is the source of surplus value. The physiocrats, Adam Smith, and David Ricardo all grasped this fact in part, but none did so consistently and none saw its implications.

Ricardo's most influential book was published in 1821. A variety of works were published in the 1820s and 1830s that, like Ricardo's, are unable to explain why the laborer sells his labor below its value. Moreover, these works share none of the scientific insights of Smith and Ricardo. They accept capitalism as it appears on the surface. They accept the common notion that land is the source of rent, capital is the source of profit, and labor is the source of wages. In contrast, classical political economists see beyond these appearances (1972:453–54, 502–3). Accordingly, Marx distinguishes between classical political economy and vulgar political economy. Classical political economy is represented by the physiocrats, Smith, and Ricardo. They at times could grasp the essence of capitalism, although they could not do so consistently. In contrast, vulgar political economists cannot see beyond the commonly accepted notions that capitalism has about itself. They see only appearances and do not grasp the essence of capitalism.

In his critique of classical political economy, Marx's conception of science as an understanding that grasps the essence of social reality as against mere appearances clearly emerges. He maintains that classical political economists "grasp the inner connection of the phenomena" (1972:453), whereas vulgar political economists accept capitalism as it appears in the surface (1972:453–54, 502–3). Moreover, Marx maintains that Smith and Ricardo both consciously operated on both levels of essence and appearance. Thus, Smith discerns the essence of capitalism, in that "he traces the intrinsic connection existing between economic categories or the obscure structure of the bourgeois economic system" (1969b:165). At the same time, he endeavors to describe the system systematically as it appears: "he simultaneously sets forth the connection as it appears in the phenomena of competition and thus as it presents itself to the unscientific observer" (1969b:165). Hence there are two conceptions operating independently and simultaneously. "One of these conceptions fathoms the inner connection, the physiology, so to speak, of the bourgeois system, whereas the other takes the external phenomena of life, as they seem and appear and merely describes, catalogues, recounts and arranges them under formal definitions" (1969b:165). These two approaches contradict one another, but this is justifiable, since Smith is consciously doing both. Smith's successors, however, mix the two together without keeping the distinction between them clearly in mind until Ricardo, who sought "to examine how matters stand with the contradiction between the apparent and the actual movement of the system. This . . . is Ricardo's great historical significance for science" (1969b:166).

For Marx, then, the task of science is to grasp the contradiction between the essence and the appearance of social reality, for in doing so, the scientist can move beyond "what merely appears to be the case" (Barbalet, 1983:25) and can grasp "essential or real relations" (1983:27).[2] Accordingly, it appears that profit emerges from the market, in circulation. The essence, however, is that profit results from unpaid labor. The scientific representatives of political economy were able to grasp to some extent this essence of capitalism.

PARTICULAR INTERESTS, COMMUNAL INTERESTS, AND IDEOLOGY

For Marx, the division of labor in an economic system creates particular interests.

For as soon as the distribution of labor comes into being, each man has a particular, exclusive sphere of activity, which is forced upon him and from which he cannot escape.

He is a hunter, a fisherman, a shepherd, or a critical critic, and must remain so if he does not want to lose his means of livelihood. (Marx & Engels, 1970:53)

At the same time, the division of labor also creates what Marx refers to as the "communal interest" (Marx & Engels, 1970:53).[3] The communal interest refers to "the mutual interdependence of the individuals among whom the labor is divided" (Marx & Engels, 1970:53). Thus, individuals in an economic system have different interests by virtue of the different work they do, but at the same time they have interests in common due to their dependency on one another in an economic system. For Marx, both particular interests and the communal interest are real, for they are created by the division of labor, and as such they are rooted in productive forces. In contrast to such real interests, the so-called "general interest" (Marx & Engels, 1970:53) does not exist in reality but exists "merely in the imagination" (Marx & Engels, 1970:53). The general interest refers to a universal interest that unites all human beings in all economic systems in all times and places. There is, for Marx, no such general interest of all humanity, any more than there is such a thing as human nature.

In their struggle to dominate other classes, dominating classes present their particular interests as general interests. "Every class which is struggling for mastery . . . must first conquer for itself political power in order to represent its interest in turn as the general interest" (Marx & Engels, 1970:54). Moreover, a new class seeking domination represents its particular interests as the communal interests. "For each new class which puts itself in the place of one ruling before it, is compelled, merely in order to carry through its aim, to represent its interest as the common interest of all the members of society" (Marx & Engels, 1970:65–66). The claim of the dominant class that its goals promote the general interest is, of course, fallacious, because there is no general interest. However, the claim of a revolutionary class that its goals promote the communal interest has some validity at first, for the revolutionary class does promote the communal interest in the sense that it promotes a further development of the productive forces. However, once a new stage in production is reached, and once the particular interests of the revolutionary class as a dominating class have taken shape, the dominating class begins to promote its particular interests at the expense of the particular interests of the non-ruling classes. As the productive forces continue to develop, this contradiction between the developing particular interests of the dominant class and the common interest of all in the society becomes manifest. At this point, the particular interests of the newly dominant class become exposed as particular interests (Marx & Engels, 1965:316–17).

In regard to the notion of communal interests, it also should be noted that, since capitalism develops productive forces that go beyond national boundaries and create a world economy, Marx sees capitalism as a force that creates universal human beings, that is, human beings who have interests in common with all other human beings in the world.

Only with this universal development of productive forces is a *universal* intercourse between men established, which produces in all nations simultaneously the phenomenon of the "propertyless" mass (universal competition), makes each nation dependent on the revolutions of the others, and finally has put *world historical*, empirically universal individuals in place of local ones. (Marx & Engels, 1970:56)

The capitalist forces of production, therefore, establish for the first time in human history a communal interest that is global in scope and unites all people in the world by virtue of their mutual dependency in the world economic system.

Marx's understanding of science and ideology is grounded in his distinctions among communal, particular, and general interests. Science promotes the communal interest. This interest is a consequence of the mutual dependency of all in the economic system, a mutual dependency created by the division of labor. This interest is a common interest that all individuals have in maximizing the productivity of the economic system that binds them together. This common interest is distinct from the particular interests that individuals have by virtue of their position in the division of labor. Science, since it is grounded in the common interest, also has an interest in productivity. The vantage point of science, therefore, is the vantage point of productivity, as distinct from the vantage point of particular classes. Moreover, since productivity develops, and since revolutionary classes for a time promote productivity, science too develops, and at particular moments in its development, it takes the vantage point of revolutionary classes. In taking the vantage point of the progressive forces of productivity and revolutionary classes, science can grasp the essence of social reality, or more precisely, the essential dynamics of a developing economic and social system.

In contrast to science, ideology is grounded in particular interests. Ideology promotes the interests of particular classes even when those interests are not consistent with the common interest in maximizing productivity. Because ideology is not rooted in the most progressive forces, it cannot grasp the essential dynamics of the developing economic and social system. It grasps only appearances, and as such, it misunderstands and distorts social reality.[4]

Although Marx believed in science as an arbiter of objective truth, and although Marx was an epistemological realist, he was not guilty of nineteenth-century scientism. Indeed, Marx's conception of science was highly sophisticated for his time. First, as Goran Therborn (1976:409–10) notes, in Marx's understanding, science does not seek to formulate universal laws. Given that the communal interest is grounded in an economic system in a historical time period, and that the communal interest is distinct from a non-existent general interest, it follows that scientific knowledge, for Marx, is historically and socially relative, in that it reflects a particular economic system in a particular stage of its development. Accordingly, Marx believes that scientific laws can be formulated, but he does not take these laws to be eternal laws (Lukács, 1971:49). He rejects any notion of truth as absolute. Rather, Marx seeks objective truth as distinct from absolute truth, and he sees objective truth as valid for a historical time period only (Parekh,

1982:199–200). He believes that scientific laws are relevant only for a particular
time period and for a particular stage of social development (Lukács, 1971:49).
As James Farr notes, Marx was not a positivist, for even though he spoke of
social scientific laws, his understanding of laws differed from that of the positivist. "Marx repeatedly states that laws in the social sciences are 'historical
laws,' that is, 'laws only for a particular historical development' " (Ball & Farr,
1984:227). Similarly, Terence Ball maintains that Marx conceives of laws as
valid only for a historical epoch (Ball & Farr, 1984:245–250).

Second, Marx rejects a copy theory of truth, in that he rejects the theory of
a " 'resemblance' between human judgments and an absolutely independent
reality" (Kolakowski, 1962:183). Accordingly, Marx was not a naive realist
(Korsch, 1970:76–84, 107–8, 117), where a naive realist "defines the truth as
the correspondence of thought to an object that is external to and 'mirrored' by
it" (Korsch, 1970:83). As Joan Cocks notes:

There is almost a new orthodoxy in philosophical circles, concerning the basic principles
of Marx's mature method. In contrast to more than a century of political and academic
opinion, it now is generally agreed that the Marx of the *Grundrisse* and *Capital* is neither
positivist nor any other variant of empiricist. He asserts, of course, that the "true scientist"
begins his social investigations by examining actual, concrete practice and that there are
correct, objectively validable explanations of social life. But he does not pretend to limit
his vocabulary to observation terms or their derivatives and in fact explicitly builds his
economic theory on concepts . . . which do not refer to observable properties or things.
He does not reduce human action to patterns of behavior, nor does he seek its explanation
in external material causes, whose relations to their effect can be subsumed under universal
causal laws. (1983:596–97)

Marx's concept of science was not only sophisticated in the sense that he
avoided the naiveté of nineteenth-century scientism, but also in that he saw the
development of scientific knowledge as interrelated with revolutionary social
movements. As Lorrain observes, "For Marx, there is no absolute truth waiting
to be unveiled, but there is an objective historical truth which deploys itself in
the historical process as men and women practically construct their social world"
(1983:214).

THE MATERIALIST BASIS FOR SCIENTIFIC INSIGHT

Marx, as is well known, had a materialist conception of history, according to
which ideas, philosophy, religion, politics, and family are understood as emerging from the material, productive foundation of society. This materialist conception is clearly seen in his critique of German philosophy in *The German
Ideology*:

In direct contrast to German philosophy which descends from heaven to earth, here we
ascend from earth to heaven. That is to say, we do not set out from what men say,

imagine, conceive, nor from men as narrated, thought of, imagined, conceived, in order
to arrive at men in the flesh. We set out from real, active men, and on the basis of their
real life-process we demonstrate the development of the ideological reflexes and echoes
of this life-process. The phantoms formed in the human brain are also, necessarily,
sublimates of their material life-process, which is empirically verifiable and bound to
material premises. Morality, religion, metaphysics, all the rest of ideology and their
corresponding forms of consciousness, thus no longer retain the semblance of independence. They have no history, no development; but men, developing their material production and their material intercourse, alter, along with this their real existence, their
thinking and the products of their thinking. Life is not determined by consciousness, but
consciousness by life. (Marx & Engels, 1970:47)

Thus, consciousness reflects social position: ''Consciousness is, therefore, from
the very beginning a social product, and remains so as long as men exist at all''
(1970:51).

   If Marx understood that consciousness reflects position, why did he believe
in the possibility of a form of knowledge that does not reflect the interests of
particular social positions but promotes the common interest of all who are
connected to one another by the forces of production? Why did he believe in
the possibility of a science of society that understood social reality not from the
limited vantage point of particular interests but from the comprehensive vantage
point grounded in common interest? Did he believe that scientists, in having a
capacity to grasp the essence of social reality as against mere appearances, were
in some sense an exception to the general law that understanding reflects social
position?

   To address these questions requires a careful examination of Marx's critique
of the political economists, which is found primarily in *Theories of Surplus
Value*, for it is in this critique that Marx's understanding of the scientific process
emerges. Through such an examination, it becomes clear that Marx did not in
any sense believe that scientific knowledge was an exception to the insight that
knowledge is shaped by social position. Rather, Marx saw the development of
the material forces of production as establishing the material conditions that
make possible scientific knowledge, a knowledge grounded in common interest,
a knowledge that grasps the essence of social reality as against what appears to
be when viewed from the vantage point of particular interests. The possibility
of science as a form of knowledge that sees beyond particular interests is established by the development of the material forces of production. That this was
Marx's view can be seen in his analysis of the mercantilists, the Physiocrats,
Adam Smith, and David Ricardo. In Marx's view, these political economists
formulated key insights in regard to the economic system, insights that were
made possible by the development of the economic system itself. At the same
time, there were important limitations in their understanding, limitations that
were reflections of the level of development of the economic system at the time
in which they wrote. Moreover, Marx viewed the further development of the
economic system in his own time as making possible previously unimagined

insights which push the science of political economy to a new stage in its development. He saw his own critique of political economy as seizing upon this possibility and as reconceptualizing political economy for this new stage.

A central theme in Marx's analysis of the political economists is the question of the origin or source of surplus value. Marx, as we have seen, believed that labor power, and more particularly, unpaid labor, is the source of surplus value. He believed that the formulation of this insight established political economy as a science. However, the political economists could not consistently grasp the implications and significance of this insight. A central theme in Marx's critique of political economy, therefore, was an analysis of the material foundations of the insights and limitations of the political economists in regard to the question of the origin of surplus value.

The Mercantilists

For Marx, the first interpreters of the modern world were the mercantilists (Marx, 1970:157–58). The mercantilists did not grasp that surplus labor is the source of surplus value. They erroneously believed that the sale of a commodity above its value is the source of surplus value (Marx, 1967:41, 178–79). Hence they believed that wealth originates in the circulation of money, especially gold and silver (Marx, 1970:158). However, Marx maintains that this error is understandable, given the limited capitalist development in the sixteenth and seventeenth centuries when the mercantilists wrote.

One has to remember that in those times national production was for the most part still carried on within the framework of feudal forms and served as the immediate source of subsistence for the producers themselves. Most products did not become commodities; they were accordingly neither converted into money nor entered at all into the general process of the social metabolism; hence they did not appear as materialisation of universal abstract labour and did not indeed constitute bourgeois wealth. Money as the end and object of circulation represents exchange-value or abstract wealth, not as any physical element of wealth, as the determining purpose and driving motive of production. It was consistent with the rudimentary stage of bourgeois production that those misunderstood prophets should have clung to the solid, palpable and glittering form of exchange-value, to exchange-value in the form of the universal commodity as distinct from all particular commodities. The sphere of commodity circulation was the strictly bourgeois economic sphere at that time. They therefore analyzed the whole complex process of bourgeois production from the standpoint of that basic sphere and confused money with capital. (Marx, 1970:158)

Thus, bourgeois production was limited at the time of the mercantilists, in that most products were not part of bourgeois production. And the circulation of money in the form of gold and silver, rather than the production of commodities, was the driving force of bourgeois economic activity at that time. Therefore, it made sense to see the source of profit in the circulation and exchange of money and other commodities rather than in the production of commodities. And in seeing the source of surplus value in circulation rather than production, the mercantilists came to the understanding that the source of surplus value lies in the exchange of commodities above their value. This formulation, Marx maintains, was valid for its time and even has some validity in a more developed capitalism in regard to certain sectors of the economy.

Political economy errs in its critique of the Monetary and Mercantile systems when it assails them as mere illusions, as utterly wrong theories, and fails to notice that they contain in a primitive form its own basic presuppositions. These systems, moreover, remain not only historically valid but retain their full validity within certain spheres of the modern economy. . . . The functions of gold and silver as money . . . are not abolished even in the most advance bourgeois economy, but merely restricted; the Monetary and Mercantile systems accordingly remain valid. (Marx, 1970:159)

The Physiocrats

Marx viewed the Physiocrats as the founders of the science of political economy. They were the first to formulate a systematic theory of capitalist production (Marx, 1933:415), and they were the first to analyze capitalism "within the bourgeois horizon" (Marx, 1969a:44). Most importantly, they "transferred the inquiry into the origin of surplus-value from the sphere of circulation into the sphere of direct production" (1969a:45), and this enabled them to grasp the fact that labor is the source of surplus-value (1969a:46). However, the Physiocrats erroneously believed that surplus value is generated only by agricultural labor. Consequently, they erroneously saw rent as the only form of surplus value and industrial profit as a form of rent.

Hence for the Physiocrats agricultural labour is the only *productive labour*, because it is the only labour that *produces a surplus-value*, and *rent* is the *only form of surplus-value* which they know. The workman in industry does not increase the material substance; he only alters its form. The material—the mass of material substance—is given to him by agriculture. . . . Because agricultural labour is conceived as the only productive labour, the form of surplus-value which distinguishes agricultural labour from industrial labour, *rent*, is conceived as the only form of surplus-value. (Marx, 1969a:46–47)

The Physiocratic understanding is related to the nature and stage of economic development. In order for surplus value to be generated, the level of productivity must be high enough to make possible production by laborers of material goods greater in value than the value of the goods which are necessary for the subsistence of the laborers. This capacity to harness the forces of nature with such power as to make surplus value possible first emerges in agriculture. Hence, the emergence of agriculture is a necessary pre-condition for the emergence of surplus value and for the insight that labor is the origin of surplus value. But although this condition is necessary, it is not sufficient. There also must emerge capitalist farmers, who engage in capitalist production in agriculture.

The representative of capitalist production, the class of capitalist farmers, directs the entire economic movement. Agriculture is carried on capitalistically, that is to say, it is the enterprise of a capitalist farmer on a large scale; the immediate cultivator of the soil is the wage laborer. Production creates not only articles of use, but also their value; its compelling motive is the production of surplus-value. (Marx, 1933:415)

Once this class of capitalist farmers emerges, it is possible to develop a "systematic conception of capitalist production" (1933:415), which is written from the vantage point of the bourgeoisie. And it is possible to grasp in such capitalist agriculture described from a capitalist vantage point the origin of surplus value in labor. This insight, impossible prior to the emergence of a class of capitalist farmers, becomes possible once such a class emerges as a significant social force. The formulation of this insight was the achievement of the Physiocrats.

At the same time, that the Physiocrats would erroneously see surplus value as generated only by agricultural labor is a consequence of the fact that the Physiocrats wrote before the emergence of large-scale industry. The production of surplus value in industry is only possible with the emergence of large-scale industry: "this utilization of the forces of nature on a large scale appears in manufacture only with the development of large-scale industry" (1969a:49). Since the Physiocrats were writing before the emergence of large-scale industry, they could not possibly grasp the origin of surplus value in its general form.

Adam Smith

Whereas the Physiocrats analyzed the economic system from the vantage point of the agricultural capitalists, Adam Smith, according to Marx, was a proponent of the industrial capitalists (Marx, 1969a:175). As a result, Smith could move political economy to a new level of understanding in regard to the question of the origin of surplus value and formulate the insight that surplus value originates not only in agricultural labor but in general social labor.

We see the great advance made by Adam Smith beyond the Physiocrats in the analysis of surplus-value and hence of capital. In their view, it is only one definite kind of concrete labour—agricultural labour—that creates surplus-value. . . . But to Adam Smith, it is general social labour . . . which creates value. Surplus-value, whether it takes the form of profit, rent, or the secondary form of interest, is nothing but a part of this labour, appropriated by the owners of the material conditions of labour in the exchange with living labour. For the Physiocrats, therefore, surplus-value appears only in the form of rent of land. For Adam Smith, rent, profit and interest are only different forms of surplus-value. (Marx, 1969a:85)

However, because Smith wrote before the emergence of large-scale industry, he could not construct a consistent theoretical system from the vantage point of the industrial bourgeoisie, and he often lapses into the Physiocratic viewpoint. Thus, for Marx, "Adam Smith still reflects the prehistory of large-scale industry and for this reason upholds the Physiocratic point of view" (1969a:60). As a result, Smith's work is full of contradictions, as the Physiocratic elements in his writing contradict his most important insights. As Marx notes, "Adam Smith is very copiously infected with the conceptions of the Physiocrats, and often whole strata run through his work which belong to the Physiocrats and are in complete contradiction with the views specifically advanced by him" (1969a:70).

The inconsistencies in Smith's analysis are especially significant in his two contradictory definitions of productive labor. The first definition is the correct one, and it follows from Smith's grasp of the origin of surplus value in unpaid labor: productive labor is that labor that produces surplus value (1969a:152–53). Consistent with this correct definition of productive labor is Smith's corresponding definition of unproductive labor as labor that exchanges not with capital but with revenue. A tailor who repairs a capitalist's trousers in exchange for money is an example of unproductive labor, because, from the point of view of the capitalist, the money is revenue and not capital, and the tailor is not producing an exchange value (1969a:157). Thus, unproductive labor is labor that provides something that the purchaser of labor power uses rather than sells. "The productive labourer produces commodities for the buyer of his labour-power. The unproductive labourer produces for him a mere use-value, not a commodity" (1969a:160), where a commodity "is never an immediate object of consumption, but a bearer of exchange-value" (1969a:159). Or again: "The same labour can be productive when I buy it as a capitalist, as a producer, in order to create more value, and unproductive when I buy it as a consumer, a sender of revenue, in order to consume its use-value" (1969a:165).

In contrast to these correct definitions of productive and unproductive labor, according to Marx, are Smith's second incorrect definitions. Smith incorrectly defines productive labor as labor that produces a quantity of labor equal to what has been paid to the laborer: "The labour of a labourer is called productive in so far as he replaces the consumed value by an equivalent, by adding to any material, through his labour, a quantity of value equal to that which was contained in his wages" (1969a:162). Here Smith has fallen back into the error of the Physiocrats: he takes industrial labor to be simply the production of the value of its own consumption, whereas agricultural labor produces surplus value. And he incorrectly defines unproductive labor as labor that does not produce material things but produces services that are consumed in their use. This is incorrect, for Marx, because providing a service involves the production of surplus value when it is purchased by a capitalist in order to sell it. This occurs, for example, when a hotel proprietor purchases the services of a cook. But a service does not involve the production of surplus value when it is purchased in order to use it, as when a capitalist pays for a meal cooked for him. Hence, for Marx, Smith's erroneous distinction between productive and unproductive labor ignores the social relation between the purchaser and the owner of labor power, and the relation of the exchange between them to capitalist production. If the purchaser of labor power uses the labor in order to produce commodities that are to be exchanged for money, then the labor is productive labor. If, on the other hand, the purchaser of labor power uses the labor to obtain goods or services for his own use, then the labor is unproductive labor. (1969a:164–67).

For Marx, Smith's correct and incorrect definitions of productive labor follow from Smith's position as a proponent of the newly emerging industrial bourgeoisie. On the one hand, by taking the vantage point of the industrial bourgeoisie, Smith was able to grasp that general social labor, not just agricultural labor, is the source of surplus value. But on the other hand, Smith's advocacy of the industrial bourgeoisie led him to polemics with the Physiocrats as advocates of the agricultural capitalists. These polemical exchanges led him into some errors that were inconsistent with his key insights. For although he lapsed into the Physiocratic viewpoint in regard to the belief that agricultural labor is the most productive, he at the same time wants to argue, against the Physiocrats, that industrial labor is productive. This leads him to the error that labor which does not produce surplus value is productive (1969a:162–63). He has lost sight of his own insight, as well as that of the Physiocrats, that productive labor produces surplus value.

His polemics with the Physiocrats aside, Smith in any event could not have developed a consistent theoretical system from the vantage point of the industrial bourgeoisie, because he was writing before the emergence of modern, large-scale industry. His distinction between productive and unproductive labor reflects the vantage point of the industrial bourgeoisie before the emergence of modern industry. To label " 'higher grade' workers" (1969a:174), such as "state officials, military people, artists, doctors, priests, judges, lawyers" (1969a:174), unproductive reflects a negative attitude toward them. Smith, in fact, advocated a reduction of the number of unproductive laborers. For their part, the unproductive laborers themselves did not approve of the label. As Marx notes, these workers "found it not at all pleasant to be relegated *economically* to the same class as clowns and menial servants and to appear merely as people partaking in the consumption, parasites on the actual producers" (1969a:175). This negative attitude that Smith adopted was, however, typical of the attitude of the industrial bourgeoisie, since these workers were under the control of the feudal aristocracy. However, as capitalism developed after Smith, the bourgeoisie transformed the state and the ideological professions, so that they began to function to promote the interests of the bourgeoisie. When this occurred, Smith's definition of unproductive labor was attacked by subsequent political economists who were proponents of the industrial bourgeoisie and of the ideological professions under its control.

It was therefore time to make a compromise and to recognise the "productivity" of all classes not directly included among the agents of material production. . . . It had to be established that even from the "productive," economic standpoint, the bourgeois world with all its "unproductive labourers" is the best of all worlds. . . . Both the *do-nothings* and their *parasites* had to be found a place in this best possible order of things. (1969a:176)

And so:

As the dominion of capital extended . . . , the sycophantic underlings of political economy felt it their duty to glorify and justify every sphere of activity by demonstrating that it was "linked" with the production of material wealth, that it was a means towards it; and they honoured everyone by making him a "productive labourer" in the "primary" sense, namely, a labourer who labors in the service of capital. (1969a:176)

Marx views these political economists who criticized Smith as second rate scientists who did not make the kind of contribution to political economy that Smith's work represents (1969a:174–77).

David Ricardo

Once modern industry emerged, the essential dynamics of capitalism could be discerned, and a more consistent theoretical analysis could be formulated. For Marx, the work of David Ricardo represented such a more insightful analysis. Ricardo's thought, Marx maintains, reflected the social position and the stage of economic development in which Ricardo wrote. In the first place, Ricardo's work focused on the period 1770–1815 (1969b:236), which was after the emergence of modern industry in England (1969a:60–61). Second, England was at that time the most advanced capitalist country in the world. Far more than any other country, it had removed the fetters of traditional feudal society. As Marx observes:

Nowhere in the world has capitalist production, since Henry VII, dealt so ruthlessly with the *traditional* relations of agriculture, adapting and subordinating the conditions to its own requirements. In this respect England is the most revolutionary country in the world. Wherever the conditions handed down from history were at variance with, or did not correspond to, the requirements of capitalist production on the land, they were ruthlessly swept away. . . . The German, for example, meets with economic relations that are determined by traditional circumstances. . . . The Englishman meets with historical conditions of agriculture which have been progressively *created* by capital since the end of the 15th century. . . . None of the conditions of production are accepted as they have traditionally existed but are historically *transformed* in such a way that under the circumstances, they will provide the most profitable investment for capital. . . . English conditions are the only ones in which *modern ownership*, i.e., landownership which has been *modified* by capitalist production, has been adequately developed. (1969b:237–38)

Writing from the vantage point of the most advanced capitalist country that had developed to the stage of modern industry, Ricardo could arrive at new insights in regard to capitalism. Earlier English political economists, writing at an earlier stage in capitalist development, were unable to grasp these insights. Similarly, political economists on the continent who were critical of Ricardo were unable to grasp the correctness of Ricardo's insights because of "the lower stage in the conditions of production from which these 'sages' start out" (1969b:240).

Given a superior vantage point rooted in advanced material conditions, Ricardo could see the correctness of Smith's first distinction between productive and unproductive labor. Moreover, he went beyond this definition and argued, against Smith, that the number of productive laborers out to be reduced.

Ricardo fully shares Adam Smith's view of the distinction between productive and unproductive labour, that the former exchanges its labour directly for capital, [the latter] directly for revenue. But he no longer shares Smith's tenderness for and illusion about the productive labourer. A productive labourer is a labourer who produces wealth *for another*. His existence only has meaning as such an instrument of production for the wealth of others. If therefore the same quantity of wealth for others can be created with a smaller number of productive labourers, then the suppression of these productive labourers is in order. (1969a:225)

Hence, Ricardo arrives at the realization that technical progress involves the reduction of the number of productive laborers.

A country is the richer the smaller its productive population is *relatively* to the total product; just as for the individual capitalist: the fewer labourers he needs to produce the same surplus, so much the better for him. The country is the richer the smaller the productive population in relation to the unproductive, the quantity of products remaining the same. For the relative smallness of the productive population would be only another way of expressing the relative degree of the productivity of labour. (1969a:227)

Thus, Ricardo was the first to grasp "the tendency of capital to reduce to a dwindling minimum the labour-time necessary for the production of commodities" (1969a:227).

However, Ricardo could not grasp the full significance of this insight, according to Marx. Because he wrote before the emergence of the proletariat as a revolutionary class, he could not see the significance of this insight from a proletarian point of view. Indeed, his work reflected contradictory tendencies in capitalism itself. On the one hand, capitalism has a tendency to reduce necessary labor time and the number of productive laborers. On the other hand, driven by profit, capitalism has the opposite tendency to maximize the appropriation of labor power and thus to increase the number of productive laborers. Reflecting this contradiction, Ricardo, on the one hand, grasps the potential of capitalism to reduce labor time to marginal time. On the other hand, Ricardo sees unlimited production as desirable, because it increases the accumulation of capital and increases employment. He therefore argues that lower wages are in the interest of workers, because lower wages lead to a greater accumulation of capital, and therefore greater employment (1969a:227–29). In this, Ricardo fails to see that the tendency of capital to reduce labor time makes possible a different type of society, a more humane society, a society characterized by the reduction of necessary labor time and by versatile labor. To see this would have required analyzing the issue from the vantage point of the proletariat, which Ricardo could not have imagined because he was writing before the conflict between the bourgeoisie and the proletariat became manifest.

As Ricardo developed a new theoretical formulation in a direction away from Smith, and given that he was unable to take a proletarian point of view, he lost sight of Smith's most important insight, namely, that unpaid labor is the source of surplus value. Thus, Ricardo overlooks the fact that the worker spends part of the working day producing the value of his own subsistence and thus working for himself, and part of the day working for the capitalist in the form of unpaid, surplus labor. And he overlooks the fact that the length of the working day is not fixed, and that, given a particular level of productivity, the length of the working day determines the amount of surplus labor and thus the amount of surplus value. Ricardo therefore overlooks the significance of the struggle over the length of the working day.

Ricardo, . . . by not *directly* showing that one *part* of the labourer's *working day* is assigned to the reproduction of the value of his own labour-power, he introduces a difficulty and obscures the clear understanding of the relationship. A twofold confusion arises from this. The *origin of surplus-value* does not become clear and consequently Ricardo is reproached by his successors for having failed to grasp and expound the nature of surplus-value. . . . But because . . . the *total working day* is regarded as a fixed magnitude, the differences in the amount of surplus-value are overlooked, and the productivity of capital, the *compulsion to perform surplus-labour* . . . are not recognized (1969b:405).

It is obvious that if the labourer needed his whole day to produce his own means of subsistence (i.e., commodities equal to the value of his own means of subsistence), there could be no surplus-value, and therefore no capitalist production and no wage labour. This can only exist when the productivity of social labour is sufficiently developed to make possible some sort of excess of the total working-day over the labour-time required for the reproduction of the wage—i.e., *surplus labour*. . . . But it is equally obvious that . . . the length of the working-day may be very different . . . The labourer must first be *compelled* to work in excess of the necessary time, and this compulsion is exerted by capital. This is missing in Ricardo's work, and therefore also the whole struggle over the regulation of the normal working-day. (1969b:406)

In Volume I of *Capital*, Marx treats the struggle of the workers to limit the working day seriously. In Marx's view, this struggle is significant, because the length of the working day determines the amount of unpaid labor that the worker is coerced to provide. The capitalist has an interest in maximizing the length of the working day, for given that necessary labor time is constant for a particular level of productivity, the way for the capitalist to increase profits is to lengthen the working day. On the other hand, from the point of view of the worker, surplus labor time contributes only to the wealth of the capitalist. Hence, it is in the interests of the workers to limit the length of the working day, and thus there emerged the historic struggle between capital and labor over the length of the working day. Ricardo, however, cannot take a proletarian point of view and so loses sight of the basic insights of political economy and fails to grasp the significance of the struggle over the length of the working day.

In Marx's view, however, Ricardo, like the Physiocrats and Adam Smith and unlike the other political economists of Ricardo's time, was a scientist. Ricardo's work, to be sure, had many inadequacies and confusions (1969b:164–66, 174–99). However, these difficulties are to a large extent consequences of the limited stage of capitalist development at the time in which Ricardo wrote. To his credit as a scientist, Ricardo was able to seize upon the possibilities for understanding that the development of the material conditions provided. Accordingly, he was able to grasp the essential dynamics of capitalism and to discern the tendency of capitalism as it develops to reduce necessary productive labor time. The key to this insight is the fact that Ricardo, writing after the emergence of modern industry and in the most advanced capitalist country, was able to analyze the development of the productive forces from the vantage point of the industrial bourgeoisie. Ricardo, Marx maintains, was scientifically justified in taking this vantage point, for at that stage of capitalist development, the interests of the industrial bourgeoisie coincided with the interests of the development of the productive forces. And science above all has an interest in maximizing productivity, because increasing productive capacity ultimately increases human well-being. Marx takes what he describes as a ruthless view in this regard. He is in favor of "production for the sake of production" (1969b:117), for "production for its own sake means nothing but the development of human productive forces, in other words the *development of the richness of human nature as an end in itself*" (1969b:118). He is opposed to the sentimentality which argues that "the development of the species must be *arrested* in order to safeguard the welfare of the individual" (1969b:118). Such sentimental arguments

reveal a failure to understand the fact that, although at first the development of the capacities of the *human* species takes place at the cost of the majority of human individuals and even classes, in the end it breaks through this contradiction and coincides with the development of the individual; the higher development of individuality is thus only achieved by a historical process during which individuals are sacrificed, for the interests of the species in the human kingdom, as in the animal and plant kingdoms, always assert themselves at the cost of the interest of individuals, because these interests of the species coincide only with the *interests of certain individuals*, and it is this coincidence which constitutes the strength of these privileged individuals. (1969b:118)

Ricardo, Marx maintains, understood this. He took the point of view of the industrial bourgeoisie because the interests of the industrial bourgeoisie, at the time in which Ricardo wrote, coincided with the interests of productivity.

Ricardo's paramount commitment was not to the industrial bourgeoisie per se, but to productivity and science. Indeed, in those circumstances where the interests of the industrial bourgeoisie were opposed to the interests of productivity, Ricardo went against the interests of the industrial bourgeoisie because of his commitment to science.

Ricardo's ruthlessness was not only *scientifically honest* but also a *scientific necessity* from his point of view. But because of this it is also quite immaterial to him whether the advance of the productive forces slays landed property or workers. If this progress devalues the capital of the industrial bourgeoisie it is equally welcome to him. If the development of the productive power of labour halves the value of the *existing* fixed capital, what does it matter, says Ricardo. The productivity of human labour has doubled. Thus here is *scientific honesty*. Ricardo's conception is, on the whole, in the interests of the *industrial bourgeoisie*, only *because*, and *in so far as*, their interests coincide with that of production or the productive development of human labour. Where the bourgeoisie comes into conflict with this, he is just as *ruthless* towards it as he is at other times towards the proletariat and the aristocracy. (Marx, 1969b:118)

Marx's critique of Ricardo reveals three aspects of Marx's conception of science. First, as was seen in Marx's critique of the mercantilists, the Physiocrats, and Smith, Marx sees a relationship between understanding and material development, according to which the stage of economic development establishes possibilities for and limitations to understanding. Second, Marx sees a scientific viewpoint as one that takes the vantage point of productivity, which has an interest in maximum productivity. This view is rooted in Marx's belief that increased productivity ultimately enhances human well-being. Third, Marx views particular class interests as coinciding with the interests of productivity. There is, for Marx, nothing eternal about this. The interests of a particular class coincide with the interests of productivity only during that time when the class is a revolutionary class. Marx's view was that in Ricardo's time the industrial bourgeoisie promoted the interests of productivity, and therefore Ricardo was scientifically justified in taking the point of view of the industrial bourgeoisie. At the same time, Marx believed that the proletariat in his own time promotes the interests of productivity. Therefore, in his time, science requires taking the point of view of the proletariat.

Vulgar Political Economy

As capitalism developed, its inherent contradictions grew deeper and became more manifest, and the contradiction between the wealth of the few and the misery of the workers became increasingly apparent (Marx, 1972:259). As a result, the working class became increasingly aware of its interests and increasingly constituted itself as a class organized to promote its interests. The manifestation of this conflict of interests established the possibility for the science of political economy to analyze itself critically from the vantage point of proletarian interests. However, such a transformation of the categories of political economy was merely a possibility. Another possibility was for political economy to constitute itself self-consciously as an apologist for bourgeois interests and thus as a defender of the established order. The first possibility represents science, the second, ideology. Thus, after the conflict between the bourgeoisie and the proletariat became manifest, political economists were forced to choose between science and ideology. As Parekh observes:

When, thanks to the inner dynamics of capitalism itself and the proletarian praxis, the falsity of the assumptions [of classical political economy] was demonstrated beyond a shadow of doubt, the classical economist was confronted with a crisis. He could no longer continue to think within the traditional framework. His "more or less" conscious assumptions had now been brought into the open and exposed; the moment of truth had arrived; and the classical economist was forced to choose between science and ideology. (Parekh, 1982:125)

The political economists who opted at this historical moment to promote the interests of the bourgeoisie created vulgar political economy. As Parekh notes, vulgar political economists "gave up all scientific pretensions and became the 'hired prize fighters' for the established order. They distorted unpalatable truths [and] employed pseudo-scientific arguments to support their thinly disguised prejudices" (1982:126).

For Marx, the emergence of vulgar political economy is inherent in the contradictions of capitalism, for given the interest of the bourgeoisie in preserving the established order, and given the use of ideology as an instrument of domination, the bourgeoisie would be expected to have its proponents in the ideological professions. Vulgar political economy had been an element in political economy since the work of Adam Smith, for insofar as classical political economy grasps the essential dynamics of capitalism, there will be those who will react to this with no pretense to science. Thus, political economy itself contains contradictions that reflect the contradictions of capitalism. As the contradictions in capitalism developed, political economy increasingly was able to grasp these contradictions. As this occurred, the number of political economists who self-consciously sided with bourgeois interests increased. Thus, political economy became increasingly characterized by a contradiction between its scientific element, which grasps the contractions of capitalism, and its opposite, vulgar political economy, which is a conscious apologist for bourgeois interests. The more political economy "penetrates its subject-matter and the more it develops as a contradictory system, the more is it confronted by its own increasingly independent, vulgar element" (Marx, 1972:501). Or again:

To the degree that economic analysis becomes more profound it not only describes contradictions, but it is confronted by its own contradiction simultaneously with the development of the actual contradictions in the economic life of the society. Accordingly, vulgar political economy deliberately becomes increasingly *apologetic* and makes strenuous attempts to talk out of existence the ideas which contain the contradictions. (Marx, 1972:501)

For Marx, the year 1830 marked the turning point for political economy, because in that year "in both England and France class antagonisms assumed serious proportions" (Bober, 1950:161). With this development, the inadequacy of analyzing capitalism from the vantage point of the bourgeoisie became manifest, and science from that moment required an analysis of political economy from the vantage point of the proletariat. But the political economists after 1830 were unwilling to take this step. Accordingly, the scientific element disappears from political economy, and the science of political economy gives way to its opposite, vulgar political economy. Marx saw his own work as a critique of political economy from a proletarian vantage point. As such, he viewed his work as science, and he saw it as belonging to the legacy of the classical and scientific political economy of the Physiocrats, Smith, and Ricardo and in opposition to the vulgar political economy of his time. As to the subsequent development of vulgar political economy, its

last form is the *academic form*, which proceeds "historically" and, with wise moderation, collects the "best" from all sources, and in doing this contradictions do not matter; on the contrary, what matters is comprehensiveness. All systems are thus made insipid, their edge is taken off and they are peacefully gathered together in a miscellany. The head of apologetics is moderated here by erudition, which looks down benignly on the exaggerations of economic thinkers. (1972:502)

Socialists, Utopian and Vulgar

As a young journalist in 1842, Marx had begun reading socialists and communists.[5] It appears to have had little effect on him at first. However, when Marx moved to Paris in October 1843, his personal contact with the working-class struggle and his study of British political economy had a profound effect on his thinking, and he became for a time an enthusiastic supporter of the socialist writers.[6] For example, in *The Holy Family*, written from September to November 1844, Marx praises Proudhon's *What Is Property?* as a scientific treatise in political economy written in the interests of the proletariat (Marx & Engels, 1975d:31–33, 41). He lends unqualified support to Proudhon against the criticisms of his work by the young Hegelian Edgar Bauer (1975d:23–54). Moreover, he cites approvingly communist and socialist writers (1975d:84), and he praises French materialism, represented by socialism and communism, as a dimension of the Enlightenment (1975d:124–26).

By the time Marx was writing *The Poverty of Philosophy* (December 1846 through April 1847), he had developed a much more critical posture toward Proudhon and other socialists. In his critique of socialist writings as found in *The Poverty of Philosophy* and *Theories of Surplus Value*, Marx distinguished between utopian socialism and vulgar socialism. Utopian socialism was written before the emergence of the proletariat as a revolutionary class. These socialists and communists, who were "the theoreticians of the proletarian class" (Marx, 1963:125), had a desire "to meet the wants of the oppressed classes" (1963:125). Unlike Ricardo, such socialists and communists were unable to take the ruthless view that the misery created by capitalism will ultimately benefit society by improving productivity. They were unable to take the view that "poverty is . . . merely the pang which accompanies every childbirth, in nature as in industry" (1963:124). Because these socialists and communists wrote before the proletariat constituted itself as a revolutionary class, they created merely utopian theoretical systems. Before the manifestation of the conflict between the bourgeoisie and the proletariat, science reflected a bourgeois point of view, and it was not possible to arrive at scientific insights from a proletarian point of view.

Distinct from utopian socialists, vulgar socialists, for Marx, were those who wrote after 1830 and who attempted to write from a proletarian point of view but who did not grasp the contradictions of capitalism. Marx maintains that as the contraction in capitalism between wealth and poverty became more apparent, "it was natural for those thinkers who rallied to the side of the proletariat to seize on this contradiction" (Marx, 1972:260). They thus proclaimed that "capital is *nothing* but defrauding of the worker. *Labour* is *everything*" (1972:260). They proposed, therefore, to "eliminate capital" (1972:260) by "transforming all men into actual workers exchanging equal amounts of labor" (Marx 1963:69). Marx maintains that in this proposal the socialists are turning the bourgeois illusion of equal exchange into an ideal, in that they are saying that the economic system ought to adopt egalitarian exchanges (1963:78). Such idealism, for Marx, ignores the fact that the bourgeoisie has an interest in preserving capital. Moreover, such idealism fails to grasp that capital is a necessary consequence of the capitalist mode of production, and capital cannot be eliminated without a transformation of the mode of production itself (1972:260). Thus, the vulgar socialists attempt to take a proletarian point of view, but their analyses are rooted in Ricardian assumptions (1972:260), which are grounded in a bourgeois point of view. As a result, they do not "*understand* the contradictions they describe" (1972:260). They have fallen short of the requirements of science for their time: they have not accomplished a transformation of the science of political economy from a proletarian point of view.

The unscientific character of vulgar socialism is illustrated by Proudhon. Proudhon, Marx maintains, misunderstood Hegel's concept of the dialectic. Proudhon writes of a contradiction between the good and the bad, where the good is equality and the bad negates equality. Proudhon wants to remove the bad and keep the good. This conception, for Marx, is static and idealistic. It does not grasp the dynamic movement of the forces of production, and therefore it does not grasp that privilege cannot be eliminated without transforming the economic system (Marx, 1963:107–22).

Summary

In Marx's understanding of science, the development of the material forces of production makes new scientific insights possible and at the same time establishes limits to scientific understanding. Accordingly, the mercantilists could not grasp that labor is the source of surplus value, because they wrote before the emergence of capitalist agriculture. Writing after the emergence of a class of capitalist farmers, the Physiocrats could grasp that labor is the source of surplus value. However, writing from the vantage point of an agricultural capitalist class, they erroneously applied these insights only to agriculture, and they could not grasp that unpaid industrial labor also creates surplus value. Adam Smith, writing from the vantage point of the industrial bourgeoisie, arrived at the insight that general social labor, and not merely agriculture labor, is the source of surplus value. However, writing before the emergence of large-scale industry, Smith lapses into Physiocratic conceptions and falls victim to many inconsistencies. David Ricardo, writing from the vantage point of the industrial bourgeoisie after the emergence of large-scale industry, was able to grasp the tendency of capitalism to reduce labor time. However, writing before the emergence of the proletarian movement, Ricardo was unable to discern the significance of this insight in relation to the possibilities for a new type of society. Writing from a proletarian vantage point, Marx saw his own work as articulating these possibilities and as moving the science of political economy to its next level of understanding. Those who continue to write from the vantage point of the industrial bourgeoisie after the emergence of the proletarian struggle create not science but either vulgar political economy or vulgar socialism, depending on their point of view.

Marx's critique of the political economists from the Physiocrats to the vulgar political economists and the vulgar socialists has left us with a powerful and useful conception of social scientific knowledge. Marx he has left us with an understanding of the connection of social science to social conflicts, according to which emerging social movements establish both possibilities for and limitations to social scientific insight. This understanding implies a moral imperative for social scientists to take seriously the interests of emerging social groups as well as to recognize the historical connectedness of any insights which might emerge. In Marx's time, this moral imperative took the form of taking seriously the interests of the proletarian class. In our own time, now that national liberation movements in the Third World have become manifest, the moral imperative takes the form of taking seriously the interests of the Third World. Such a new vantage point constitutes the foundation for a transformation of the categories of classical Marxism. Such a transformation of classical Marxism is most consistent with Marx, for it follows Marx's understanding concerning the process through which one comes to scientific insight. These issues will be explored more fully in subsequent chapters.

NOTES

1. For Marx's formulation of his thesis that labor power is the source of value and surplus labor is the source of surplus value, see Marx, 1967:177–230.

2. Lorrain (1983:223) and Cohen (1978:326–36) also argued that Marx believed that science grasps essential relations behind appearances.

3. This is rendered in the German as "gemeinschaftlichen Interesse" (Marx and Engels 1932:22).

4. Some scholars reject the notion that Marx saw ideology as a distortion of social reality. Lenin and Lukács, for example, have a positive concept of ideology, and they refer to a proletarian scientific ideology (Lorrain, 1983:69). Lorrain notes, however, that because neither had access to *The German Ideology*, they "were not acquainted with Marx's and Engel's most forceful thesis in favor of a negative concept of ideology" (1983:54). In a similar vein, Sprinzak maintains that ideology, for Marx, is not false knowledge, for Marx accepted a positive interpretation of ideology, according to which all thought is ideological, in that it reflects material conditions (1975:395–400). Marx, according to Sprinzak, did not contrast ideology with science, for science, as all thought, emerges from material conditions (1975:409). However, most recent interpretations of Marx maintain that Marx had a negative view of ideologies as distortions of social reality. Lorrain, for example, maintains that Marx saw ideologies as distortions, as misrepresentations of social contradictions in the interests of the ruling class (1983:25–30; 1979:46–52). Similarly, for Althusser, history is difficult to explain scientifically, because of the ideologies generated by the ruling class, and the function of science is to see through ideology (1976:55–56). He maintains that ideology is not necessarily error as against knowledge, but rather, more precisely, ideologies are ideas which function to perpetuate class domination (1976:154–56). In a similar vein, Schaff maintains that, for Marx, ideology is a distortion of understanding due to the influence of class interests (1976:137). Therefore, Marx did not refer to a scientific ideology or a proletarian ideology (1976:137). He did not view his own theory as "ideology" (1976:138). Finally, Parekh writes that, for Marx, ideology is a "body of thought resulting from the universalization of a partial and narrow point of view" which is grounded in a particular social group (1982:29). Ideologies obscure conflicts of interest and present the existing social order as natural (1982:57–58).

5. McLellan maintains that "the words socialism and communism were used almost interchangeably about this time [1844]. The word 'socialism' first became current among the Owenites in the 1820s; 'communism' was a more particular term of recent French origin, applying the doctrines of men such as Cabet and Dezamy and involving especially the abolition of private property" (1970:183–84).

6. See Chapter 5.

4

THE PROLETARIAN
POINT OF VIEW

Taking the proletarian point of view is a central dimension of Marx's effort to move the science of political economy to a level of understanding appropriate for a time of proletarian struggle. Marx believes that doing so makes possible insights previously unknown in the science of political economy. But what precisely does Marx mean by taking the proletarian point of view? This chapter endeavors to explore this question fully.

BOURGEOIS AND PROLETARIAN VIEWPOINTS IN POLITICAL ECONOMY

In his critique of political economy, Marx maintains that the political economists had mistakenly taken capitalist production to be eternal. They recognized that there is historical variation in economic systems in human history, but they viewed the variable dimensions as belonging to the realm of circulation. They thus viewed production itself as unchanging and eternal. Marx writes in the *Grundrisse*: "Note the fatuitousness of all bourgeois economists, including e.g. J. St. Mill, who considers bourgeois relations of production as eternal, but their forms of distribution as historical" (1973:758–59). Accordingly, the political economists did not grasp that production and circulation form a systemic unity and that production is the foundation from which circulation emerges.

The conclusion that we reach is not that production, distribution, exchange, and consumption are identical, but that they all form the members of a totality, distinctions within a unity. Production predominates not only over itself, in the antithetical definition of production, but over the other moments as well. The process always returns to production to begin anew. That exchange and consumption cannot be predominant is self-evident.

. . . A definite production thus determines a definite consumption, distribution and exchange as well as *definite relations between these different moments*. (1973:99)

In viewing production as eternal, the political economists have failed to distinguish those characteristics that are common to all forms of production from those characteristics that are particular to the capitalist mode of production. For "all elements of production have certain common traits, common characteristics" (1973:85). But "the elements which are not general and common must be separated out from the determinations valid for production as such, so that in their unity . . . their essential difference is not forgotten" (1973:85). The political economists do not attempt to make this distinction, and the result is that they view capitalist production as eternal, unchanging, and a natural dimension of the human condition. For political economists,

the aim is . . . to present production . . . as distinct from distribution etc., as encased in eternal natural laws independent of history, at which opportunity *bourgeois* relations are then quietly smuggled in as the inviolable natural laws on which society in the abstract is founded. (Marx, 1973:87)

In *Theories of Surplus Value*, Marx maintains that the work of even the most scientific representatives of political economy makes the error of assuming capitalist production to be eternal (1972:500–501). For example, Ricardo, the most advanced of the political economists who wrote from the vantage point of modern industry, assumes capitalist production to be eternal in that he assumes that capitalism can never fetter production (1972:55; 1970:59–60). The Ricardians also assume capitalism to be eternal (1972:259), and the opponents of the Ricardians who are defenders of the proletariat assume capitalist production to be eternal (1972:260). Thus, the error of taking capitalist production as natural and inevitable for human economic systems is widely accepted in political economy, for· it is present not only in vulgar political economy but in its scientific form, not only among the defenders of the bourgeoisie but also among the defenders of the proletariat.

In taking capitalist production to be eternal, political economists, according to Marx, are looking at the history of economic systems from a bourgeois point of view. For in the wake of the emergence of the bourgeoisie as a revolutionary class, it becomes possible to see in past economic forms the earlier formations of the capitalist mode of production. Indeed, it is in the interests of the bourgeoisie to do so. And given this reinterpretation of the history of economic systems from a bourgeois vantage point, it appears that economic systems always will be capitalist. This appearance obscures the essence of reality, namely, that capitalism is merely a passing historical phase. For Marx, an analysis of the economic system from a bourgeois point of view, prior to the emergence of the proletarian struggle, is scientific. But, as we have seen in the previous chapter, once the proletarian struggle emerges, such a vantage point ceases to be scientific. As Marx notes in the Preface to the second German edition of *Capital*,

As soon as these [modern economic] conditions did come into existence, they did so under circumstances that no longer allowed of their being really and impartially investigated within the bounds of the bourgeois horizon. In so far as Political Economy remains within that horizon, in so far, i.e., as the capitalist regime is looked upon as the absolutely final form of social production, instead of as a passing historical phase of its evolution, Political Economy can remain a science only so long as the class-struggle is latent or manifests itself only in isolated and sporadic phenomena. (1967:14)

For Marx, then, in the wake of the emergence of the proletarian struggle, science requires a movement beyond the bourgeois horizon to a point of view that does not assume capitalism to be eternal but views capitalism as a passing historical stage. Such a new point of view will lead to a transformation of the categories of political economy, for as Engels maintains in the preface to the English edition of *Capital*,

it is . . . self-evident that a theory which views modern capitalist production as a mere passing stage in the economic history of mankind, must make use of terms different from those habitual to writers who look upon that form of production as imperishable and final. (Marx, 1967:5)

For Marx, by taking a proletarian point of view, the political economist adopts a vantage point that enables him to discern that capitalism is a passing stage. For from a proletarian vantage point, one can discern the contradiction between the wealth of the few and the misery of the many, and one can discern that these contradictions are leading to the development of a new type of society, communism, in which the interests and human needs of the proletarian class are attained. Hence, from a proletarian vantage point, one can see in the contradiction of capitalism the seeds of the destruction of capitalism. Therefore, one can understand that capitalism is a passing stage in human history. Accordingly, in the wake of the proletarian struggle, the true scientists are those who consciously take a proletarian point of view. As he wrote in *The Poverty of Philosophy*, once the proletariat constitutes itself as a revolutionary class, science allies itself with this class and becomes revolutionary:

The *Socialists* and the *Communists* are the theoreticians of the proletarian class. So long as the proletariat is not yet sufficiently developed to constitute itself as a class, and consequently so long as the struggle itself of the proletariat with the bourgeoisie has not yet assumed a political character, and the productive forces are not yet sufficiently developed in the bosom of the bourgeoisie itself to enable us to catch a glimpse of the material conditions necessary for the emancipation of the proletariat and for the formation of a new society, these theoreticians are merely utopians who, to meet the wants of the oppressed classes, improvise systems and go in search of a regenerating science. But in the measure that history moves forward, and with it the struggle of the proletariat assumes clearer outlines, they no longer need to seek science in their minds; they have only to take note of what is happening before their eyes to become its mouthpiece. So long as they look for science and merely make systems, so long as they are at the beginning of the struggle, they see in poverty nothing but poverty, without seeing in it the revolutionary, subversive side, which will overthrow the old society. From this moment, science, which is a product of the historical movement, has associated itself consciously with it, has ceased to be doctrinaire and has become revolutionary. (Marx, 1963:125–26)

But what exactly is a proletarian point of view, and how does a scientist construct one? Marx's approach to this question was sophisticated, and it is easy to miss the subtleties of his approach, thereby reducing his view to the rather banal position that taking the proletarian point of view involves thinking as workers do, on the grounds that only the proletariat understands the essence of capitalism. But this was not what Marx meant by taking the proletarian point of view. As McBride observes, the standpoint of the proletariat

certainly cannot be equated with some non-existent, imagined empirical consensus of the social views and aspirations of all propertyless, subsistence-salaried industrial workers (the group that most clearly counts as "the proletariat" in Marxian usage) at a given time in the nineteenth century. (1977:17)

If this were Marx's position, one could ask, how could any scientist who is not a worker understand the social world as workers do? As Parekh observes, if "only the proletariat can grasp the truth about capitalism" (1982:165), then this "rules out all but the proletariat from understanding capitalism, and disqualifies not only Marx and Engels but also his commentators, many of whom come from the ranks of the petty bourgeoisie" (1982:165). But clearly, Marx does not take the banal, simplistic, and indefensible position that taking the proletarian point of view involves thinking as workers do.

To understand what Marx means by taking the proletarian point of view, let us examine Marx's use of points of view in *Capital*, where Marx often illustrates his arguments by showing that the point of view of the capitalist on any particular question is different from that of the worker. In Volume III of *Capital*, for example, Marx discusses the difference between the cost price and the actual cost of a commodity. The cost price is what the capitalist pays for the production of a commodity. It includes what the capitalist pays for wear and tear on instruments of production, for materials of production, and for labor. Since the cost price is what the capitalist pays, it appears to the capitalist that the cost price is the actual cost. And since the capitalist does not pay for unpaid labor, this surplus labor is not included in the cost price. Thus, Marx argues that from the capitalist point of view, the cost price appears to be the actual cost, but in fact, the actual cost is the cost price (what the capitalist pays) plus the surplus labor (for which the capitalist does not pay).

Why would Marx argue that the cost price appears to be the actual price *from the capitalist point of view*? Why does he not simply describe this view as a mistaken view rather than a view of the capitalist? Clearly, Marx's example indicates that there is an objective aspect of the capitalist's situation that makes it appear to him that the cost price equals the actual price. Namely, in the process of production, the capitalist pays the cost price. The cost price appears to be the actual price to the capitalist because the cost price is what he actually pays. Thus, the capitalist viewpoint on the question of the actual cost of a commodity is grounded in the *objective condition of a capitalist* as one who pays the cost price in order to produce the commodity. The capitalist therefore does not have a mistaken view, but a view that is grounded in his objective condition.

But the objective condition of the worker is entirely different, for what the worker provides in the productive process is not capital but labor. From the vantage point of one who provides labor, the actual cost of the product lies in the amount of labor expended. Hence from the vantage point of the worker, one arrives at the insight that "the capitalist cost of the commodity is measured by the *expenditure of capital*, while the actual cost of the commodity is measured by the *expenditure of labor*" (Marx, 1909:39).

Hence, by taking the point of view of the proletariat, Marx means describing the productive process from the vantage point of the *objective condition of the laborer* as one who provides labor power. Just as a scientist can take a bourgeois vantage point by assuming or taking as given the objective condition of the capitalist, so a scientist can take a proletarian vantage point by assuming or taking as given the objective condition of the worker. To take a proletarian vantage point, then, is not to endeavor to think as workers think, but to take as given the objective conditions of the proletariat in an analysis of capitalism.

A second illustration is found in Volume II of *Capital*. Here Marx discusses the payment of money by the capitalist to the worker in exchange for labor power. In this exchange, the money serves two functions. For the capitalist, the money functions as capital, because the capitalist is advancing the money to produce a commodity that is to be sold for profit. For the worker, the money functions as revenue, because he spends it to preserve labor power and thereby to live (1933:437–38, 511). Since the money serves different functions for the capitalist and the worker, they have different points of view on the money. From the capitalist's point of view, the money is capital advanced for profit, and from the worker's point of view, the money is revenue spent in order to live (1933:437).

Marx, therefore, describes two ways of viewing money when money is exchanged for labor. His position is not simply that one of these ways is correct and the other is incorrect. Rather, his position is that each view reflects one of the two different functions which the same money serves. Which function can be discerned depends on one's vantage point, and differing points of view are rooted in different positions in the system of capitalist production. The objective condition of the capitalist is that of a purchaser of means of production. As such, he advances the money as capital, and, for him, the money functions as capital. Accordingly, the money is viewed by the capitalist as capital. In contrast, the objective condition of the worker is that of a seller of labor power. The worker thus spends the money as revenue. The money functions as revenue for the worker and is therefore viewed as revenue by the worker. Thus, there is a proletarian point of view and a bourgeois point of view, and these points of view are rooted in objective conditions.

The political economists, Marx maintains, have described the exchange of money for labor power from the vantage point of the capitalist. Accordingly, they describe the money as capital and the labor as a commodity that is exchanged for capital. In describing the exchange in these terms, the political economists are turning the worker into a capitalist (1933:512). However, the exchange can be described from the vantage point of the seller of labor power, in which case the exchange is viewed as labor power for revenue. Moreover, from the vantage point of the seller of labor power, it can be seen that this revenue is created by labor power. For

the money which the laborer receives from the capitalist is not given to him until after he has given the capitalist the use of his labor-power, after it has already been realized in the value of the product of the labor. The capitalist holds this value in his hands, before he pays for it. . . . Labor-power first supplies, in the form of commodities, the equivalent which is to be paid to the laborer, and then only is it paid by the capitalist to the laborer in money. In other words, the laborer himself creates the fund out of which the capitalist pays him. (1933:439)

Accordingly, in looking at the exchange from the vantage point of the seller of labor power, it can be seen that the worker creates value, whether this value be value equivalent to necessary labor or surplus value (1933:445–46). Thus, in taking the vantage point of the seller of labor power, one is led to a reaffirmation of the most important insight of political economy, namely, that labor is the source of value.

In examining in detail these illustrations from *Capital*, what Marx means by taking the point of view of the proletariat emerges. He certainly does not mean adopting a point of view which is commonly held by workers. Rather, he means assuming or taking as given the objective conditions of the workers. Such objective conditions include the fact that the worker provides labor power to the productive process and is a seller of labor power. This objective condition is fundamentally different from that of the capitalist, who advances capital. The science of political economy has assumed the vantage point of an advancer of capital. From that vantage point, it was difficult to see that the cost price is different from the actual price, and that money exchanged for labor is revenue to the worker. Such oversights made it difficult to develop a theory that consistently grasped the origin of surplus value in surplus labor. Accordingly, the time has arrived, Marx maintains, to push the science of political economy forward by taking as given the objective conditions of the workers, the sellers of labor power. When an analysis of the process of production attempts to look at the process from this vantage point, it makes possible the insights that the actual cost is the cost price plus surplus labor and that the money exchanged for labor power is not capital but revenue. These insights are consistent with and reinforce the fundamental insight of political economy that labor is the source of value. Therefore, an analysis of political economy constructed from such a vantage point makes possible a consistent theory that grasps the implications of the origin of value in labor and the origin of surplus value in surplus labor.

Further, Marx maintains that the emergence of the proletarian movement makes possible an analysis of capitalism that takes as given the objective conditions of the worker and analyzes capitalism from this vantage point. The proletarian movement has focused on limiting the length of the working day. This movement has provoked a conflict between the capitalist and working classes, a conflict that has made manifest the opposed interests inherent in capitalism. On the one hand, the worker has an interest in limiting the working day to a normal length. If the working day extends beyond a normal length, the workers find that their capacity to work deteriorates. This is opposed to their interests, for the workers sell their labor power as a commodity.

By an unlimited extension of the working-day, you may in one day use up a quantity of labour-power greater than I can restore in three. . . . You pay me for one day's labour-power, whilst you use that of 3 days. That is against our contract and the law of exchanges. I demand, therefore, a working-day of normal length. (1967:234)

On the other hand, the capitalist has an interest in extending the working day, even if this shortens the laborer's life. For from the point of view of the capitalist, profits are maximized by maximizing the amount of surplus labor that can be harnessed in a single day. Accordingly, from a capitalist point of view,

it is not the normal maintenance of the labour-power which is to determine the limits of the working-day; it is the greatest possible daily expenditure of labour-power, no matter how diseased, compulsory, and painful it may be, which is to determine the limits of the labourers' period of repose. Capital cares nothing for the length of life of labour-power. All that concerns it is simply and solely the maximum of labour-power, that can be rendered fluent in a working day. It attains this end by shortening the extent of the labourer's life, as a greedy farmer snatches increased produce from the soil by robbing it of fertility.

The capitalistic mode of production . . . produces thus, with the extension of the working-day, not only the deterioration of human labour-power by robbing it of its normal, moral and physical, conditions of development and function. It produces also the premature exhaustion and death of this labour-power itself. It extends the labourer's time of production during a given period by shortening his actual life-time. (1967:265)

Marx maintains, however, that the capitalist is within his rights to pursue his interests in this way: "The capitalist maintains his rights as a purchaser when he tries to make the working-day as long as possible, and to make, whenever possible, two working-days out of one" (1967:235). At the same time, the worker is within his rights to attempt to prevent this extension of the working day beyond its normal length. "The labourer maintains his right as a seller when he wishes to reduce the working-day to one of definite normal duration'' (1967:235). Hence, there emerges the struggle over the length of the working day, a struggle that pits right against right and which only force can decide: ''There is here, therefore, an antinomy, right against right, both equally bearing the seal of the law of exchanges. Between equal rights force decides'' (1967:235). The struggle over the length of the working day is inherent in capitalism, for it pits the rights and interests of the workers against the rights and interests of the capitalists. This struggle makes it possible to discern that the bourgeoisie and the proletariat have different and opposed interests and vantage points. As a result, this struggle establishes the possibility that political economists can grasp that the proletariat has an objective position and vantage point different from the bourgeoisie and that the process of capitalist production can be described from this vantage point. Therefore, the struggle over the length of the working day makes it possible for political economists to view the capitalist process of production from a vantage point that takes as given the objective conditions of the proletariat. However, the political economists, Marx maintains, have not understood the significance of the struggle over the length of the working day, and they have not seized upon this possibility.

THE POINT OF VIEW OF SOCIETY

For Marx, however, to take as given the objective conditions of the worker is not sufficient for science. The scientist must also take the point of view of society. Thus, in taking a vantage point based on the objective conditions of the worker, the task is to construct an analysis not from the vantage point of the individual worker, but from the vantage point of society as a whole. In Chapter 20 of Volume II of *Capital*, Marx discusses in a critique of Adam Smith the importance of taking a social point of view. Marx here is addressing the question: What are the component parts of the value of a commodity? And Marx maintains that one arrives at a different answer to this question according to whether one takes an individual or a social point of view. Marx maintains that Smith erred on this question because he addressed it from the vantage point of the individual rather than of society. From the point of view of the individual worker, part of the labor is labor for which the capitalist has paid (necessary labor), and part of the labor is labor for which the capitalist has not paid (surplus labor). Accordingly, from an individual point of view, labor can be reduced to necessary labor plus surplus labor. However, there is the vantage point of the society as a whole, which looks at ''the labor expended by the entire working class during the whole year'' (1933:594). From this vantage point, it can be seen that part of the labor is devoted to the production of commodities that are part of the means of production of other commodities, which are ultimately consumed by individuals. While from an individual point of view, all products that produce surplus value are equivalent, from a social point of view, a distinction can be made between articles for production and articles for consumption. In taking a social point of view, Marx can make some distinctions that Smith cannot make. Accordingly, Marx distinguishes two departments of production. First, there is the production of means of production, the production of commodities that are used in the production of other commodities. Production in this Department I thus involves production for "productive consumption" (1933:457). Department II, however, involves the production of commodities which "pass into the individual consumption of the capitalist and working classes" (1933:457).

Moreover, from the social point of view, one can discern the component parts of capital in each department, for since there is awareness of the production of means of production from the social point of view, this makes possible a recognition that the means of production are part of capital. Moreover, it can be seen that some of this capital is used up and some of it is not in the process of production. Accordingly, by taking a social point of view, Marx can distinguish, in each department, between variable capital and constant capital. The variable capital consists of the labor for which the capitalist pays. The constant capital "is the value of all the means of production" (1933:457). The constant capital consists of fixed capital, which includes machines, tools, buildings, and laboring animals; and circulating capital, which is the raw material out of which the commodities are made. Now as commodities are produced, some of the constant capital is used up in the form of wear and tear, and this constant capital must be replaced. Therefore, from the vantage point of society, it can be seen that the value of the commodity is not reduced to variable capital plus surplus labor, as Smith thought, but to variable capital plus surplus labor plus constant capital. In other words, from the point of view of society, the production of constant capital can be seen as part of the working day. From the social point of view, one can see that a "portion of the social working day . . . produces means of production, . . . creates nothing new but *constant* capital" (1933:503). Smith, however, looked at the question only from the point of view of the individual and therefore did not grasp that the production of constant capital is part of the working day.

Marx's concept of taking the point of view of society underscores the fact that by taking the proletarian point of view, Marx does not mean thinking as workers do, for the task is not to learn the vantage point that workers have developed by virtue of their position in the economic system. Rather, the task is to construct an analysis of capitalism from the vantage point of the society as a whole and from a vantage point based on the objective conditions of the worker. This analysis is very different from the commonly accepted understanding of workers.

THE POINT OF VIEW OF PRODUCTIVITY

Marx also describes the scientific point of view as the point of view of productivity. This is clear from Marx's critique of Ricardo in *Theories of Surplus*

Value, where Marx praises Ricardo for placing the interests of the productivity above those of the industrial bourgeoisie. Ricardo, according to Marx,

> wants *production for the sake of production* and this with *good reason*. To assert, as sentimental opponents of Ricardo's did, that production as such is not the object, is to forget that production for its own sake means nothing but the development of human productive forces, in other words the *development of the richness of human nature as an end in itself*. (Marx, 1969b:117–18)

This support of productivity is, for Marx, a "scientific necessity" (1969b:118), and Ricardo's position reflects "scientific honesty" (1969b:118). Thus, Marx maintains that the scientific vantage point is that of the development of productive forces, for such development ultimately promotes "the development of the individual" (1969b:118). At a certain stage in historical development, the interests of productivity coincide with the interests of the bourgeoisie as they did during the time when the Physiocrats, Smith, and Ricardo wrote. Since 1830, however, the proletarian struggle has emerged, and the interests of productivity have coincided with the interests of the proletariat.

The task of the scientist in Marx's time, then, is to recognize that, since the proletariat has constituted itself as a revolutionary force, the proletariat has become a progressive force that pushes productivity, and therefore the potential for individual development, forward. In grasping this, scientists recognize the scientific necessity of analyzing capitalism from the vantage point of the objective conditions of the proletariat and at the same time, from the vantage point of the society as a whole.

By the proletarian point of view, then, Marx means a vantage point that takes as given the objective conditions of the proletariat. These conditions are themselves interpreted from a social point of view. Accordingly, the objective conditions of the proletariat refer to the objective conditions of the proletariat as a social group and not to the objective conditions of the individual worker. For Marx, therefore, adopting the proletarian point of view involves adopting a vantage point which takes as given the objective conditions of the proletarian social class.

INTERPRETATIONS OF MARX

There are a number of difficulties in Marxist interpretations of Marx's concept of taking the proletarian point of view. For the most part, these interpretations have not seen the real strengths and limitations in Marx's concept. Some of these interpretations (Georg Lukács, Ernst Bloch, and Adam Schaff) are reductionist: they reduce the concept of the proletarian point of view to the simplistic notion that the proletariat understands social reality better than other classes, and that the task of the scientist is to adopt this more insightful proletarian standpoint. Other interpretations (Louis Althusser, William McBride, and Bhikhu Parekh) recognize that the reductionist view is an oversimplification of Marx, but these interpretations have a variety of difficulties in their own right. Finally, Goran Therborn's and Norman Geras' interpretations begin to grasp the essence of Marx's concept of science; these interpretations will be developed further in subsequent chapters.

Let us first review the reductionist interpretations. Lukács maintains that the bourgeoisie has a vested interest in deceiving itself and other classes in its understanding capitalism, for it must deceive itself in order to support with a clear conscience the economic system that serves only its interests. In contrast, it is in the interests of the proletariat to discern the truth about the system that undermines its interests. Thus the proletariat, and only the proletariat, can understand the essence of capitalism because it, and only it, has an interest in doing so (1971:61–69). Accordingly, Lukács interprets Marx as believing that the understanding of the proletariat is an objective understanding (1971:149–50). This objective understanding of the proletariat is rooted in the objective conditions of the proletariat. The fundamental condition of the worker is that of exploitation: "He is no more than a cipher reduced to an abstract quantity, a mechanized and rationalized tool" (1971:166). But the relations of capitalist production have an impersonal quality: the personalities of the workers are not transformed into commodities, only their work. As a result of this impersonality, the workers can be aware of their exploitation. This is in contrast to pre-capitalist production, in which personality was imbedded in work, and consequently, laborers could not reflect clearly about their own situation (1971:167–68). Thus, the objective condition of the proletariat involves exploitation in an impersonal system, which makes possible, for the first time in history, understanding by the exploited of exploitation.

The objective conditions of the bourgeoisie, however, do not make possible its understanding of exploitation in capitalism. The bourgeoisie and the proletariat do share the same objective reality, and as a result, "for the capitalist also there is the same doubling of personality, the same splitting up of man into an element of the movement of commodities" (1971:166). However, this phenomenon impacts differently upon the capitalist than it does upon the worker: to the capitalist "it necessarily appears as an activity . . . in which effects emanate from himself" (1971:166). Accordingly, the capitalist, unlike the worker, cannot grasp the fact that the worker is reduced to a tool in a mechanized and rationalized system of commodity production and market exchange. The capitalist illusion of himself as an actor who is the author of his own actions "blinds him to the true state of affairs, whereas the worker, who is denied the scope for such illusory activity, perceives the split in his being preserved in the brutal form of what is in its whole tendency a slavery without limits" (1971:166). Thus the bourgeoisie is unable to understand objectively the capitalist system: "mere immediacy adheres to its thought, constituting its outermost barrier, one that cannot be crossed" (1971:164). But the same objective reality that imprisons the bourgeoisie within immediacy drives the proletariat beyond immediacy: "The same reality employs the motor of class interests to keep the bourgeoisie imprisoned within this immediacy while forcing the proletariat to go beyond it'' (1971:164). Thus, the proletariat is driven by a quest for truth and "authentic objectivity" (1971:164). And this is why Marx believed that "the knowledge yielded by the standpoint of the proletariat stands on a higher scientific plane objectively; . . . it provides the adequate historical analysis of capitalism which must remain beyond the grasp of bourgeois thinkers'' (1971:163–64).

Another interpretation of Marx as maintaining that the proletariat has a scientific understanding is that of Ernst Bloch. Paralleling Lukács, Bloch maintains that Marx sought to establish "universally valid truth" (1971:148) in the proletarian revolution. The working class is the only class capable of understanding its condition because it is the first class in history to have an interest in understanding its condition.

For as Marx opined, . . . the working class is the *only* one hitherto whose *very interest* is not compatible with mystification and false consciousness whether subjective or objective, but only with a fully objective and universally valid analysis and examination of their condition. . . . For the first time, it was now the *interest* of a class itself to get to know its condition clearly (Bloch, 1971:148–49).

Lukács and Bloch, then, interpret Marx as maintaining that the objective conditions of capitalism make possible an objective understanding *by the proletariat*. Against this interpretation, however, I would argue that, although Marx did believe that the proletariat understands more than the bourgeoisie due to its objective conditions, this is not a central dimension of Marx's concept of *science*. For Marx, as we have seen, a scientific understanding is attained by analyzing capitalism from a vantage point that takes as given the objective conditions of the proletariat. At the same time, it should be acknowledged that there is some ambiguity in Marx's writing. He frequently, for example, referred to taking a proletarian point of view, without explaining what he meant by this. Because of the complexities of Marx's thought and because of some ambiguity in his formulation, there are difficulties in interpreting Marx on this question. To resolve some of these difficulties, in Chapter 5 I will endeavor to move beyond what Marx wrote to an analysis of what Marx did and experienced in the formulation of his science. This will constitute further evidence, above and beyond what he wrote, in support of the interpretation of Marx's concept of science as involving not taking a proletarian understanding but adopting a vantage point that takes as given the objective conditions of the proletariat.

In addition to Lukács and Bloch, Adam Schaff also has a reductionist interpretation of the meaning of the proletarian point of view. Schaff, however, presents his views as an interpretation of Marxism, rather than as an interpretation of Marx. Schaff defines ideology as "the term for views on problems of a desired purpose of social development which are shaped on the basis of definite class interests and serve their defence'' (1976:140). According to this definition, ideologies are class-conditioned. But even though ideologies are class-conditioned, not all ideologies are false or are distortions of social reality. Schaff does not presume that ''ideology must imply a cognitive deformation ('false consciousness')'' (1976:140). ''There is no reason why we may not consider class-conditioned truth to be true'' (1976:140). This definition of the term ideology, Schaff notes, is different from the definition of Marx and his contemporaries. But Marxists since Lenin have defined the terms in this way and hence refer to a ''scientific ideology'' (1976:141). A scientific ideology is possible because ''class interests and their defence may be linked with science and be based on scientific foundations'' (1976:141).

Having defined the possibility of a scientific ideology, Marxism further distinguishes, according to Schaff, between revolutionary classes and conservative classes. Revolutionary classes ''are classes which struggle in accord with their interest for the abolishment of the existing order'' (1976:142). Conservative classes are ''classes struggling, in accord with their interests, for the maintenance of the existing social order which is the foundation of their rule and the privileges derived therefrom'' (1976:142). Because of the interest of the revolutionary classes in social change, they are better able than conservative classes to understand social change.

In a fashion which is most often unconscious but, at times, also fully conscious, the members and supporters of a class which finds itself objectively in a revolutionary situation, since their group and individual interest coincides with the developmental trend in society, are not subject to the mechanism of psychic restraints when it comes to reflecting in cognition that which is actually taking place in society; on the contrary, their interest leads to a more acute observation of the phenomenon of changes, of the disintegration of the old order and the manifestation of the birth of a new order whose victory they are expecting. Their cognition of social processes and their ideology, which is the groundwork of their social action, are a true, accurate reflection of reality since, in this respect, they do not encounter the restraints and obstacles derived for a corresponding social conditioning. (1976:142–43)

So the proletarian ideology, accepted by members of the revolutionary class, is an objective and true understanding of social reality. The proletarian ideology is therefore a scientific ideology.

In order to attain scientific truth, therefore, one must, according to Schaff, adopt the understanding of the proletariat. ''We say to students of social phenomena: 'If you wish to attain objective truth in your studies, then consciously adopt class and party positions which are in accord with the interests of the proletariat' '' (1976:245–46). The knowledge attained in this way is not absolute, but relative to social conditions, for it represents ''the highest achievement of the human mind in *given* conditions'' (1976:246). Nonetheless, this knowledge has an objective character, for it is superior to the knowledge attained by taking the standpoint of conservative classes. Accordingly, the result is "relative objective truth" (1976:250).

As Schaff notes, this use of the terms science and ideology in Marxism begins with Lenin and is different from Marx's usage. For Schaff, the proletarian ideology, which is the understanding of the members of the proletarian class, is a scientific understanding. Similarly, Lenin maintains that "Marxism . . . is . . . the ideology of the laboring class" (1960:394). Such a conception is fundamentally different from that of Marx. Marx does not argue that the proletariat has a scientific understanding, but that the scientist who takes a vantage point based on the objective conditions of the proletariat can develop a scientific understanding. Schaff's arguments thus are not incorrect as long as it is kept in mind that his concepts of science and ideology are not interpretations of Marx but interpretations of Marxism since Lenin.

Alongside the reductionist interpretations, which maintain that the proletariat itself has an objective understanding, there are the interpretations of Althusser, McBride, and Parekh, which seek to go beyond this simplistic and problematic interpretation. However, these interpretations also have their difficulties.

Louis Althusser maintains that science "reveals the mechanisms of class exploitation, repression and domination, in the economy, in politics and in ideology" (1971:8). And he maintains that Marx's achievement was to formulate such a science. In doing so, Marx was able to expose the ideologies of his time as ideologies, that is, to expose widely accepted conceptions as false conceptions that function to preserve the economic system (1976:154–56). Thus, Marx, in formulating science, could formulate a body of thought characterized by an "epistemological break [with] its *ideological* prehistory" (1976:154). Central to this achievement was Marx's "*conjunction* of different and independent theoretical" (1976:156) traditions, namely, German philosophy, English political economy, and French socialism. But what enabled Marx to move beyond the ideology of his time and to formulate science through the synthesis of divergent intellectual traditions? For Althusser, the key here was the fact that Marx took a proletarian point of view: "it was by *moving* to take up absolutely new, proletarian class positions that Marx realized the possibilities of the theoretical conjunction from which the science of history was born" (1976:157). By adopting the point of view of the proletariat, Marx could formulate the new science:

In order to fulfill the conditions that govern the science of history, Marx had to abandon his bourgeois and then petty-bourgeois class positions and adopt the class positions of the proletariat. . . . It is only from the point of view of the exploited class that it is possible to discover, against all bourgeois ideology and even against classical Political Economy, the mechanisms of those relations of exploitation, the relations of production of a class society. (1971:8)

Moreover, Althusser maintains that Marx could not have taken the standpoint of the proletariat if the proletarian struggle had not emerged: "Without the proletariat's class struggle, Marx could not have adopted the point of view of class exploitation, or carried out his scientific work'' (1971:9). Hence, as a result of the emergence of the proletarian struggle and Marx's ''ever deeper engagement in the political struggles of the proletariat'' (1976:160), Marx was able to take the standpoint of the proletariat and to formulate a synthesis of German philosophy, English political economy, and French socialism in a scientific critique of ideology.

By taking the class position of the proletariat, Althusser does not interpret Marx to mean assuming the understanding of the working class. Rather, it involves assuming a point of view that recognized the objective significance of the proletarian struggle: ''A proletarian *class position* . . . is the consciousness and practice which conform with the objective reality of the proletarian class struggle'' (1971:13). Thus, to take a proletarian point of view is different from having a class instinct, which is an understanding rooted in the experience of exploitation. The class instinct of the workers needs to be educated (1971:13). Althusser views Marx's science as science for the proletariat, not only because it debunks bourgeois ideologies, but also because it functions to educate the proletariat to an understanding beyond that instinctive understanding that is rooted in the direct experience of exploitation. Thus, Marx's science received its inspiration from the political struggle of the proletariat; yet, it draws upon the culture of scientific inquiry in order to give to the workers an understanding that would not be possible on the basis of the experience of exploitation alone. ''In this scientific work, which bears the mark of all his culture and genius, he has given back to the Workers' Movement in a theoretical form what he took from it in a political and ideological form'' (1971:9). On the other hand, because the workers do have the direct experience of exploitation, they are more able than members of the bourgeoisie to understand Marxist science. ''If the workers have 'understood' *Capital* so easily it is because it speaks in scientific terms of the everyday reality with which they are concerned: the exploitation which they suffer because of the capitalist system'' (1971:73). Thus, although the workers are unable to formulate science on the basis of the direct experience of exploitation, they are better able than the bourgeoisie to understand it once it has been formulated by a scholar who draws upon a scientific culture and who takes a vantage point that takes as given the significance of the proletarian struggle.

There is much merit in Althusser's analysis, and his interpretation of Marx's concept of science is in important respects consistent with the interpretation of this book. For example, Althusser recognizes that Marx was above all a scientist who sought to formulate a scientific critique of bourgeois political economy and bourgeois ideology. Second, Althusser is aware of the importance of the emergence of the proletarian struggle in establishing the conditions that made possible Marx's scientific formulation. Third, Althusser recognizes that Marx's concept of taking the standpoint of the proletariat cannot be reduced to thinking as workers do, for the analysis of capitalism from a proletarian standpoint is formulated by scientists and plays an educative role in regard to proletarian consciousness.

However, there are difficulties in Althusser's formulation. The first difficulty concerns Althusser's discussion of taking the proletarian point of view. Althusser maintains that what Marx did was "to adopt the class positions of the proletariat" (1971:8), which involves adopting a position that conforms with "the objective reality of the proletarian class struggle" (1971:13). However, Althusser does not explain what this method involves. In this chapter, I have examined Marx's use of points of view in *Capital* in order to explain his method more fully. Such an explication is absent in Althusser's work.

Second, Althusser maintains that Marx drew upon a scientific culture to formulate a scientific understanding from a proletarian point of view. Again, his observations here need further elaboration. What are the elements of a scientific culture that make possible understandings that cannot be formulated on the basis of direct experience of exploitation? How can a scientist, who is typically (as in the case of Marx) not a worker, integrate the elements of a scientific culture with the workers' experience of exploitation in order to formulate a scientific critique from the standpoint of the worker? Indeed, the answers to these questions are not fully developed in Marx's own work. But precisely such questions must be addressed for the further development of Marxism. Subsequent chapters will reconstruct Marx's concept of science in light of twentieth-century philosophy. This reconstruction will endeavor to address these questions.

The first two difficulties in Althusser's work can be overcome through further elaboration. However, a third difficulty is more fundamental; it concerns Althusser's application of Marx's concept of science to scientific inquiry today. Althusser maintains that just as the proletarian struggle established the conditions for Marx's scientific achievement, so in our own time the further development of social conditions establishes new possibilities for science that go beyond the formulations of Marx. He writes:

In order to defend Marx's work, in order to develop and apply it, we are subject to the same class conditions in theory. It is only on the positions of the proletariat that it is possible to provide a radical critique of the new forms of bourgeois ideology, to obtain thereby a clear view of the mechanisms of imperialism and to advance in the construction of socialism. (1971:9)

The difficulty here is Althusser's notion that the standpoint of the proletariat continues to be the basis for scientific achievement in the twentieth century. This notion fails to grasp the far-reaching implications of Marx's concept of science, for in Marx's understanding, the bourgeois revolution had established possibilities for scientific insight from the bourgeois vantage point. This in turn gave way to the possibilities for scientific insight established by the proletarian revolution. Accordingly, Marx's concept of science suggests the possibility of entirely new vantage points as new social movements emerge. And as we look retrospectively at the twentieth century, it is clear that the emergence of social movements that defined themselves as other than working-class movements has been a significant social fact. These movements include national liberation move-ments in the Third World and civil rights movements of minorities in the United States. They also include the struggle of women for equal rights. Now, these movements can be dismissed on the grounds that they do not challenge the fundamental premises of capitalism and thus are co-opted by capitalism, but that criticism can also be voiced against the workers' movement in Marx's time as well as in the twentieth century. Or it could be argued that these movements are dimensions of the proletarian struggle, and that they thus do not have theoretical implications beyond that of the working-class struggle itself. But this argument simply interprets these movements from the vantage point of the proletariat. It fails to take a vantage point that takes as given the objective conditions of these subjected groups. Such an argument, therefore, is inconsistent with Marx's concept of science. These movements have the same political significance in our time as the proletarian struggle had in Marx's time. Therefore, to be consistent with Marx's method, we must recognize the theoretical significance of these twentieth-century social movements. They establish the possibility for new in-sights through vantage points that take as given the objective conditions of these subjected groups that have constituted social movements in the twentieth century. All of this will be discussed at further length in Chapter 7. For the moment let us simply note that Althusser fails to see these implications of Marx's concept of science.

William Leon McBride believes that there is ambiguity in the notion that Marx took the standpoint of the proletariat. And he asserts:

the ambiguity involved in designating Marxism's standpoint as that of the proletariat cannot satisfactorily be eliminated, as Lenin and others later attempted to do, by iden-tifying the interests of the proletariat with the goals formulated by its 'vanguard' Party, for this simply raises new questions about the validity of the Party's claims. (1977:17)

McBride endeavors to resolve this ambiguity in a different way, namely, with reference to Marx's concept of the proletariat as a universal class. Marx took from Hegel "the notion that a single social class, distinguishable from the other classes by differences in sets of interests and specifically in its relationship to property, could be at least potentially 'universal' " (McBride, 1977:18). Against Hegel, who had seen government bureaucrats as a universal class, Marx con-sidered the proletariat to be a universal class. It was a universal class in that it "held no part of the riches of modern society and thus had 'nothing to lose' " (1977:18). Because of its "position of extreme subordination" (1977:18), it would act to "abolish the existing power relationships" (1977:18) and to "put an end to private ownership of the means of production and to class divisions as such" (1977:18).

There are many difficulties in McBride's analysis. Leaving aside difficulties in his interpretation of Marx's concept of a universal class, we turn to the issue more central to our purposes. McBride has here explained the objective conditions that make the proletariat a revolutionary class. This explanation does nothing to explain the connection of this revolutionary class to Marx's understanding. Is Marx's viewpoint the same as that of the revolutionary proletariat as it struggles to attain its interests? If so, how is it possible for Marx, who was not a worker, to develop such revolutionary consciousness? If not, what are the differences between Marx's viewpoint and proletarian consciousness, and what are the connections between the two? McBride's explanation raises more questions than it answers, and it does nothing to resolve ambiguities in the notion of the viewpoint of the proletariat.

Bhikhu Parekh rejects the notion that Marx took a proletarian point of view in his analysis of capitalism. He maintains that "Marx cannot be seen as a proletarian social theorist" (1982:175). He writes:

We must, for analytical convenience, distinguish between Marx's political support of the proletariat, and his epistemological appreciation of its point of view. . . . As a scientist Marx was not a class theorist, but a "free agent of thought". He aimed to study the capitalist mode of production and human history form the most comprehensive and self-critical point of view possible. Accordingly he studied them not from the proletarian point of view, but from the standpoint of the social whole, critically constructed out of all the standpoints available to him, including the proletarian. (1982:175)

Marx, according to Parekh, believed that German philosophy and English political economy were characterized by narrow and partial viewpoints. He therefore endeavored to avoid such one-sided understanding in his analysis of capitalism.

Marx was convinced that, in order to study society critically, he must investigate it not from a partial and narrow, but the widest point of view available to him, from the "standpoint of the whole" as he called it. . . . Accordingly Marx went on to develop the most comprehensive and self-critical point of view possible. (1982:176)

According to Parekh, there were three reasons why Marx could not take a proletarian point of view. First, "there are many questions about capitalism that do not get asked from the proletarian point of view" (1982:182), such as questions concerning international trade and colonialism. Second, "the proletariat is not generally able to see through the ideologically constituted social world, and asks for such things as fair wages rather than the very abolition of the wage slavery" (1982:182). Third, "the questions posed by the proletariat are not scientific, and must be transposed into the scientific language before they can be accepted as genuinely theoretical questions" (1982:183).

There are difficulties in Parekh's interpretation of Marx. In the first place, to assert that Marx did not take a proletarian point of view in his analysis is difficult to reconcile with the texts. We have seen examples of Marx looking at several issues from a vantage point based on the objective conditions of the proletariat in order to reformulate the concepts of classical political economy. Although

Marx does not attempt to adopt the understanding of the workers, he clearly does endeavor to analyze capitalism from a vantage point based on the objective conditions of the workers. Moreover, although Marx does write in Volume II of *Capital* of the importance of taking the vantage point of society, for the most part in his work he endeavors to formulate an understanding of capitalism from a vantage point based on the objective conditions of the workers. Accordingly, his discussion of taking the point of view of society cannot reasonably be interpreted as evidence that he did not seek to take an interpretation based on the objective conditions of the proletariat, for this would involve ignoring a great deal of his writing on the issue. Rather, his discussion of taking the vantage point of society can more reasonably be interpreted as a method that he used as a dimension of taking a vantage point based on the objective conditions of the proletariat, in which such conditions refer to the proletariat as a social group and not to the conditions of the individual worker.

A second difficulty with Parekh concerns the three reasons he gives as to why Marx could not be a theorist for the proletariat. Parekh makes a distinction between the argument that ''only the proletariat can grasp the truth about capitalism'' (1982:165) and the argument that ''the truth about it can only be grasped from the *standpoint* of the proletariat'' (1982:165). Although Parekh does not explain what taking the standpoint of the proletariat involves, I take him to be making a distinction similar to the one I have made between thinking as workers do and taking a vantage point based on the objective conditions of the workers. Parekh argues that those who argue that Marx took a proletarian view mean to say that Marx took a proletarian standpoint.[1] Parekh argues against this interpretation and maintains that Marx did not take a proletarian standpoint. However, Parekh loses sight of his distinction between the proletarian understanding and taking the proletarian standpoint in his discussion of the three reasons (quoted above) as to why Marx could not be a proletarian theorist. For example, when Parekh argues that the proletariat does not raise questions about colonialism and that it has merely trade union consciousness, this shows that Marx did not take the understanding of the proletariat. It does not show that Marx did not take the standpoint of the proletariat, if this is meant as taking a vantage point based on the objective conditions of the proletariat.

A third difficulty with Parekh's analysis concerns his references to Marx's texts. For example, in support of the notion that Marx does not take a proletarian point of view but takes the point of view of society, Parekh cites *Grundrisse*, where Marx notes that circulation is a social process and that the totality of this process establishes alienation (Marx, 1973:196–97). However, Marx is simply arguing here that an economic system must be understood as a total social process in order for its dynamics to be fully understood. This is very different from arguing that an economic system must be understood from the point of view of society. Indeed, one can understand an economic system as a total social system from a variety of points of view, including the point of view of a dominant class, of a subjected class, or of society as a whole. Parekh also cites observations by Marx written in 1842, where Marx defends two articles he wrote as a newspaper correspondent. Marx here argues that the press gradually gets at the truth by a division of labor, in which a number of different individual points of view are presented, establishing the material that enables one member of the press to "create a single whole" (Marx & Engels, 1975a:333). However, these observations of the youthful Marx, written in relation to Marx's work as a journalist, cannot reasonably be cited as justification for the claim that Marx, as a scientific analyst of the economic system and the science of political economy, did not believe that one gets at the truth by taking the standpoint of the proletariat. Still other references by Parekh to Marx contain observations by Marx that are not entirely clear. In short, the references do not always mean precisely what they should mean in order to support Parekh's interpretation of Marx; still other references are vague and elusive. This is especially problematic given the far-reaching and somewhat unorthodox and controversial claims that Parekh is making.

In spite of these difficulties, Parekh has some important observations in regard to the issue of the proletarian point of view. One of them is Parekh's observation, referred to above, that questions raised by the proletariat must be transposed into scientific language. It is indeed the case that Marx's method brings to the quest for truth a scientific understanding that places the proletarian experience into a scientific context. This interrelation of science and proletarian consciousness needs further elaboration, and this will be attempted in subsequent chapters. But even more important is Parekh's notion that the contribution of the proletariat to the quest for truth is to raise questions. Parekh writes that Marx maintains that the proletariat

is compelled by its conditions of existence to ask questions which the dominant class cannot or will not. It has a distinct pool of negative experiences, and the consequent interests and needs. As such it asks disturbing questions, challenges the basic assumption underlying the dominant universe of discourse, questions the prevailing social arrangement, and wonders it there are no better alternatives. Since its experiences and interests are different, it does not share the biases of the dominant class. It is therefore particularly sensitive to the biased assumptions of the current views of man and society and forms of inquiry. As such it finds problematic what the dominant class takes for granted. It asks how private property is justified, why there should be classes, why society collectively cannot regulate production, why production should be for profit rather than the satisfaction of human needs, why some should work when others do not, why one should respect the established authority when it preserves a social order unable to guarantee one even a decent livelihood, and so on. These and other fundamental and subversive questions directly grow out of its experiences and are a matter of life and death to it. (1982:181)

In contrast to the proletariat, the bourgeoisie is unable to ask such fundamental questions about the social order:

Unlike the proletariat, the dominant class is not compelled by its conditions of existence to ask radically novel questions. It has created the social order in its own image, and shares its basic biases. As such it is inherently incapable of raising fundamental questions about it. (1982:181)

Further, the questions raised by the proletariat make possible the expansion of horizons:

By continually raising [questions] in one form or another, the proletariat places new items on the intellectual and political agenda, extends the limits of the dominant horizon of thought and opens up a whole new way of looking at man and society. (1982:181)

Although my formulation of the issue will be somewhat different, my reconstruction of Marx's concept of science will use and further develop this notion of subversive questions. In my formulation of the issue, I will draw upon the cognitional theory of Bernard Lonergan to maintain that scientists discover relevant questions through encounter with revolutionary struggles constituted by subjected groups. Often, such relevant questions are subversive in regard to prevailing understandings in social science and society.

Finally, there are the interpretations of the proletarian point of view found in Therborn and Geras. These interpretations constitute a good beginning, and they will be developed further in subsequent chapters. Therborn maintains that there were three important political developments that provided the background for the creation of Marxism as a system of thought. First, there was the emergence of the industrial bourgeoisie as the dominant social force in England and France (1973:8). Second, there was the failure of the bourgeois revolution in Paris and the subsequent repression of radical democratic intellectuals by the Prussian king (1973:8–9). Third, there was the emergence of the proletarian struggle, for "this was also the period in which the working-class movement made its decisive appearance" (1973:8). Therborn maintains that these political factors combined to make possible the formulation of Marxism by Marx and Engels, for given the successes of the bourgeois revolutions in England and France, the radical democratic intellectuals in Germany had every expectation for a similar success in Germany. Instead, they experienced repression, which led to their radicalization and an increasing sense of alienation. As Therborn observes.

The Young Hegelians—especially after the betrayal they experienced from the bourgeois liberals in the face of Prussian repression—were not simply a bourgeois intelligentsia. Socially, in the strategic years of 1842 to 1845, they were a *déclassé* and radicalized section of the petty bourgeoisie. (1973:9)

Given these experiences of the German radical democratic intellectuals, the emergence of the proletarian struggle at precisely this time was bound to have a decisive impact. This was especially true for Marx and Engels because of their personal contact with the workers' movement in Paris. Accordingly, Therborn argues, they created a system of thought that is orientated to the liberation of the workers, a system of thought that reflects a union between its creators and the workers' movement.

The decisive difference in the social situation of Marxism . . . was, of course, the union between its founders and the revolutionary workers' movement. The earliest intellectual interests of both Marx and Engels were the same as those of many left-wing *Kulturkritiker* of the 20th century—philosophy, poetry, journalism, belles-lettres in general. But although both Marx and Engels kept and nourished these cultural interests, what they · created was . . . "the doctrine of the conditions of the liberation of the proletariat," concentrating by necessity on the "critique of political economy." Moreover, as they say in the *Communist Manifesto*, their theoretical conclusions "express, in general terms, actual relations springing from an existing class struggle, from a historical movement going on under our very eyes." (1973:8)

Because of this "union" of Marx and Engels with the working-class movement, they could learn from the proletariat. In particular, they learned two things:

First of all, they had to learn the concrete materiality of the real social world, beyond all problems of theology or the rational state. Secondly, they had to learn the class struggle, learn to see the proletariat not just as the most suffering class—as did the utopian socialists—but to discover "the proud, threatening and revolutionary proletarian." (1973:10)

Accordingly, they were able to arrive at the insight that communism would require "the organized, revolutionary struggle of the working class" (1973:13). But even though Marx and Engels learned from the proletariat, they also contributed to the proletarian struggle, for they developed a scientific theory of history.

Marx and Engels, after having *unlearnt* their "German ideology," could contribute something to the proletarian movement that even the best theorists from the proletariat itself, such as the German tailor Wilhem Weitling, could not; a scientific theory of history and a revolutionary strategy based on it. (1973:14)

Thus, Marx did not simply adopt the understanding of the proletariat. Rather, he learned from the proletariat, and he developed a scientific understanding of the proletarian struggle that was based on what he had learned from it.

There are some strong points in Therborn's interpretation of the origins of Marxist analysis. For example, he avoids the simplistic argument that Marx in his original formulation adopted the workers' understanding. He recognizes that there is an important connection between Marx and the working-class movement as Marx is developing his understanding. And he recognizes that Marx is developing a scientific understanding that is different from and goes beyond the understanding of the workers. Not even the most theoretically advanced workers can arrive at this scientific understanding insofar as they are disconnected from scientific understandings.

In the next chapter, we shall develop further Therborn's notion of a ''union'' between Marx and the working-class struggle by examining in detail Marx's intellectual development during the time when he first developed his theoretical system. An understanding of Marx's intellectual development will enable us in subsequent chapters to develop further Therborn's notion that Marx's scientific understanding goes beyond that of workers. In doing so, we shall address the questions, What precisely can science contribute to understanding that cannot be known through the direct experience of exploitation? And how can scientists claim to develop an understanding that grasps more about exploitation than can be grasped by those who have directly experienced exploitation? In addressing these questions, we will be able to formulate an explanation of the relationship between science and the working class as exemplified in the life and work of Marx. This explanation will formulate in precise terms the elements of the union between Marx and the working class.

Like Therborn, Geras maintains that, in the creation of Marxism, Marx and Engels learned from the working class and yet produced a scientific understanding that the working class itself was incapable of formulating. Geras rejects any interpretation in which Marxism is created outside the working class and independent of its political struggles. He maintains that even though Marxism was created by bourgeois intellectuals, it was created by intellectuals who linked their fate to the working class and who, accordingly, were prepared to learn from the working class. Geras writes:

Marxist theory was not produced *outside* the working class movement. It was produced *inside* the working class movement. True, it was produced by intellectuals, and these intellectuals were most often of bourgeois or petty-bourgeois origin. But that is another matter. For these were not just any bourgeois intellectuals. They were precisely those who linked their fate with that of the working class, formed organizations to institutionalize that union, and participated in the class struggle for socialism. What they brought to the working class movement was not a well-formed science elaborated elsewhere, but the theoretical training and the elements of scientific culture essential to the production of such a science, things which their position as intellectuals had enabled them to acquire and which cannot emerge spontaneously from experience on the factory floor, or from participation in strikes and demonstrations. At the same time, what they gained from the working class were a number of experiences not readily available to most bourgeois intellectuals and which do not emerge spontaneously from the activity of theoretical work: the experience of exploitation and repression, the experience of the struggle against these realities, the experience of the successes and failures of that struggle. The theoretical practice by which Marxist theory, as such, was founded and developed . . . was . . . a theoretical practice interior to the working class movement, and which could only teach the masses something because it also knew how to learn from them. (1972:84)

So the proletariat does not itself produce Marxism. Marxism is produced by intellectuals who defend the interests of the proletariat in such a clear and consistent manner that their fate becomes tied to the fate of the working class.

Thus, if the working-class revolution succeeds, such intellectuals would come to occupy a position of prestige and influence in the new society. On the other hand, if the revolution does not succeed, such intellectuals would continue to have a marginal status. In linking their fate to that of the proletarian struggle, the personal status of such intellectuals becomes tied to the fate of the proletarian struggle. Such intellectuals, in effect, escaped their own class origins. "They had ceased to be bourgeois intellectuals, abandoned their class origins and interests, and risked all the refusals and ridicule of official culture to espouse the interests, perspectives and struggles of the working class" (1972:85).

Even though the proletariat did not produce Marxism, it does, unlike the bourgeoisie, have the capacity to understand Marxism, for the proletariat has an interest in understanding Marxism.

Marxism is not a science just like any other. . . . If it can claim for the knowledges it produces the same validity and objectivity claimed by the other sciences for theirs, it cannot claim for them the same universal recognition. These knowledges are anathema to the bourgeoisie and its ideologues (some of whom are also scientists): by disclosing the mechanisms and contradictions of its power, they call into question the permanence of that power. Since it is precisely permanent power that the bourgeoisie wishes and thinks for itself in one ideological form or another, it cannot but refuse to look at this question and the theory which contains it. The proletariat, on the other hand, can look at this question because it has a direct interest in looking at it. (1972:85)

Thus, Marxism, for Geras, was produced by intellectuals who in their work so clearly espoused proletarian interests that their fate became tied to the proletarian struggle. And it was formulated by intellectuals who learned from the proletarian struggle. Therefore, even though Marxism was formulated by intellectuals and not workers, Marx has important historical connections to the workers' struggle. Moreover, because it is in their interests to do so, the workers are more capable than capitalists of understanding Marxism. This connection between the creation of Marxism and the working-class movement is an important point that will be elaborated more fully in subsequent chapters.

NOTE

1. This is not always true. We have seen that Lukács and Bloch have taken the position that the working class has a valid and objective understanding rooted in the condition of exploitation. They interpret Marx as adopting this valid and objective working-class understanding.

5

MARX'S INTELLECTUAL DEVELOPMENT

The philosopher Bernard Lonergan writes of the phenomenon of conversion in one's development. "Conversion involves a new understanding of oneself because . . . it brings about a new self to be understood. It is putting off the old man and putting on the new. It is not just a development but the beginning of a new mode of developing" (1971:33–34). Conversion has three dimensions, for Lonergan, the intellectual, the moral, and the religious. "Conversion is three-dimensional. It is intellectual inasmuch as it regards our orientation to the intelligible and the true. It is moral inasmuch as it regards our orientation to the good. It is religious inasmuch as it regards our orientation to God" (1971:34).

In the period of October 1843 through August 1844, Marx experienced, in Lonergan's terminology, an intellectual and moral conversion. For most of 1843, Marx was a radical democrat who was a product of the left-wing Young Hegelian school in German philosophy. But after his move to Paris in October 1843, Marx experienced personal encounter with the working-class struggle, and he also undertook a study of the intellectual tradition of classical political economy. These personal and intellectual experiences enabled Marx to forge an analysis of political economy, an analysis that was distinctive in two ways. First, it synthesized political economy, Hegelian philosophy, and socialism. This synthesis crossed not only the boundaries of intellectual traditions but also national cultures, combining the most advanced thought of England, Germany, and France. Second, the analysis was undertaken from a unique point of view, in that it took as given the objective conditions of the working class. This creative synthesis was formulated in its fundamentals as early as the writing of the *Economic and Philosophic Manuscripts*, from April through August 1844. Let us look in detail at this remarkable intellectual conversion.

MARX'S IDEAS BEFORE PARIS

David McLellan (1970:10–14, 25–26) distinguishes liberalism, radicalism, and socialism according to their usage in European social thought in the 1830s and 1840s. Liberalism advocated freedom of the individual, whereas radicalism advocated popular sovereignty. The two strains of thought were similar, and indeed radicalism "only gradually separated itself from liberalism and did not achieve a complete break until the early 1840s" (1970:12). However, there was a difference in emphasis. Liberals were in favor of checks and balances, such as bi-cameral parliament, and could accept class inequality as natural. Radicals, in contrast, were opposed to checks and balances and would not accept inequality as inevitable. Distinct from radicals and liberals were the socialists. Socialists emphasized the radical concern with inequality and added proposals to reduce inequality, such as collective ownership of economic enterprises. Socialists believed that the extremes of inequality were leading to a polarization of classes and to a proletarian revolution.

Marx's pre-Paris writings clearly show that Marx prior to Paris should be categorized as a radical, but in no sense a socialist, in McLellan's definition of the terms.[1] For example, in "Contribution to the Critique of Hegel's Philosophy of Law," written in the spring and summer of 1843, Marx analyzes Hegel's concept of the state. According to Marx, Hegel's concept of sovereignty had led him to endorse monarchy (Marx & Engels, 1975c:20–28). Against Hegel's defense of monarchy, Marx defends democracy:

Democracy is the *essence of all state constitutions*. . . .

Only democracy, therefore, is the true unity of the general and the particular. . . .

In democracy the constitution, the law, the state itself, insofar as it is a political constitution, is only the self-determination of the people. . . .

All forms of state have democracy *for* their truth and . . . they are therefore untrue insofar as they are not democracy. (1975c:30:31)

Similarly, in a series of articles written in October 1842, when Marx was editor of the *Rheinische Zeitung*, he takes the utopian position that the state ought to promote the interests of all citizens. The articles concerned a proposed law on the theft of wood, which would allow the forest owner to determine the value of the stolen wood. Marx and other critics saw this proposed law as promoting the interests of the forest owners. Marx argues that the state ought to promote the common good and not the interests of the forest owners (Marx & Engels, 1975a:236, 239:40, 245, 248, 261–62). He asserts that the members of the Rhine Provincial Assembly, which approved the proposal,

are legally entrusted not only with the representation of particular interests but also with the representation of the interests of the province, and however contradictory these two tasks may be, in case of conflict there should not be a moment's delay in sacrificing representation of particular interest to representation of the interests of the province. (Marx & Engels, 1975a:262)

This type of moral argument, which proclaims what individuals ought to do in a manner that is disconnected from material interests, is exactly the kind of argument that Marx would scornfully reject as he formulated his theoretical system after his move to Paris. However, at this stage in his development, he continued to have such utopian conceptions. Indeed, he presented a similar type of argument in "Contribution to the Critique of Hegel's Philosophy of Law," written just months before his move to Paris. Here Marx, under the influence of Feuerbach, critically analyzes Hegel's idealism, but in his critique he accepts Hegel's understanding that the state ought to promote general interests and to conserve particular interests within the context of general interests (Marx & Engels, 1975c:5, 16, 18, 28–30).

Prior to his move to Paris, Marx had also written in defense of freedom of the press (Padover, 1978:131–33). In the year before Marx's move to Paris, his feelings in this regard were strengthened by his own daily experiences with censorship as editor of the *Rheinische Zeitung*, in which capacity he served from October 15, 1842, to March 17, 1843 (Padover, 1978:143–50). Indeed, he resigned from his position in part because of censorship restrictions. During his tenure as editor, the paper boldly proclaimed the free press as "an indispensable organ of a people's needs and grievances" (Padover, 1978:146).

Thus, in the months immediately prior to his move to Paris, Marx was not a socialist or a communist in any sense of these terms. He was an outspoken defender of popular sovereignty and of freedom of the press as an important element in rule by the people. He believed that through adherence to these principles, the state would do what it ought to do, namely, to promote the interests of all citizens. These ideas were widely current in Germany in the 1830s and 1840s as liberalism and radicalism. His ideas in 1842 and 1843 were not different from other German radical intellectuals of his time, although he did express his views with forthrightness and with a flare for polemics.

Indeed, Marx in 1842 and 1843 specifically distanced himself from socialist and communist ideas, which were gaining currency at the time. For example, in an article on communism published in the *Rheinische Zeitung* the day after Marx took over as editor, Marx maintains that communism ought to be studied and criticized, but he is not prepared to admit that communism has any validity.

The *Rheinishce Zeitung*, which does not admit that communist ideas in their present form possess even *theoretical reality*, and therefore can still less desire their *practical realisation*, or even consider it possible, will subject these ideas to thoroughgoing criticism. ... Such writings as those of Leroux, Considerant, and above all the sharp-witted work by Proudhon, cannot be criticized on the basis of superficial flashes of thought, but only after long and profound study. (Marx & Engels, 1975a:220)

Here Marx seems intrigued by communism, indicating that it must be seriously studied and not superficially addressed, but he nonetheless in no sense considers himself a proponent of such ideas. Indeed, he is suspicious that these ideas are not valid even in theory, much less in reality.

Six weeks later, on November 30, 1842, Marx makes a similar observation in a letter to Arnold Ruge. He writes:

I regard it as inappropriate, indeed even immoral, to smuggle communist and socialist doctrines, hence a new world outlook, into incidental theatrical criticism, etc., and . . . I demand a quite different and more thorough discussion of communism, if it should be discussed at all. (Marx & Engels, 1975a:394)

Nine months later, in September 1843, Marx was to take a similar position on communism, even though he had in the intervening months read communist writings (Padover, 1978:595). The occasion was a letter to Ruge, with whom Marx was to publish the *Deutsch-Französische Jahrbücher*.[2] Marx expressed to Ruge his intentions for the journal:

I am not in favour of raising any dogmatic banner. On the contrary, we must try to help the dogmatists to clarify their propositions for themselves. Thus, *communism*, in partic-ular, is a dogmatic abstraction. . . .

And the whole socialist principle in its turn is only one aspect that concerns the *reality* of the true human being. But we have to pay just as much attention to the other aspect, to the theoretical existence of man, and therefore to make religion, science, etc., the object of our criticism. . . . In the first place religion, and next to it, politics, are the subjects which form the main interest of Germany today. We must take these, in whatever form they exist, as our point of departure, and not confront them with some ready-made system such as, for example, the *Voyage en Icarie*.[3] (Marx & Engels, 1975c:142–43)[4]

These words were written in September 1843. In late October 1843, Marx moved to Paris to serve as co-editor of the journal.

It is clear, therefore, that prior to Marx's move to Paris, his ideas were fairly typical of German radical intellectuals. They were basically consistent with the current of radicalism. He was interested in communism and socialism, and indeed he studied them in the fall of 1842 and the winter of 1843, but he was not sure of the validity of their claims. He certainly was not prepared to embrace their ideas. He was highly intelligent, scholarly, outspoken, witty, arrogant, and given to polemics, all of which was earning him a reputation as an outstanding advocate of radical ideas, but there was no hint of the theoretical system that he was to express so profoundly in *The German Ideology* in 1846 and that was to attain fairly widespread distribution in *The Communist Manifesto* in 1848.

Although the key to Marx's conversion was his experience in Paris, his ex-periences before he moved to Paris were important in setting the stage for his conversion. Especially important here was his experience of repression as an academic and a journalist. The repressive atmosphere in Germany in 1842–1843 deeply affected many intellectuals. As Goran Therborn writes:

The pious hopes of liberal bourgeois and Young Hegelians that the new Prussian king, Frederick William IV, would effect a revolution from above, were stifled in the winter of 1842–43 by a wave of press censorship and academic dismissals, and the democratic intellectuals were rapidly radicalized, one way or the other. (1976:325)

Marx experienced this general phenomenon of repression personally in a number of ways. Because of the movement against academics who were atheists, Marx's mentor at the University of Berlin, Bruno Bauer, was forced out of the academic profession (Padover, 1978:127–28). Marx himself could not obtain his Ph.D. at the University of Berlin and was forced to submit his dissertation at the University of Jena, where there was greater tolerance (Padover, 1978:124–25). And because of this repression, a university career, on which Marx had planned, was now closed to him (Padover, 1978:127–28). For this reason Marx undertook a career in journalism (Padover, 1978:129–30). And here, as we have seen, Marx experienced on a daily basis the restrictions of the censor (Padover, 1978:143–50).

As a result of these experiences, Marx was feeling an increasing alienation from the German national culture. And contributing to this alienation, above and beyond the repressive atmosphere, were his growing differences with the Young Hegelians, who had been Marx's closest friends and intellectual contacts during the years when he was a student at the University of Berlin (Padover, 1978:113–16). Marx's differences with the Berlin Young Hegelians were both political and theoretical. Politically, Marx believed that "their uncompromising attacks on liberal initiatives for reform were inimical to good relations with the progressive movement being mounted by the Rhineland bourgeoisie, which Marx supported" (Barbalet, 1983:35). Theoretically, the Young Hegelians were "attempting to work out 'revolutionary' principles derived from Hegel" (Barbalet, 1983:35). Marx, however, "regarded such projects poorly and was himself attempting to develop a total critique of Hegel" (Barbalet, 1983:35). These political and intellectual differences grew during Marx's tenure as editor of the *Rheinische Zeitung* in Bonn, in which capacity he was actually participating in the progressive movement in the Rhineland. He was beginning to view the concerns of the Young Hegelians as overly abstract. At this time, he became close to Ruge, and he became an admirer of Feuerbach, both of whom believed that philosophy must take elements not only from German thought but also from France.

Given Marx's increasing alienation from the political culture and philosophy of Germany, when the decision was made to publish the *Deutsch-Französische Jahrbücher* in Paris, he was pleased, for he was happy for "the opportunity to leave his native country" (Padover, 1978:172). He wrote to Ruge, "The atmosphere here is enslaving and I see absolutely no room in Germany for any free activity'' (quoted in Padover, 1978:172). The journal itself was envisioned to have pieces from German and French contributors, for the idea was to synthesize the best elements of German and French cultures. Thus, although Marx's ideas at the time of his move to Paris were very much a product of German philosophy and German intellectual currents, Marx left Germany as a marginal person who had found that his ideas were beyond the limits of tolerance in higher education and in journalism and who was increasingly questioning the premises of German philosophy.

At the end of October 1843, Marx moved to Paris in order to assume the editorship with Ruge of the *Deutsch-Französische Jahrbücher*. This move to Paris was to stimulate Marx to a critical reassessment of his assumptions and to lead him to the formulation of ideas beyond the horizon of German philosophy. There were two important elements in this transformation: Marx's encounter with the working-class struggle and his study of political economy.

MARX ENCOUNTERS THE WORKING-CLASS STRUGGLE

In Paris Marx encountered activists in the working-class struggle. These working-class activists were of three types: artisans, workers, and intellectuals. An artisan was a ''master craftsman who worked in his own home and employed 'companions' '' (McLellan, 1970:5). In the beginnings of capitalism, merchants contracted with artisans. However, as capitalist production developed, it became increasingly located in factories and increasingly centralized and mechanized. Accordingly, capitalist development led to increasing control of the process of production by the capitalist class and to the corresponding displacement of the artisan with the industrial worker. The artisans, therefore, were of somewhat higher status than industrial workers. They were skilled craftsmen who had greater control of their work than the industrial worker. And whereas the primary interest of the industrial worker was in shortening the working day and increasing compensation, the primary interest of the artisan was in the preservation of his craft. Artisans and industrial workers had in common an opposition to the capitalist class, rooted in the fact that the capitalist drive for profits was in opposition to the fundamental interests of both artisans and industrial workers. In contrast to the artisans and industrial workers, the intellectuals in the working-class struggle, although activists on behalf of the working class, were not themselves members of the working class, in that they were neither artisans nor industrial workers. They were primarily professionals, including journalists, writers, university professors, and physicians (Padover, 1978:224–25).

A number of scholars have noted that in Paris Marx had frequent contact with the artisans, industrial workers, and intellectuals who were working-class activists; that these working-class activists included socialists of various forms and members of socialist organizations, such as the Communist League; and that Marx's contact with such working-class activists had a profound effect on his intellectual development. Alex Callinicos, for example, maintains that in Paris, Marx encountered the German and French communists. There were some 40,000 German immigrants in Paris in 1844, the overwhelming majority of them artisans. Among them the League of the Just, driven underground for its role in the abortive 1839 insurrection of Blanqui and the *Société des saisons*, exercised a growing influence. Marx's contacts with this group, whose ideas were a mixture of the Utopian socialism of Fourier, the social Christianity of Lamennais, and the conspiratorial putschism of Blanqui, and his contacts with their French counterparts, were his first experience of working-class organization. The impact was profound. (1983:36)

Similarly, Saul Padover notes that Marx's meeting of workers in Paris had a significant influence on his development. Padover maintains that the workers in Paris in 1843–1845 were discontented and intelligent, and they are ''seething with radical idealism'' (1978:181). He maintains that ''class divisions were palpable, sharp and uncompromising. Marx did not have to imagine or invent the class struggle; he only had to look around him'' (1978:181). Moreover, Padover maintains that Marx in Paris came to personally know many working-class activists. He writes:

Paris provided Marx with the opportunity of getting to know real proletarians. He was introduced to working class radicals by a few men from the circle of German refugee intellectuals centered around Moses Hess, his friend and admirer from Cologne. . . .
   Paris had a colony of about 10,000 German artisans and journeymen—''shoemaker'' was then virtually synonymous with ''German''—with strong communist leanings. . . . Marx was introduced to the German artisans by a refugee physician, August Hermann Ewerback, who was both a member of the *Bund der Kommunisten* [Communist League] and chief of the secret society, *Bund der Gerechten* [League of the Just]. (1978:181–82)

Marx's contacts included not only German socialists but also French socialists. Padover notes that ''a police spy (Paris was then teeming with them) reported that in the summer of 1844 he often saw Marx visiting the meetings of the French communist groups in the Barrière du Trone, on the Rue de Vincennes'' (1978:183).
   McLellan also notes that the key to Marx's intellectual transformation in Paris was his personal contact with activists in working-class organizations. He maintains that prior to moving to Paris, Marx had studied the writings of socialists and communists. However, their work had little effect on his thinking. But in Paris, personal contact with radical intellectuals active in the working-class cause had a profound impact on his thinking. McLellan writes:

Far from being elaborations of bookish material studied at second or third hand, Marx's sudden espousal of the proletarian cause can be directly attributed to his first-hand contacts with socialist intellectuals in France. Instead of editing a paper for the Rhenish bourgeoisie or sitting in his study in Kreuznach, he was now at the heart of socialist thought and action. From October 1843 Marx was breathing a socialist atmosphere and even living in the same house as Germain Maurer, one of the leaders of the League of the Just whose meetings Marx frequented.It is not surprising that his surroundings made a swift impact on Marx. (1970:156—57)

Similarly, Therborn maintains that "it was in Paris . . . that Marx . . . underwent the decisive experiences that led [him] to break with Left Hegelian philosophy and radical-liberal politics" (1976:318). According to Therborn, what was important here was Marx's study of political economy as well as his encounter with working-class activists. He writes that in Paris Marx "came into contact with revolutionary workers from the French and German secret communist societies" (Therborn, 1976:319).

Various scholars, then, have noted that Marx in Paris encountered intellectuals, artisans, and industrial workers who were socialists and activists in the working-class struggle. There is an important issue at stake for these scholars. Marxism, as we have seen, claims to be an analysis of capitalism that has a special historic connection to the working class. Some Marxists have claimed that Marxism is written from a proletarian point of view. Others have claimed that Marxism is a scientific analysis that has been formulated by intellectuals who are united with (Therborn, 1973:8) and who have linked their fate with (Geras, 1972:84) the proletarian class. Given this claim of a historic connection between Marxism and the working class, it is important for Marxists to demonstrate that Marx, although not a worker, was personally connected to workers and to the workers' struggle. Yet the empirical claim for a personal connection between Marx and workers has been disputed. Tucker maintains, for example, that "the only proletarians which Marx knew were those in books" (quoted in McLellan, 1970:157). More recently, Alvin Gouldner has presented a similar argument. He writes:

Marx and Engels were never leaders of working-class parties, nor even editors of socialist newspapers; they were basically respected "consultants" to various working-class movements and parties. They were never on a picket line; they were never factory workers. . . . Marx lived much of his adult life a scholar in libraries, and he died at his desk. As he said, he was "a machine condemned to devour books." (Gouldner, 1985:20)

In regard to such arguments by Tucker and Gouldner, the claims of Padover are very important. Padover is primarily a biographer who has written biographies of a number of diverse figures, Marx among them. He is not a Marxist in any sense, and he does not have a theoretical interest in defending Marxism's historic connection to the working class. His biography of Marx, which is subtitled "An Intimate Portrait," is full of many detailed observations of Marx's personal life, and it is an important source for the issue of the connection of Marx's ideas to his personal life. In regard to the question of Marx's connection to the working-class struggle, Padover believes that Marx for most of his life was connected primarily to socialist intellectuals and artisans and not industrial workers (1978:224–25, 376–80). However, according to Padover, Marx's experiences in Paris involved an intense contact with socialist industrial workers as well as socialist artisans and intellectuals, and this contact profoundly affected his understanding.

Thus, in response to the arguments of Tucker and Gouldner, to assert that Marx in Paris was connected to industrial workers is an oversimplification. Rather, given the observations of Padover as well as Therborn and Callinicos, the more reasonable claim is that Marx was connected in Paris to working-class activists, and that these activists included industrial workers, artisans, and intellectuals. These workers, artisans, and intellectuals were socialists who were committed to the working-class cause and who participated in an organized struggle on behalf of the interests of the working class. It is clear that Marx was particularly affected in this experience by the conditions of the industrial worker. His focus on the conditions of the industrial worker can be seen in his writings in 1844 on the problem of alienation. Here he writes of the separation of the worker from the process and product of production, a separation that results from the impact of capitalism on the industrial worker. Moreover, for many years Marx was to write of the importance of the struggle for a limit to the working day, an issue of importance to the industrial worker as against the artisan. Thus, Marx clearly sought to understand capitalism from a point of view that takes as given the objective conditions of the industrial worker, and he saw the working-class struggle primarily as a struggle of industrial workers. The evidence is not, however, that Marx only encountered industrial workers in Paris. Rather, he encountered intellectuals, artisans, and industrial workers, who were socialists and activists on behalf of the working class. In short, he encountered the *working-class struggle*.

As a result of this encounter with the working-class struggle, Marx came to understand the proletariat as a revolutionary force. This was an idea that he took from socialism but transformed in accordance with his own developing understanding. At first, his conceptions of the role of the proletariat reflected the elitism of German philosophy: The workers were to transform the world under the guidance of philosophy; hence, Marx's well-known assertion in 1844 that philosophy is the head of the revolution, and the proletariat is the heart. However, as Marx developed his understanding, he came to the view that the proletariat not only acts but also is integrally involved in the development of revolutionary consciousness. Hence, Marx arrived at the notion that the proletarian struggle transforms not only society but also social consciousness.

Marx's new understanding of the role of the proletariat can be seen in his writings of 1844. In "Contribution to the Critique of Hegel's Philosophy of Right: Introduction," which was written a few months after Marx's arrival in Paris (McLellan, 1977:63), Marx proclaims that the proletariat is a universal class that can emancipate society. He writes:

So where is the real possibility of a German emancipation?
We answer: in the formation of a class with radical chains, a class in civil society that

is not a class of civil society, of a social group that is the dissolution of all social groups, of a sphere that has a universal character because of its universal sufferings and lays claim to no particular right, because it is the object of no particular injustice but of injustice in general. This class can no longer lay claim to a historical status, but only to a human one. It is not in a one-sided opposition to the consequences of the German political regime, it is in total opposition to its presuppositions. It is, finally, a sphere that cannot emancipate itself without emancipating itself from all other spheres of society and thereby emancipating these other spheres themselves. In a word, it is the complete loss of humanity and thus can only recover itself by a complete redemption of humanity. This dissolution of society, as a particular class, is the proletariat. (McLellan, 1977:72–73)

These are powerful words, full of compassion, anger, and hope. Marx is outraged by what he sees as the intense exploitation and degradation of the working class. It is a class with "radical chains." It has experienced its dissolution as a social group and the complete loss of its humanity. The exploitation of this class is so great that it represents "injustice in general." The suffering of this class is so great that its sufferings are universal. Yet this extreme degradation is the basis for hope, for the universal character of its suffering makes it possible for this class to emancipate and redeem all of humanity. With these words, Marx for the first time "proclaims his adherence to the cause of the proletariat" (McLellan, 1977:63). The proletariat has become for him the object of his compassion as well as the source of his hope for humankind. The sufferings of the proletariat have become the symbol of the human capacity for evil. The proletarian struggle has come to represent the human capacity to strive for justice in the midst of human degradation.

Marx's enthusiasm for the proletariat as the source of the human hope for social justice can be seen in his letter to Feuerbach, written August 11, 1844.

You would have to attend one of the meetings of the French workers to appreciate the pure freshness, the nobility which burst forth from these toil-worn men. . . .
It is among these "barbarians" of our civilized society that history is preparing the practical element for the emancipation of mankind. (Marx & Engels, 1975c:355)

And Marx's recognition of the role of the proletariat as a revolutionary force can be seen in the following passage in *The Holy Family*, written from September to November 1844.

The proletariat . . . is compelled as proletariat to abolish itself and thereby its opposite, private property, which determines its existence, and which makes it proletariat. It is the *negative* side of the antithesis, its restlessness within its very self, dissolved and self-dissolving private property. (Marx & Engels, 1975d:36)

It is clear that Marx also is wrestling here with an understanding of the proletariat in the context of a materialist re-interpretation of the Hegelian dialectic. This quest is even more pronounced in the following passage from the same work:

Indeed private property drives itself in its economic movement towards its own dissolution, but only through a development which does not depend on it, which is unconscious and which takes place against the will of private property by the very nature of things, only inasmuch as it produces the proletariat *as* proletariat, poverty which is conscious of its spiritual and physical poverty, dehumanisation which is conscious of its dehumanisation, and therefore self-abolishing. The proletariat executes the sentence that private property pronounces on itself by producing the proletariat, just as it executes the sentence that wage-labour pronounces on itself by producing wealth for others and poverty for itself. (Marx & Engels, 1975d:36)

The impact of Marx's encounter with the working-class struggle also can be seen in his reflections on socialism. Marx had studied French socialists in late 1842 and early 1843 (Padover, 1978:144, 595). However, as we have seen, as late as September 1843, Marx clearly was not a socialist and was not very sympathetic to their claims. However, his attitude toward socialist writings was to change dramatically after his move to Paris. This change of mind can be seen in his writings in 1844. In the *Economic and Philosophic Manuscripts of 1844*, written between April and August, Marx acknowledges his debt to French, English, and German socialists in his analysis of political economy (Bottomore, 1964:63–64). In *The Holy Family*, written from September through November 1844, Marx praises Proudhon's widely read socialist tract *What Is Property*? as a scientific treatise in political economy written from a vantage point that takes as given the interests of the proletariat (Marx & Engels, 1975d:31–33, 41).[5] In *The Holy Family* Marx also defends socialist writers for ascribing a revolutionary role to the proletariat (Marx & Engels, 1975d:36–37). And in the same work he offers the following observations on communists and socialists:

All communists and socialist writers proceeded from the observation that, on the one hand, even the most favourably brilliant deeds seemed to remain without brilliant results, to end in trivialities, and, on the other, *all progress of the Spirit* had so far been *progress against the mass of mankind*, driving it into an ever more *dehumanised* situation. They therefore declared "*progress*" (see *Fourier*) to be an inadequate, abstract *phrase*; they assumed (see *Owen* among others) a fundamental flaw in the civilized world; that is why they subjected the *real* foundations of contemporary society to incisive *criticism*. This communist criticism had practically at once as its counterpart the movement of the *great mass*, in opposition to which history had been developing so far. One must know the studiousness, the craving for knowledge, the moral energy and the unceasing urge for development of the French and English workers to be able to form an idea of the *human nobility* of this movement. (Marx & Engels, 1975d:84)

Marx is here praising socialist and communist writers for focusing, unlike German philosophy, on the real foundations of human history and for developing an understanding that is the theoretical counterpart to the working-class struggle. In *The Holy Family*, Marx, in addition, praises communism and socialism as the culmination of the Enlightenment. Marx saw the Enlightenment as an attack on seventeenth-century metaphysics, and he views nineteenth-century German philosophy as a restoration of metaphysics. In contrast to German philosophy, socialism and communism, especially in France and England, are carrying on the Enlightenment legacy (Marx & Engels, 1975d:124–25).

. As we have seen, by 1847 Marx moved beyond this identification with and support of the socialism and communism of his time, and had formulated his own theory of communism, a scientific communism that integrated the insights of political economy, German philosophy, and socialism in an analysis that takes as given the objective conditions of the working class.[6] As he developed his scientific theory of communism, he began to see ways in which the socialism and communism of his time were utopian and unscientific. However, in 1844, utopian and unscientific socialism were important elements in his thought. They provided for him key insights, such as the concept of the proletariat as a revolutionary force. Thus, in light of his encounter with the working-class struggle in 1843–1844, he had begun to re-evaluate his earlier understanding of socialism and to use socialist insights in his writings.

We see, then, that Marx experienced a remarkable intellectual development in a relatively short period of time. Less than a year after he distanced himself from socialism and communism, Marx writes that the bourgeoisie creates its own destruction by creating the proletariat, which, conscious of itself as poor and dehumanized, abolishes private property. He has become a champion of the proletarian cause and has moved from liberalism and radicalism to socialism, as the terms were then defined.

LUDWIG FEUERBACH

The impact of Marx's encounter with the working-class struggle on his intellectual development can be seen in the evolution in Marx's use of the ideas of Ludwig Feuerbach. Feuerbach was a native of Bavaria who had studied under Hegel at the University of Berlin (Padover, 1978:69) and who had a strong impact on the Young Hegelians in the 1840s. Marx had read Feuerbach's *Essence of Christianity* in 1841 (Padover, 1978:135). However, the book did not have a great effect on him. "The chief subject of the book, its critique of religion, was not of paramount interest to Marx, as he had already learned atheism from Bruno Bauer" (McLellan, 1969:96). Accordingly, "the articles that Marx wrote for the *Rheinische Zeitung* in 1842 show no trace of Feuerbach's influence" (McLellan, 1969:97). However, Feuerbach published two articles in 1843, and these two articles were to have a strong influence on Marx's writings during 1843–1845 (McLellan, 1969:97–133). Especially important in this regard were the "Contribution to the Critique of Hegel's Philosophy of Law" (written in the spring and summer of 1843), the *Economic and Philosophic Manuscripts* (written from April to August 1844), and *The Holy Family* (written from September to November 1844).

The strong influence of Feuerbach on Marx's writings of 1843 and 1844 has been clearly demonstrated by McLellan. However, McLellan does not address an important question from our point of view, namely, the contrast in Marx's use of Feuerbach's concepts in his writing prior to October 1843 as against his writing of 1844. In "Contribution to the Critique of Hegel's Philosophy of Law," written before Marx moved to Paris, Marx uses Feuerbach's concepts to criticize Hegel's turning the idea into a subject and thus inverting the ideal and the real. For Hegel, according to Marx, civil laws and the family are determined by the state (Marx & Engels, 1975c:5–6). In fact, Marx maintains, the state arises from family and civil society (Marx & Engels, 1975c:7). This confusion results from assuming the idea to be the subject. Marx writes:

The idea is made the subject and the *actual* relation of family and civil society to the state is conceived as its *internal imaginary* activity. Family and civil society are the premises of the state; they are the genuinely active elements, but in speculative philosophy things are inverted. When the idea is made the subject, however, the real subjects, namely, civil society, family, "circumstances, caprice, etc.", become *unreal* objective elements of the idea with a changed significance. (Marx & Engels, 1975c:8)

As McLellan notes, this critique of Hegel for inverting reality by making the idea the subject is taken from Feuerbach. Especially important here was Feuerbach's "Vorlaufige Thesen zur Reform der Philosophie," which was published in April 1842. McLellan writes:

The "Thesen" are a general criticism of Hegelian philosophy: Marx applies this same criticism to Hegel's political philosophy. Some of Marx's most characteristic terminology is taken over straight from the "Thesen." For example,. . . . Marx accused Hegel of having reversed the proper relation of subject and object, by making the idea or the state the cause instead of the effect: "The important thing is that Hegel everywhere makes the idea into the subject and thus the real, proper subject into the predicate." This makes specific Feuerbach's criticism at the beginning of the "Thesen": "We need only make the predicate into the subject and thus reverse speculative philosophy in order to arrive at the unconcealed, pure and naked truth." (1969:103)

Thus, Marx used Feuerbach in his critique of Hegel's inversion of the actual relation between the idea and reality and between the state and civil society. Marx at this stage in his development is becoming increasingly critical of German philosophy as speculative and wedded to the mistaken premise that ideas shape history. As was noted above, this increasing disaffiliation with German philosophy was in part a result of his experiences as an editor of the *Rheinische Zeitung*, in which capacity he participated in liberal and radical movements calling for a free press and popular sovereignty. But in this critique of German philosophy in the "Contribution to the Critique of Hegel's Philosophy of Law," Marx is still in no sense a socialist, and he certainly has not yet arrived at the conclusion that the proletariat is an agent of revolution. Therefore, his use of Feuerbach in his pre-Paris writings is limited to the purpose of criticizing Hegel's idealism. However, once he encounters the working-class struggle and begins to see the proletariat as an agent of social change, he begins to see in Feuerbach new possibilities, and he begins to use Feuerbach's concepts to articulate the socialist notion of the proletariat as an agent of social change. This new and very different use of Feuerbach can be seen in his writings of 1844.

As we have seen, Marx first proclaimed the cause of the proletariat in "Towards a Critique of Hegel's Philosophy of Right: Introduction," which was written early in 1844. In the "Introduction," Marx expresses a complementary relation between the proletariat and philosophy in the revolutionary struggle: "As philosophy finds in the proletariat its material weapons, so the proletariat finds in philosophy its intellectual weapons" (McLellan, 1977:73). Expanding upon this notion, Marx summarizes the possibilities for the liberation of Germany:

The emancipation of Germany is the emancipation of man. The head of this emancipation is philosophy, its heart is the proletariat. Philosophy cannot realize itself without transcending the proletariat, the proletariat cannot transcend itself without realizing philosophy. (McLellan, 1977:73)

McLellan notes that such a distinction between head and heart in a revolutionary philosophy is taken from Ludwig Feuerbach.

Feuerbach declared that the two essential tools of philosophy are the head, source of activity and idealism, and the heart, source of passivity and feeling. Truth and life were only to be found where "the sanguine principle of French sense-perception and materialism is united to the phlegm of German metaphysics". Thus the philosopher who really wished to be in touch with life and mankind would have to be of Gallo-Germanic blood. The heart, the feminine principle and seat of materialism, is French; the head, the masculine principle and seat of idealism, is German. The heart is essential, being the source of all revolution and movement. (McLellan, 1969:105)

But in using this idea from Feuerbach, Marx at the same time transformed it. The head is no longer represented by German philosophy, but by philosophy as a whole. And the heart is no longer represented by French materialism, which is itself a way of thinking. Rather, the heart is represented by a real materialist force, namely, the proletarian struggle. Thus, he is using Feuerbach's distinction in his formulation of a theory of proletarian revolution, thereby placing Feuerbachian concepts into a socialist context.

In a similar way, Marx takes Feuerbach's terms "species-life" and "species-being" and gives them a new meaning in light of his concern for the conditions of the working class. As Bottomore [7] notes:

The terms "species-life" (*Gattungsleben*) and "species-being" (*Gattungswesen*) are derived from Feuerbach. . . . Feuerbach discusses the nature of man, and argues that man is to be distinguished from animals not by "consciousness" as such, but by a particular kind of consciousness. Man is not only conscious of himself as an individual; he is also conscious of himself as a member of the human species, and so he apprehends a "human essence" which is the same in himself and in other men. According to Feuerbach this ability to conceive of "species" is the fundamental element in the human power of reasoning: "Science is the consciousness of species." Marx, while not departing from this meaning of the terms, employs them in other contexts. (1964:13)

Let us examine the different context in which Marx uses these terms. In the *Economic and Philosophic Manuscripts* of 1844,'' Marx's analysis has a special concern for the situation of the industrial worker. As a dimension of this concern, Marx formulated the concept of alienated labor.[8] For Marx, the worker in capitalism is alienated in four respects. First, the worker is alienated from the product that labor produces. "The object produced by labour, its product, now stands opposed to it as an *alien being*, as a *power* independent of the producer" (Bottomore, 1964:122). Second, the worker is alienated from the process of production. "Alienation appears not merely in the result but also in the *process of production*, within *productivity* itself" (Bottomore, 1964:124). Accordingly, the worker "does not fulfill himself in his work but denies himself . . . [and] does not develop freely his mental and physical energies" (Bottomore, 1964:125). Third, labor in capitalism is alienated in the sense that capitalism converts labor to a means for individual existence; as such, labor ceases to be an activity that expresses the individual's consciousness of belonging to a species. Marx here uses Feuerbach's concept of species-life to make this point. He writes that alienated labor

makes *species-life* into a means of individual life. In the first place it alienates species-life and individual life, and secondly, it turns the latter, as an abstraction, into the purpose of the former, also in its abstract and alienated form.

For labour, *life activity, productive life*, now appear to man only as *means* for the satisfaction of a need, the need to maintain his physical existence. Productive life, is however, species-life. It is life creating life. (Bottomore, 1964:127)

Accordingly, "alienated labor turns the *species-life of man* . . . into a *means* for his *individual existence*" (Bottomore, 1964:129). Moreover, as a consequence of this alienation from species-life, there is a fourth dimension to alienation: "*man is alienated* from other *men*" (Bottomore, 1964:129).

Although the language is somewhat obscure, it is clear that Marx is arguing that labor in capitalism negates the consciousness of belonging to a species, a consciousness that is a distinctive characteristic of humans as against animals. Labor in capitalism thus reduces the laborer to an animal-like struggle for existence. In using Feuerbach's concept of species-life in this way, Marx is placing the concept into the context of the development of systems of production, for he is recognizing that a system of production can undermine such consciousness of belonging to a species, and he is arguing that such is indeed the situation that the worker confronts in a capitalist system of production. This new context, very different from Feuerbach's intention, reflects Marx's attention to the objective conditions of the working class in light of his experience of encounter with the working-class struggle.

Not only does Marx use Feuerbach's concepts in a new way in the wake of his encounter with the working-class struggle, but he also came to a new understanding of Feuerbach's work as a whole, in that he sees Feuerbach's work as providing a philosophical foundation for socialism. With reference to the two articles that Feuerbach wrote in 1843, Marx writes to Feuerbach: "In these writings you have provided—I don't know whether intentionally—a philosophical basis for socialism and the Communists have immediately understood them in this way" (Marx & Engels, 1975c:354). This assessment, written August 11, 1844, was very different from Marx's interpretation of the work when he originally read it in 1843, several months before his move to Paris.

Even though Marx significantly used Feuerbach's concepts during the time when he was experiencing an intellectual and moral conversion, in many ways Marx's conversion rendered Feuerbach's ideas less useful to Marx than they had been when Marx was a political radical dissatisifed with the speculativeness of German philosophy. At the time of his conversion, Marx's initial strategy was to transform Feuerbach's concepts in order that they could be used to express his new ideas. But as he continued to search for ways to formulate his new ideas, he would rapidly find other sources more fruitful, and he would quickly move beyond Feuerbach. In *The German Ideology*, which he wrote with Engels from September 1845 to the summer of 1846 (Padover, 1978:597), Marx and Engels argue that Feuerbach has failed to escape the idealism of German philosophy. With reference to a book that Feuerbach published in 1845, they write:

It is also clear from these arguments how grossly Feuerbach is deceiving himself when . . . he declares himself a communist. . . . .Feuerbach's whole deduction with regard to the relation of men to one another goes only so far as to prove that men need and *always* have needed each other. He wants to establish consciousness of this fact, that is to say, like the other theorists, merely to produce a correct consciousness about an *existing* fact; whereas for the real communist it is a question of overthrowing the existence state of things. (Marx & Engels, 1970:60)

As Barbalet observes, in *The German Ideology* Feuerbach is "counted as merely another representative of modern German philosophy. . . . Marx's political use of Feuerbach, therefore, ranges from 1843 to 1845, and abruptly ends with a theoretical critique of him the following year" (1983:37).

MARX'S STUDY OF POLITICAL ECONOMY

Just as Marx was transformed by his encounter with the working-class struggle in Paris, so was Engels transformed by his encounter with the working-class struggle in England. Friedrich Engels went to England in 1842 at the age of twenty-two. Although German by birth and education, he had an excellent command of English, and he quickly made an effort to meet leaders and activists in the working-class struggle (Cameron, 1985:10–11). England was at that time the most advanced country in radical thought and working-class activity (Cameron, 1985:9). Engels was particularly influenced by the Chartists, for this was the group that most impressed him and with which he had the most personal contact in Manchester. The Chartists were so called because of their support of the People's Charter, drawn up in 1835 by the General Workingman's Association of London. The Charter contained six points, including universal manhood suffrage and the abolition of property qualifications for candidates to the House of Commons (Cameron, 1985:10–11). Even though the focus of the Chartists was on the radical proposal of universal suffrage, the program of social change that they advocated was essentially socialist. Their analyses understood the exploitation of the worker by the capitalist class and the need for a working-class struggle. They proposed working-class control of society and the nationalization of land, railroads, and other forces of production (Cameron, 1985:14–15). In these ideas, they pre-dated and anticipated Marx. They were, however, utopian socialists, in that they "adhered to the simplistic idea that one should abstractly draw up a plan for socialism and then work to achieve it" (Cameron, 1985:16). They fell short of the later historical materialism of Marx, in that they did not see socialism as emerging from the unfolding of contradictions in the system of production.

Engels was impressed and moved by the Chartists. He wrote, "In every town, the Chartists have shown more activity than all the German political, socialist and religious parties taken together" (quoted in Cameron, 1985:11). Along with his encounter with the Chartists, Engels in England began to study English political economists and socialists (McLellan, 1970:164) and to accumulate data on the conditions of the working class (Cameron, 1985:12). His first work on political economy, "Outlines of a Critique of Political Economy," was published in Marx and Ruge's *Deutsch-Französische Jahrbücher* in February 1844. It was a critical analysis of English political economy, focusing on the connection of political economy to the interests of the bourgeoisie (see Marx & Engels, 1975c:418–43). Engels's clasic work, *Condition of the Working Class in England*, was completed in March 1845 (Cameron, 1985:12).

Engels was to be important to Marx's intellectual development, primarily because Engels stimulated Marx to a serious study of political economy. Marx and Engels had first met in 1842, but the meeting had little impact on Marx. As McLellan observes, "The two had met . . . in Cologne in Novemebr 1842, but Marx had received Engels coldly, seeing in him a representative of the Berlin *Freien*[9] with whom he had just broken" (1970:163). However, in late 1843 or very early 1844, Marx read Engels's "Outlines of a Critique of Political Economy" (Oakley, 1984:10; Marx & Engels, 1975c:375–76). The article "was the first work on economics from which Marx took notes" (McLellan, 1970:163). Marx was very impressed by it, referring to it in the Preface to *A Contribution to the Critique of Political Economy* as a "brilliant essay on the critique of economic categories'' (Marx & Engels, 1975c:615). The article stimulated Marx to initiate a study of political economy. ''Engels' passionate critique of man's material situation under capitalism is the most likely intellectual catalyst that drew Marx towards a study of political economy'' (Oakley, 1984:10; see also McLellan, 1970:164). Marx and Engels met for a second time on August 28, 1844, at which time they began their lifelong relationship as collaborators and friends (Padover, 1978:183–85, 595–96; McLellan, 1970:164). This association with Engels reinforced Marx's turn early in 1844 to the study of political economy.

The study of political economy was an important part of Marx's intellectual development during the first months of 1844. Early in 1844, Marx copied excerpts from and made critical commentaries on political economists, all of which were recorded in a series of nine notebooks. In these Paris Notebooks are found notes by Marx on seventeen political economists, including the English political economists Adam Smith, David Ricardo, and James Mill, and the French political economist Jean-Baptiste Say (Oakley, 1984:10).[10] This study became the basis of the *Economic and Philosophic Manuscripts* of 1844 (also known as the *Paris Manuscripts*), which were written during the period of April through August of that year (Oakley, 1984:10–11; Padover, 1978:190; Callinicos, 1983:37). In the manuscripts, one finds the basic elements of the analysis of political economy that Marx was to formulate in his later works.

In the Preface to the *Paris Manuscripts*, Marx notes that his ''conclusions are the fruit of an entirely empirical analysis, based upon a careful critical study of political economy'' (Bottomore, 1964:63). He also acknowledges his debt to French, English, and German socialists, and he notes his appreciation for Feuerbach's critique of Hegel (Bottomore, 1964:63–65).

Marx begins the manuscripts by expressing his concern for the condition of the worker. He notes that in a situation in which wealth is decreasing, the workers will be especially hard hit. ''If the wealth of society is diminishing, . . . *none suffers so cruelly from its decline as the working class*'' (Bottomore, 1964:71). Moreover, even in situations when wealth is increasing, the workers will suffer, because greater demands will be placed upon their labor time, and this will lead to a shortening of their lives. And increasing wealth means expansion of capital and thus a greater dependency of the worker on the mechanized labor of capital. And as more workers are thrown into such dependency, there is greater competition among workers, thereby lowering their wages. Accordingly,

even in the state of society which is most favourable to the worker, the inevitable result for the worker is overwork and premature death, reduction to a machine, enslavement to capital which accumulates in menacing opposition to him, renewed competition, and beggary or starvation for a part of the workers. (Bottomore, 1964:73)

In noting the connection between overwork and premature death, Marx here anticipates the fuller discussion in his later works of the significance of the length of the working day.

Marx next proceeds to attempt to use the concepts of political economy to formulate his understanding of the essential dynamics of capitalism. Here he discusses concepts and issues that were to be central in *Capital*. He defines necessary labor time, capital, and profit (Bottomore, 1964:69–70, 85–89). He discusses competition among capitals, and its tendency to give way to the concentration of capital (Bottomore, 1964:89–94). He describes the emergence of large-scale landed property and its tendency to lead to the decline of feudalism and the feudal aristrocracy and to the emergence of the bourgeoisie and the proletariat as the only two classes (Bottomore, 1964:113–15, 140–41). Marx summarizes his use of political economy with these words:

We have begun from the presuppositions of political economy. We have accepted its terminology and its laws. We presupposed private property; the separation of labour, capital and land, as also of wages, profit and rent, the division of labor; competition; the concept of exchange value, etc. From political economy itself, in its own words, we have shown that the worker sinks to the level of a commodity, and to a most miserable commodity; that the misery of the worker increases with the power and volume of his production; that the necessary result of competition is the accumulation of capital in a few hands, and thus a restoration of monopoly in a more terrible form. (Bottomore, 1964:120)

Thus, Marx uses the concepts of political economy, but he seeks to go beyond them, and in particular he seeks to discern a meaning in the concepts of political economy from a vantage point which examines the impact of the system of production on the conditions of the worker.

Marx, then, is formulating a critique of political economy. He maintains that heretofore political economy has examined capitalism from the point of view of the capitalist: "When, for example, the relation of wages to profits is defined, this is explained in terms of the interests of capitalists" (Bottomore, 1964:120). As a result, political economy sees only external appearances and does not understand the essential dynamics of private property or its laws (Bottomore, 1964:120). Moreover, political economy treats the worker merely as a worker and not as a human being. In Marx's words:

It is self-evident that political economy treats the *proletarian*, i.e. one who lives, without capital or rent, simply from labour, and from one-sided, abstract labour, merely as a *worker*. It can, therefore, propound the thesis that he, like a horse, must receive just as much as will enable him to work. Political economy does not deal with him in his free time, as a human being, but leaves this aspect to the criminal law, doctors, religion, statistical tables, politics and the workhouse beadle. (Bottomore, 1964:76)

In other words, "political economy conceives the worker only as a draught animal, as a beast whose needs are strictly limited to bodily needs" (Bottomore, 1964:79). Accordingly,

The needs of the worker are thus reduced to the need to maintain him *during work*, so that the race of workers does not die out. Consequently, wages have exactly the same significance as the *maintenance* of any other productive instrument, and as the *consumption of capital* in general so that it can reproduce itself with interest. They are like the oil which is applied to a wheel to keep it running. Wages thus form part of the necessary *costs* of capital and of the capitalist, and they must not exceed this necessary amount. (Bottomore, 1964:138)

But Marx seeks to "rise above the level of political economy" (Bottomore, 1964:76). He seeks to grasp the essential dynamics of private property by taking as given the objective conditions that confront the working class. In Marx's words:

We shall begin from a *contemporary* economic fact. The worker becomes poorer the more wealth he produces and the more his production increases in power and extent. The worker becomes an ever cheaper commodity the more goods he creates. The *devaluation* of the human world increases in direct relation with the *increase in value* of the world of things. (Bottomore, 1964:121)

Thus, Marx is endeavoring to use a point of view that takes as given the objective conditions of the working class. These objective conditions are that the working class creates its own poverty by creating wealth and becomes a cheaper commodity by creating commodities.

In taking this point of view, one can see that the working class experiences alienation. The contemporary economic fact that the working class creates its own poverty "simply implies that the object produced by labour, its product, now stands opposed to it as an *alien being*, as a *power independent* of the producer" (Bottomore, 1964:122). As we have seen, alienation has four dimensions: the worker is alienated from the product, the process of production, from a consciousness of himself as capable of fully human life, and from other men (Bottomore, 1964:122–29). These dimensions of alienation can be discerned from a vantage point that takes as given the objective conditions of the working class. But political economy, which examines capitalism from the point of view of the interests of capitalists, does not understand the phenomenon of alienation. To some extent, alienation is obscured by political economy: "*political economy conceals the alienation in the nature of labour in so far as it does not examine the direct relationship between the worker (work) and production*" (Bottomore, 1964:124). Moreover, to the extent that political economy is aware of alienation, it sees alienated labor as a consequence of private property. However, Marx argues, this is not so:

Through alienated labor the worker creates the relation of another man, who does not work and is outside the work process, to this labour. The relation of the worker to work also produces the relation of the capitalist (or whatever one likes to call the lord of labour) to work. *Private property* is, therefore, the product, the necessary result, of *alienated labour*, of the external relation of the worker to nature and to himself. (Bottomore, 1964:131)

In this error, political economy has grasped only appearances: "although private property appears to be the basis and cause of alienated labour, it is rather a consequence of the latter" (Bottomore, 1964:131). But from a point of view that takes as given the objective conditions of the working class, the essence of private property and alienation can be understood, and it can be seen that private property is a consequence of alienated labor.

In the *Paris Manuscripts*, Marx also anticipates themes that were to be central in *Theories of Surplus Value*. He anticipates, for example, his later discussion of the Physiocrats. He notes that the Physiocratic system reflects "the economic decomposition of feudal property" (Bottomore 1964:149). Accordingly, the Physiocrats seek to re-establish feudal property, but to do so in the language of modern economics. In the process, the Physiocrats arrive at the insight that agricultural labor is the source of wealth. However, they cannot see the implications of this insight for labor in general. They do not grasp that "agriculture does not differ from any other industry; and that it is . . . *labour in general* which is the *essence* of wealth" (Bottomore, 1964:150). That the Physiocratic theory would appear before the scientific political economy of Smith parallels historical development, for "labour appears at first only as *agricultural labour* but later establishes itself as *labour in general*" (Bottomore, 1964:151).

Marx further observes that as political economy develops from Smith to Ricardo, it increasingly describes the workers as a worker devoid of all human qualities. But this cynical view of the workers is scientific, for in the first place, it shows "with greater logic and clarity, that *labour* is the sole *essence of wealth*" (Bottomore, 1964:148). Second, this increasing cynicism is increasingly scientific because it reflects the increasing alienation and objectification of the capitalist system of production (Bottomore, 1964:148–49). Indeed, the contradiction in political economy between the insight, on the one hand, that labor is the source of value, and the claim, on the other hand, that private property is everything, is in reality nothing other than "the contradiction of *alienated labour* with itself" (Bottomore, 1964:132). Therefore, in Marx's view, "political economy has merely formulated the laws of alienated labour" (Bottomore, 1964:132). However, Marx argues, it is now possible to move to a new understanding of alienation. This new understanding does not take as given the concept of private property. Rather, it understands the secret of private property, namely, that it is a consequence of alienation. This secret is revealed as the system of production develops:

Only in the final stage of the development of private property is its secret revealed, namely, that it is on one hand the *product* of alienated labour, and on the other hand the *means* by which labour is alienated, *the realization of this alienation*. (Bottomore, 1964:131)

Thus, the development of the system of production makes it possible to understand that alienation is the source of private property.

In this discussion of the Physiocrats and the development of political economy from Smith to Ricardo, Marx is suggesting some ideas that he will formulate in a much more developed form in the *Theories of Surplus Value*. Particularly important here is his discussion of the relationship between the development of science and the development of material conditions. He clearly has begun an analysis that will consume much of his energy in the 1850s and 1860s, namely, an analysis of the development of theories of political economy and the connection of their insights and oversights to the development of the system of production. Ultimately, his analysis will include the dimension of revolutionary struggle in making possible such insights, an element that is lacking in these brief fragments. But it is clear that in 1844 he has begun to address this issue and that some of the basic ideas of his later formulation have begun to take shape.

In the *Paris Manuscripts*, Marx uses socialist writers in his effort to go beyond political economy. Thus, he quotes socialist writers who argue that workers are degraded and made dependent by capitalism and, as a result, are compelled to sell their labor power (Bottomore, 1964:77–84). Yet, in the manuscripts, Marx is clearly moving toward a critique of socialism and toward his own definition of communism and socialism. He writes that communism is the abolition of both alienation and private property (Bottomore, 1964:155–56, 159–60). He criticizes the socialists Étienne Cabet and Francois Villegardelle for advocating a crude form of communism in which private property becomes general. In this form, all people are workers and all workers are owners of private property. This crude communism does not grasp that emancipation requires the abolition of private property itself and therefore of the alienation that is its source (Bottomore, 1964:153, 155–56). Moreover, Marx argues that Cabet and Villegardelle refer to historical examples in order to justify communism. They do not see that a fully developed communism does not replicate past historical forms but can only emerge as a resolution of the antagonisms in the system of alienation (Bottomore, 1964:155–56). In the same vein, Marx criticizes Proudhon for taking the side of labor in the context of a system of private property. Proudhon's proposals for an enforced increase in wages and equality of incomes cannot restore "human significance and worth" (Bottomore, 1964:132) to work or to the worker. The socialist perspective that Marx is formulating recognizes the importance of a "new mode of production" (Bottomore, 1964:168). Thus, in the *Paris Manuscripts*, Marx anticipates the criticisms of utopian and vulgar socialism that he will formulate in a more developed form in *Theories of Surplus Value*.

In the *Paris Manuscripts*, Marx continues to be influenced by the tradition of German philosophy, a tradition that constitutes his intellectual roots. As we have seen, he uses Feuerbach's concept of species-being in order to formulate the concept of alienation. Yet he continues his critical posture toward Hegel and the Young Hegelians. In Hegel's system, emancipation from alienation "occurs in *consciousness*, in *pure thought*, i.e., in abstraction'' (Bottomore, 1964:201) because "Hegel has merely discovered an *abstract, logical* and *speculative* expression of the historical process" (Bottomore, 1964:198). German philosophy since Hegel, moreover, has for the most part not escaped this limitation. Strauss and Bruno Bauer, he writes, remain "ensnared in Hegelian logic" (Bottomore, 1964:195). Among the German philosophers, only Feuerbach has developed "a *serious* and *critical* relation to Hegel's dialectic" (Bottomore, 1964:197). Feuerbach's achievement is "to have founded *genuine materialism* and *positive science* by making the social relationship of 'man to man' the basic principle of his theory" (Bottomore, 1964:197). Thus, Marx in the *Paris Manuscripts* continues to stand in the tradition of German philosophy. He rejects the work of the Young Hegelians, including his former mentor, Bruno Bauer. But he identifies with the materialist critique of Hegel associated with Feuerbach. And he specifically uses Feuerbach's concepts in his critique of political economy.

In the *Economic and Philosophic Manuscripts of 1844*, then, Marx has a critical relationship to the three intellectual traditions of political economy, socialism, and German philosophy. He is attempting a critique of political economy, and he uses concepts from all three intellectual traditions in his critique. At the same time, he adopts a critical posture toward all three traditions. He maintains that political economy writes from a capitalist point of view and fails to understand the essence of alienation or private property; that socialism has failed to grasp the insights of political economy, and thus is utopian or vulgar; that German philosophy has understood only the history of consciousness, and not real human history. Marx seeks to go beyond these limitations, to synthesize the insights of each of the traditions, and to formulate a critique of political economy from a vantage point which takes as given the objective conditions of the working class.

Clearly, Marx's thinking has developed to an astonishing extent from October 1843 to August 1844. In less than a year, Marx has come to think in a completely different way. He has experienced a moral and intellectual conversion, prompted by his study of political economy and his encounter with the working-class struggle.

Moreover, much of this new way of thinking would define his world view for the rest of his life. In the *Economic and Philosophic Manuscripts of 1844*, Marx begins to address issues that were to be central in *Capital, Theories of Surplus Value*, and *Contribution Toward a Critique of Political Economy*. And although the later formulation would address these issues in a much more developed form, his subsequent intellectual development would to a large extent follow the basic ideas developed in the horizon shift of 1843–1844. He would, of course, continue to develop in his ideas. In 1846, Marx would reject Feuerbach in *The German Ideology* and the "Thesis on Feuerbach." And in *The Poverty of Philosophy*, written in 1847, he would dismiss socialism as utopian. Furthermore, he ultimately would more fully articulate the notion of the role of the revolutionary struggle of the proletariat in the development of scientific insights. But his subsequent development would not involve the kind of intellectual transformation which occurred during the moral and intellectual conversion of 1843–1844. His subsequent development would occur within the context of the horizon which he creatively forged in the midst of the profound personal and intellectual experiences of 1843–1844.

GERMAN PHILOSOPHY

To what extent did Marx continue to be influenced by German philosophy after 1844? In *The German Ideology*, written during 1845–1846, Marx and Engels deliver a scathing and irreverent critique of German philosophy. In this critique, does Marx put German philosophy to rest, never to return to it again? Althusser believes that he does. Althusser maintains that in *German Ideology*, Marx announces his intention to turn away from philosophy and to turn to the construction of a new science of history or historical materialism (Althusser, 1971:35–40, 67–68). Like Althusser, William LeoGrande is an advocate of what Barbalet (1983:1) calls the discontinuity thesis on the relationship between the young and the mature Marx. LeoGrande maintains that the Marx of 1846 is very different from the Marx of 1844. In 1844, in *The Holy Family*, Marx praises Feuerbach; in contrast, in 1846, Marx attacks Feuerbach in the "Theses on Feuerbach" and in *German Ideology*. Moreover, *German Ideology*, according to LeoGrande, differs in other important ways from the *Paris Manuscripts*. "Man's species being, which served in the early works as the basis of man's communal character, is replaced in the *German Ideology* and subsequent works by a material connection" (LeoGrande, 1977:140). Further, in the *German Ideology*, "Capitalism is doomed as a social system not because it generates life conditions that violate man's essence; it is doomed because it generates conditions that negate its *own* mode of operation" (1977:142).

In my view, however, the interpretations of Althusser and LeoGrande are questionable. Hegelian philosophy clearly constitutes the foundation of Marx's critique of political economy, especially the notion, so central to his historical materialism, of a dialectical development in human history, according to which human history is driven by contradictions in the system of production. Marx's historical materialism is of course a materialist transformation of Hegel, but the legacy of Hegel is unmistakable. Many scholars have taken this interpretation and have argued in favor of the continuity thesis. Karl Korsch (1970:30–45, 66–68, 83–85), for example, stresses the philosophical foundation of scientific Marxism. Korsch acknowledges that Marx's scientific socialism ceases to be philosophy and is the annihilation of philosophy (1970:43–45). However, this abolition of philosophy does not involve simply rejecting philosophy (1970:68). "It is incorrect to say that Marx's materialist theory is no longer philosophical because it has an aim that is not simply theoretical but is also a practical and revolutionary goal" (1970:67). In his abolition or negation of philosophy, Marx does not reject philosophy. Rather, he rejects only that philosophy which is not also practice, for "theoretical criticism and practical overthrow are inseparable activities" (1970:83). In the same vein, Aldolfo Vazquez notes that the concept of praxis is strongly rooted in German philosophy (1977:25–26). Vazquez argues against the notion of a discontinuity between the Marx of the *Paris Manuscripts* and the Marx of *German Ideology*. "The fundamental thesis of the *Manuscripts*– that man transforms himself and the world through labour–comes to be the key to the subsequent development of Marx's thought" (1977:110). Similarly, Sidney Hook in *From Hegel to Marx*, stresses the continuity of Marx and Hegel, especially in the fact that Marx applies the Hegelian dialectic to human history and to the revolutionary consciousness of the proletariat. For Hook, the heart of the dialectical notion in Hegel is the idea that contradiction drives the social system: "The driving force in the development of a dialectical situation is derived from the conflict and opposition of the elements within it" (1958:67). In Marx's hands, consciousness, especially class consciousness, and even more particularly, the revolutionary class consciousness of the proletariat, is essential to the dialectical process:

It is in the field of history, however, that the principle of dialectic becomes vitally relevant for Marx. . . . Through *class* consciousness society attains self-consciousness. Consciousness implies activity. As a result of the activity of class consciousness the interacting social whole becomes transformed. The class is the subject of the historical process, the carrier of the transformative principle. (Hook, 1958:74)

Roger Garaudy also stresses the foundation of Marx's analysis in Hegelian dialectics. Hegelian dialectics focuses on contradictions which set the whole in motion and foster its development (1976:92–93). Marx effected a "materialist reversal of Hegelian philosophy and the transition from speculation to science [which] enabled him to work out a dialectical method related to the valid method of science" (1976:95). In a similar vein, Scott McNall maintains that "Marx preserved a Hegelian view of the structure of history but provided a different content" (1984:477). Indeed, he argues that the entire debate over continuity versus discontinuity in Marx was unnecessary and related to the availability of texts. Ronald Kieve also argues that Marx's materialist dialectic is grounded in Hegel's idealism. He notes that the "first fully materialist formulation of the dialectical method" (1983:50) is found in *The Poverty of Philosophy*. In addition, Joan Cocks (1983) stresses the debt of Marx to Hegel. Finally, David McLellan (1970:214– 20) and Terrel Carver (Carver, 1975:38–39) stress the continuity of the young and the mature Marx. There is, therefore, an emerging consensus among scholars that there is continuity between the Marx of 1844 and the Marx of 1846 and after. This consensus view is entirely consistent with my point of view, because the timing of Marx's horizon shift of 1843–1844 would imply such a continuity.

There is a second disagreement among scholars concerning Marx's intellectual development. Scholars agree that Marx underwent a shift or a turn in his intellectual development, but the point at which they place this turn varies according to which aspects of the work of the mature Marx they attach most significance. Vazquez notes that some place the turn at the "Contribution to a Critique of Hegel's Philosophy of Right," for here is a rejection of idealism. Some place the turn at the "Introduction to the Contribution to a Critique of Hegel's Philosophy of Right," for there the role of the proletariat is proclaimed. Others place it at the *Paris Manuscripts*, for they "discuss human labor as an essential dimension of man" (1977:96). Others place it at *German Ideology*, for "Marx first formulated there the laws of correspondence between productive forces and the relations of production" (1977:96). Some place it at the *Communist Manifesto*, "where Marx set out clearly and explicitly the theory of the revolutionary action of the proletariat" (1977:97). Some place it at the 1859 Prologue to the *Contribution to the Critique of Political Economy*, for it was here that the full dimensions of the materialist conception of history were expressed. Vazquez himself place the break at the *Communist Manifesto*, for "Marxism becomes a philosophy of praxis with the *Manifesto*" (1977:97), and in the *Communist Manifesto*, "the foundations are laid for the meeting of thought and action" (1977:97). Vazquez maintains that in the "Introduction," a scientific understanding of the role of the proletariat is not yet developed; and that the revolutionary role of the proletariat is not at this point seen as a consequence of its socio-economic position, but as a consequence of the fact that it is a negation of the universally human (1977:101–2). Marx had not yet discovered the idea that revolutionary praxis emerges from human labor (1977:102–3).

I have difficulty with all these interpretations, for they attempt to establish the time of the turn on the basis of intellectual content alone. This amounts to nothing more than designating what one takes to be the central idea in Marx's corpus and showing when that idea first appeared. Such designations are thus unrelated to events in Marx's life. Taking into account the impact of events in Marx's life, the period of 1843–1844 clearly marked a significant turn in Marx's thought, for during that period Marx intensively studied political economy and personally encountered the working-class struggle. As a result of these experiences, Marx during that period developed in basic form the theory that he would both defend and further develop for the rest of his life.

Thus, I would make the following observations in regard to the scholarly controversies involving Marx's intellectual development. First, Marx experienced a turn in his development, or a moral and intellectual conversion, during 1843–1844. This conversion was stimulated by his encounter with the working-class struggle and by his study of political economy. Moreover, given that this conversion occurred during 1843–1844, there is continuity between the Marx of 1844 and the Marx of 1846 and after. However, the conversion of 1843–1844 in one sense does create discontinuity between the Marx of 1844 and the Marx of pre-October 1843, not discontinuity in the sense that Marx ceased to be profoundly influenced by German philosophy, but discontinuity in the sense that Marx developed a completely different view of the world, and as a result, any quotation without qualification of Marx's writing prior to October 1843 is very misleading.

THE UNION OF MARX AND THE WORKING-CLASS STRUGGLE

In our examination of Marx's intellectual development during the pivotal year of 1843–1844, we have seen that the union of Marx and the working class was forged through his encounter with the working-class struggle. In this encounter, Marx confronted ideas that were widely discussed in the working-class struggle: that capitalism leads to premature death; that capitalism mechanizes labor; that the working day ought to be shortened; that private property ought to be abolished; that agriculture and industry ought to be collectivized and nationalized; and that a working-class struggle was necessary to attain the interests of the working class. And Marx also encountered the workers themselves, and, as we have seen, was impressed and moved by their courage and dignity. As he encountered the people and ideas of the working-class struggle, he took both seriously. He did not examine them from his own social position as an educated member of the German middle class. Rather, he demonstrated an openness and acceptance of both the people and ideas of the working-class struggle, even though these people and ideas were different from those of his own social background. On the other hand, he did not accept the ideas of the working-class struggle at face value. Rather, he transformed these ideas as he developed his own understanding, an understanding that was influenced by German philosophy and by the science of political economy as well as by the working-class struggle. The result, as we have seen, was a profound synthesis of political economy, German philosophy, and socialism, a synthesis forged from a vantage point that takes as given the objective conditions of the working class.

Our examination of Marx's intellectual development during 1843–1844 enables us to push our understanding of Marx's concept of science beyond his writing on the subject. From his writing we have seen that Marx's view was that economic development establishes possibilities for and limitations to understanding, that revolutionary movements enable the social scientist to grasp the essence of an economic system by taking as given the objective conditions of the revolutionary class, and that this understanding of the essential dynamics of an economic system promotes not particular interests but the common interest of all who are bound by an economic system. *In light of Marx's own intellectual development, we are now able to formulate what the social scientist must do in order to construct a vantage point which takes as given the objective conditions of the revolutionary class. To wit, the social scientist must encounter the revolutionary movement, take seriously its insights, yet transform these insights in light of existing theoretical insights, including those of science and philosophy.*

In the process, social scientists formulate insights which transform science and move it to a more advanced level of understanding.

NOTES

1. For similar observations, see Callinicos (1983:34), McLellan (1973:75–77; 1970:184; 1969:34), Johnson (1983:67–82), Althusser (1976:158–59), and Padover (1978:140–43).

2. For an account of this short-lived journal, which was the immediate reason for Marx's move to Paris, see Padover (1978:172–77).

3. A book written by the socialist Étienne Cabet.

4. The letter to Ruge can also be found in Padover (1979).

5. Marx's views on Proudhon are discussed in more detail in Chapter 3.

6. See Chapter 3.

7. Excerpts from *Karl Marx: Early Writings* edited by T. B. Bottomore. Published by McGraw-Hill, 1964. Used by permission.

8. McLellan (1970:168, 170) also interprets Marx's concept of alienated labor to be expressing Marx's concern for the dehumanization, poverty, and mutilation of the worker.

9. The Young Hegelians centered at the University of Berlin.

10. Marx read French translations of the English political economists (Padover, 1978:189).

6

THE COGNITIONAL
THEORY OF BERNARD
LONERGAN

Bernard Lonergan (1904–1984) was a Catholic philosopher of the neo-Thomist school. The basic thrust of neo-Thomism has been to endeavor to reconstruct classical Thomist Catholic theology in a manner that is appropriate and meaningful for modern consciousness. Lonergan has focused on the philosophical components of this task. As a twentieth-century philosopher, he accepted an idea that had a wide following in his time: that understanding is influenced by social position. But as a Catholic philosopher with intellectual roots in classical Thomism, Lonergan was also committed to the notion that some things could be known. His task, then, was to formulate an understanding of the process through which the "subject" (that is, the person seeking truth) can come to know, given the fact that knowing proceeds in a horizon context.

Lonergan's task has important similarities to that of Marx. As a product of the nineteenth century and its faith in reason and science, Marx took as given that the scientific endeavor establishes a correct and true understanding of reality. Yet Marx understood that reality shapes consciousness. He was thus among the first to grasp the common twentieth-century notion that understanding is influenced by social position. Accordingly, he had to reconcile his faith in science with his awareness that knowledge is rooted in social position. Both Marx and Lonergan, therefore, sought to formulate an understanding of truth, given the fact that knowledge reflects social position. Their analyses represent the most penetrating formulations of their respective traditions. Although their terminologies differ, reflecting the different intellectual traditions upon which they draw, their meanings overlap to a considerable extent. But there are significant differences. Especially important here is the fact that Lonergan understates the role of power in social position, and Marx does not make explicit the role of what Lonergan calls "relevant questions."

GENERAL COGNITIONAL STRUCTURE

Lonergan's major works are *Insight: A Study of Human Understanding*, a lengthy manuscript originally published in 1957, and *Method in Theology*, originally published in 1972. Lonergan's goal in *Insight* is to formulate an understanding of the process of knowing in all fields of human thought. He attempts to formulate the cognitional structure that is common to acts of understanding in all fields of inquiry, including such diverse fields as mathematics, science, and common sense. He does not seek to explicate what is known by the mathematician, scientist, and person of common sense; rather, he seeks to explicate the process by which the mathematician, scientist, and person of common sense come to know. Lonergan's goal, therefore, is to formulate an understanding of understanding itself, to achieve "insight into insight" (1958:ix). Further, he views a valid understanding of understanding as an invariable understanding, for what is known by the scientist, mathematician, or person of common sense is modified by new insights; but the attainment of further insights in mathematics, science, and common sense does not modify an understanding of insight itself. Accordingly, Lonergan seeks to formulate what he calls an invariable cognitional structure (1958:xxvi).

Lonergan's investigation of the general cognitional structure is empirical in two ways. First, Lonergan constructs his explanation of cognitional structure through empirical observation of insight as it occurs in the various fields of human inquiry. Thus, in his account Lonergan appeals "not to philosophers, not metaphysicians, but to the insights, methods, and procedures of mathematicians, scientists, and men of common sense" (1958:xii). Second, Lonergan calls upon the reader to verify his cognitional theory by reflecting upon the reader's own knowing. If readers reflect upon their own acts of understanding, they will be able to discover and identify the cognitional structure in their own attainments of insight. This is referred to by Lonergan as the appropriation of cognitional structure, and it involves a process of "one's own rational self-consciousness clearly and distinctly taking possession of itself as rational self-consciousness" (1958:xviii).

In his formulation of the general cognitional structure, Lonergan maintains that the subject progresses through three levels of consciousness. First is the level of experience in which the subject experiences data that are present to consciousness. On this first level of experience, the data, which can be the data of sense or of imagination, are not in any way operated on by the subject; they are simply given as data. However, although the data are simply given, the data are in no sense independent of the subject, for the subject must be conscious of the data. Accordingly, it is entirely possible for two subjects to be observing the same event or thing, and by virtue of the fact that they have differing foci of attention, they experience differing data. But even though the data experienced by the subject are relative to the subject by virtue of this process of selection on the basis of orientation, it remains that once the subject becomes conscious of the data, it is simply given as data on the first level of experience.

On the second level of consciousness, the level of understanding, subjects operate on the data. Subjects cannot remain satisfied with mere experiential consciousness of data, and hence, they attempt to move beyond experience by attempting to make sense out of what they experience. What they seek is a grasping of understandable relations among elements in the data. Hence, subjects seek what Lonergan calls an intelligibility in the data. Driven by this quest, subjects first grasp a hypothetical intelligibility in the data and next articulate this hypothetical intelligibility. Both the grasping and the articulating occur on the second level of consciousness. Lonergan refers to the former as insight and the latter as formulation.

But subjects cannot rest satisfied with a hypothetical insight and hypothetical formulation. They seek to determine if the insight is correct. Hence, subjects move to the third level of consciousness, the level of reflection and judgment, where they raise questions relevant to the issue at hand and gather the evidence that is established through their answers. An incorrect judgment or oversight occurs because relevant questions do not appear to consciousness. On the other hand, if all questions pertinent to a single insight have been asked, a correct judgment will occur, because the questions coalesce around a single issue, and their answers modify and reinforce one another. If subjects, then, are to make a correct judgment, they must raise all relevant questions. As subjects find that their answers reinforce one another, they are in a position to know that it is possible that all pertinent questions have been addressed. When this occurs, subjects are in a position to make what Lonergan calls a probable judgment, which is the judgment that the insight has a high probability of being correct. Subjects cannot make the judgment with certitude, for they cannot be certain that there are not further relevant questions. If at some future time, new developments bring to consciousness further relevant questions, the insight is likely to be modified, but not completely rejected.

Accordingly, Lonergan sees the process of knowing as involving a movement through three levels of consciousness: experience, understanding, and reflection. This cognitional process is dynamic, for subjects move step-by-step to the attainment of knowledge. The key to the dynamics of the cognitional process is that subjects are driven through the levels of consciousness by what Lonergan calls a "pure desire to know" or an unrestricted desire to understand. "Deep within us all, emergent when the noise of other appetites is stilled, there is a drive to know, to understand, to see why, to discover the reason, to find the cause, to explain" (1958:4). Thus, whenever individuals are presented in experience with what they do not understand, the desire to know pushes them to seek an understanding of it; and they will continue to seek to know until they come to an understanding. But even an insight formulated in this process cannot completely satisfy the desire to know, and hence subjects are driven to ask: Is the insight correct? Complete satisfaction only comes in the judgment that affirms the insight.

Lonergan's claim for the existence of a desire to know in the subject is based, as are other aspects of his account of the general cognitional structure, upon empirical observation of insight as it occurs in various fields of human intellectual activity. It is not a claim, it should be noted, that the desire to know exists as a predominant force in most people. For Lonergan, there are desires other than the desire to know, such as desires for power, privilege, status, or comfort. These other desires can subvert the desire to know. But in spite of these other desires, there are persons who at times succeed in stilling other desires, and hence, permit the desire to know to become the predominant driving force. Indeed, there are persons who spend immense amounts of time, consumed and pushed by the desire to know, preoccupied with the pursuit of answers to a set of related questions in their field, both in the world of scholarship and the world of practical affairs. The desire to know

is beyond all doubt. It can absorb a man. It can keep him for hours, day by day, year after year, in the narrow prison of his study or his laboratory. It can send him on dangerous voyages of exploration. It can withdraw him from other interests, other pursuits, other pleasures, other achievements. It can fill his waking thoughts, hide him from the world of ordinary affairs, invade the fabric of his dreams. It can demand endless sacrifices that are made without regret though there is only the hope, never a certain promise, of success. (1958:4)

The pure desire to know, therefore, is the source of knowing, for without its capacity to drive the subject, he or she could not move through the levels of consciousness. As the source of knowing, the desire to know exists prior to knowing (1958:637). It exists along with other desires and can emerge to drive the subject through the process of knowing. Since the desire to know exists prior to knowing, the desire is not itself an element of cognitional process, apart from its role in driving the subject through the levels of consciousness; it is the levels of consciousness that constitute such elements of cognitional process. Accordingly, when Lonergan speaks of a detached, disinterested, unrestricted desire to know (1958:636), it is erroneous to interpret this to mean that Lonergan understands the process of knowing to be detached or disinterested, in the sense, for example, of being unrelated to the social location of the knower. To the contrary, and as we shall see, in Lonergan's account of cognitional structure, experience of the data is relative to the subject's orientation, and insight is relative to intellectual perspective and social location. It is only on the level of reflection and judgment that knowing becomes independent of the orientation, perspective, and social location of the subject. The disinterested desire to know, then, is disinterested as desire, and it exists prior to cognition along with other desires; it is the source of the drive of the subject through the process of knowing, a process that itself can be described as fundamentally influenced by social location at the levels of experience and understanding. Let us now examine in more detail Lonergan's understanding of the process of knowing at each of the three levels.

THE LEVEL OF EXPERIENCE

On the level of experience the data of sense or imagination is present as simply given to the consciousness of the subject. Because data are simply given, they are distinct from facts, for data consists in those elements of the empirical and imaginable of which the subject is conscious, and facts are affirmed as true by the subject on the level of reflection and judgment. In order to attain knowledge of facts, the subject must operate on the data, and these operations involve the movement of the subject through the levels of understanding and reflection. But unlike facts, data are simply given, simply presented to the consciousness of the subject in sense or imagination.

However, the subject does not simply experience data that are in some sense out there in the real world. Rather, data possess a relativity to the subject, for data are experienced by the subject, and each subject experiences different data. In the realm of the imaginable, for example, each subject possesses different capacities for imagination, and hence, data present to the consciousness of the subject in imagination vary from subject to subject. Moreover, in regard to the realm of sense, what data are present to consciousness of the subject vary with each subject's spatio-temporal location and capacities for hearing, seeing, smelling, touching, tasting. But beyond this, even given similar spatio-temporal location and powers of sense among subjects, subjects can sense differing data by virtue of their having differing orientations. We do not at any given time sense all the objects that it is possible for us to sense because many aspects of the sensible world that are within the range of our senses are not the object of our attention. Thus, "Thales was so intent upon the stars that he did not see the well into which he stumbled. The milkmaid was so indifferent to the stars that she would not overlook the well" (1958:182). What we experience, then, is a function of the orientation of our "conation, interest, attention, purpose" (1958:182).

Because orientations vary from subject to subject in accordance with their varying interests and purposes, Lonergan distinguishes four "patterns of experience" (1958:182). The biological pattern of experience involves an attention upon that which is necessary for the survival of the individual and species, such as food, drink, and sex. The aesthetic pattern of experience involves attention to those symbols which express the liberation of men and women from the humdrum of mere survival in a biological sense as well as from "the wearying constraints of mathematical proofs, scientific verification, and common sense factualness" (1958:185). The dramatic pattern of experience involves a focus upon the drama of social interaction. It is characterized above all by a desire to obtain the esteem and admiration of others. The intellectual pattern of experience involves an interest in knowing in one or more of its various forms, and hence it is characterized by an accommodation to the pure desire to know. This is the pattern of experience in cases of insight. Thus, individuals are attentive to differing aspects of the world of common sense in accordance with their varying interests and purposes. All of us are attentive to these various dimensions some of the time, and thus each of us exhibit each pattern of experience at various times. When studying, we may conform to the pure desire to know. When we study to the point of hunger or exhaustion, the biological pattern may come to the fore. When we attempt to publish the results of our study, perhaps the desire to obtain the esteem of others is an important motivation. On the other hand, one pattern can be predominant in the life of an individual. The true scholar or artists accommodates other interests to the overriding orientation, and there are those whose primary goal in life is to have a position of higher status in society.

In Lonergan's account of the level of experience, then, we see that data are simply given, for they are not yet operated on by the subjects, and hence, they are distinct from facts. Yet the data that subjects experience are relative to their spatio-temporal location, their powers of sense and imagination, and their orientation.

THE LEVEL OF UNDERSTANDING

Having experienced the data, subjects move to the level of understanding. At the level of understanding, subjects endeavor to make sense of the data by selecting and organizing it in a way that makes it comprehensible to them. At this level, subjects arrive at insights into the data and formulate these insights.

In order to illustrate this level of understanding, Lonergan explains in detail a number of cases of genuine insight, beginning with the famous example of Archimedes, and continuing with illustrations from mathematics, natural science, and common sense.

Natural science, for Lonergan, involves prescinding from the empirical residue through generalization. By empirical residue, Lonergan means that aspect of empirical data which is incapable of being conceptualized or given theoretical explanation. Differences in particular times and places, for example, are differences that lack theoretical significance. Science prescinds from "the empirically residual difference between individuals" (1958:29) and constructs explanations based upon common or general universal elements possessed by individuals of the same class. Scientific explanation, therefore, is not an explanation of individuality, for it ignores individual differences, and these must, therefore, be viewed as aspects of the empirical residue. Scientific explanation involves generalization, and thus it involves "an explanation of a singular combination of common properties" (1958:29) of a class.

Scientific explanation, moreover, involves prescinding from the empirical residue through abstraction. To Lonergan, "to abstract is to grasp the essential and to disregard the incidental, to see what is significant and set aside the irrelevant, to recognize the important as important and the negligible as negligible" (1958:30). But by what criteria does the scientist grasp the essential and recognize the significant? For Lonergan, the essential or the significant is selected in relation to any insight or cluster of insights, or in relation to a fully developed science. Accordingly, from the data that are presented to the scientist in experience, the scientist selects what are relative to previously accumulated insights that are the possession of a science.

Thus science selects data in accordance with theoretical concepts, and in this respect science is like other forms of knowing. For knowing in all forms occurs within a perceptual context. Any act of observation, that is, any "act of seeing, hearing, touching, tasting, smelling" (1958:73), does not occur in a "cognitional vacuum" (1958:73). Rather, observation occurs "within a context that is determined by interests and preoccupations" (1958:73). Accordingly, each person is differentiated from another by virtue of the fact that each possesses a flow of perceptions, which, in Lonergan's usage, emerges from "the flow of sensations, as completed by memories and prolonged by imaginative acts of anticipation" (1958:73). Such differences in perceptual flow reflect individual differences in occupations, cultures, and periods of history, for such differences in social location give rise to differing patterns of "interests and objectives, desires and fears, that emphasize elements and aspects of receivable presentations, enrich them with the individual's associations and memories, and project them into future courses of possible, fruitful activity" (1958:73). For Lonergan, scientific observation is not in principle different from this process of perceiving. Accordingly, the detachment and disinterestedness of science does not refer to a process in which the scientist puts aside or brackets and, therefore, escapes the influence of perceptions. Rather, the detachment and disinterestedness of science refers to scientists putting aside perceptions grounded in the interests of everyday living and taking for themselves the interests of science.

Hence, to become a scientific observer is, not to put an end to perception, but to bring the raw materials of one's sensations within a new context. The interests and hopes, desires and fears, of ordinary living have to slip into a background. In their place, the detached and disinterested exigencies of inquiring intelligence have to enter and assume control. Memories will continue to enrich sensations, but they will be memories of scientific significance. Imagination will continue to prolong the present by anticipating the future, but anticipations of a practical moment will give way to anticipations that bear on a scientific issue. (1958:73–74)

Lonergan further maintains that as scientists select what is significant in accordance with the interests of science, scientists are oriented to the grasping of "the intelligibility immanent in the immediate data of sense" (1958:77). Such intelligibility "resides in the relations of things, not to our senses, but to one another" (1958:78). In anticipating such intelligibility in the data, when scientists observe a failing object, for example, they are not concerned with what use knowledge of free fall might have for us in terms of practical application. Rather, their quest is solely that of the relation of distance and time, for this relation expresses the relation of things to one another. Further, Lonergan maintains that this intelligibility that expresses the relations of things to one another and is immanent in the immediate data of sense is hypothetical, for the correlation or function or law or theory that explains the relation of things to one another is not a necessary explanation, but a possible one. Hence, the intelligibility that science seeks is that of possibility. Therefore, in sum, "there is . . . an intelligibility immanent in the immediate data of sense; it resides in the relations of things, not to our senses, but to one another; it consists not in an absolute necessity, but in a realized possibility" (1958:78).

Natural scientists, therefore, select from the data that which has significance in light of scientific interest. They prescind from the data those aspects that are relevant to the grasping of an immanent intelligibility in the data, immanent not in the sense that such intelligibility is the necessary expression of the data, but immanent in the sense that the intelligibility expresses relations of things to one another, and not to our senses. As scientists approach the data, they anticipate an immanent intelligibility in the data. In all this, the scientist's orientation to the data is distinct from that of the person of practical affairs, who is vulnerable to a type of misunderstanding that has its roots in a phenomenon which Lonergan calls group bias. Group bias refers to the spontaneous feeling of identification with, sympathy for, and interest in the social group, an interest which takes priority over the demands of detached intelligence and the good of order (1958:222–23).

THE LEVEL OF REFLECTION AND JUDGMENT

On the third level of consciousness, the subject marshals the evidence in reflection in order to affirm or deny in judgment that the understanding or insight is correct. But when is the evidence sufficient to make such a judgment? Lonergan maintains that in the process of reflection on insights, the subject initially makes a prospective judgment that the insight is correct. This judgment is not final, for it is conditioned. However, if those conditions have been satisfied, then the judgment must be made that the insight is correct. When this occurs, what had previously been a prospective judgment is now grasped by the subject as "virtually unconditioned" (1958:280). Here Lonergan distinguishes between the formally unconditioned, which "has no conditions whatever" (1958:280) and the virtually unconditioned, which "has conditions indeed but they are fulfilled" (1958:280). Accordingly, a prospective judgment is at first conditioned, but if and when it is known that the fulfilling conditions exist, then the judgment can and must be made that the insight is correct, for the judgment has been transferred from the status of a conditioned to the status of a virtually unconditioned. "To grasp evidence as sufficient for a prospective judgment is to grasp the perspective judgment as virtually unconditioned" (1958:28). To make a judgment that the insight is correct is to grasp that the conditions exist which make necessary such a judgment.

But how does the subject know if such conditions exist? Lonergan formulates an answer through an illustration of a concrete judgment of fact. A man returns home to find that there is smoke in the air and water on the floor, and he makes the concrete judgment of fact that something has happened. The conditioned is the judgment, something has happened. The fulfilling conditions are two sets of data: the house as remembered by the subject and the home as now present to the subject in sense. The fulfilling conditions are present to the subject in experience, for it requires no insight or reflection for him to see and smell water and smoke and to remember that he did not see and smell water and smoke when he left. Thus, the two sets of data appear to consciousness at the level of experience. Because this is a concrete judgment of fact, a relatively simple class of judgments, the mere presentation of the data in experience constitutes sufficient conditions for the judgment to be made. Note that the mere existence of the smoke and water does not make necessary the judgment, for the smoke and water must be experienced by the subject. But if the smoke and water exist, and if they are experienced by the subject, he must make the judgment that something has happened. Once he sees and smells the house, the judgment must follow.

Lonergan proceeds to an illustration of insight into a concrete situation, a more complex case where mere presentation of data in experience is not sufficient. In such a case, judgment does not immediately follow from mere experience of the data. Rather, judgment follows an insight which grasps an intelligibility in the data, and it is a judgment concerning the correctness or incorrectness of such an insight. In such cases, the fulfilling conditions for making the judgment that an insight is correct include the condition that the insight be correct. For Lonergan, an insight is correct when it is invulnerable, which occurs when all the relevant questions have been asked.

Insights are vulnerable when there are further questions to be asked on the same issue. For the further questions lead to further investigations that certainly complement the initial insight, that to a greater or less extent modify its expression and implications, that perhaps lead to an entire new slant on the issue. But when there are no further questions, the insight is invulnerable. For it is only through further questions that there arise the further insights that complement, modify, or revise the initial approach and explanation. (1958:284)

But how does the subject know if all the relevant questions have been asked? Lonergan maintains that the subject knows that all the relevant questions have been asked when responses to relevant questions reinforce one another.

Lonergan illustrates the invulnerable insight by looking again at the case of the man who arrives home to find smoke in the air and water on the floor. Going beyond the judgment that something has happened, he now has the insight that there has been a fire. As an insight, the idea that there has been a fire suggests itself to the subject as a hypothesis, and he must now gather evidence to determine if the insight is correct. Now in marshaling the evidence, there are a number of relevant questions that can be asked. And there is a point at which all possible questions that deal with the issue of whether or not there has been a fire have been asked. Pushed by the desire to know, the subject raises and formulates answers for the various relevant questions concerning the issue of whether there has been a fire. He approaches the point where all of the relevant questions have been asked, where there are no further pertinent questions to be put. He knows he is approaching this point because he finds answers to questions beginning to coalesce about one another and reinforce one another; where at first further relevant questions may have revised the formulation of the insight, he now sees that further relevant questions reinforce and do not modify the insight. At this point, the subject is in a position of mastery of a concrete situation, and his mastery can be so great that he knows that there are no further relevant questions. Thus, he is able to accurately make the judgment that there has or has not been a fire.

Note that the key criterion for correct insight is not that no further relevant questions appear to the consciousness of the subject; rather, the invulnerable insight is an insight in relation to which there are in fact no further relevant questions to be asked. Furthermore, relevant questions are distinct from questions that are related to the issue at hand but not directly relevant. In the case of the issue of whether or not there has been a fire, the question ''Where is my cat?'' is a related but not directly relevant question.

In the case of the invulnerable insight into concrete situations, the subject knows with certainty that he has raised the relevant questions. Many insights, of course, concern problems that are far more complex than that posed by the concrete situation. Further, for some insights, relevant questions have for the moment been addressed, but future insights lead to new facts that bring to light relevant questions that could not previously have been known. These difficulties apply, for example, to insights in science, and the scientist, therefore, cannot know with certainty that there are no more relevant questions that would modify the insight. Apart from this difference, the movement of the subject through reflection and judgment is essentially the same in science as in the concrete situation: scientists raise relevant questions, and through them, they modify the insight; they become more and more familiar with the problem, and thus they know they are moving closer and closer to an invulnerable insight as they increase mastery of the issue. The difference is that the scientist cannot know with certainty that there are no further relevant questions; hence, *the judgment of the scientist is a probable judgment, according to which it is probable but not certain that there are no more pertinent questions*. Thus, the scientist makes the probable judgment that he or she very probably but not certainly has attained an invulnerable insight.

The probable judgment involves grasping the virtually unconditioned, and accordingly, the probable judgment is a conditioned whose conditions have been fulfilled, for if subjects through raising relevant questions in regard to a complex issue move to a position of mastery of the issue and discern that answers to relevant questions do not modify but reinforce the insight, they are in a position to know that they are approaching an invulnerable insight. They cannot know for certain that there are no further relevant questions, but they are in a position to make the judgment that very probably there are no further relevant questions that would modify the insight. They are, thus, in a position to judge the insight correct; they do not judge the insight certain or invulnerable, but they judge it to be correct. Again, this judgment is virtually unconditioned; the conditioned is the judgment that the insight is correct; the conditions are that there very probably are no further relevant questions; through mastery of an issue, the subject discerns that there very probably are no further relevant questions, and, therefore, the judgment must of necessity be made that the insight is correct.

According to Lonergan's formulation in *Insight*, then, a correct judgment is a judgment that is virtually unconditioned; it is a judgment that must be made because certain conditions are met. In the case of a concrete judgment of fact, the condition is the presentation of data in experience. In the case of insight into concrete situations, the condition is the awareness that all relevant questions have been raised. In the case of insight into complex issues, the condition is the awareness that there is a high probability that all relevant questions have been raised. When such conditions are met, the judgment that the insight is correct must be made by the subject, for to fail to do so would be to ignore experience in the first case, to violate logic in the second case, and to violate the canons of science in the third case. Inasmuch as the judgment is necessary when such conditions are met, the judgment is characterized by an independence from the subject who makes the judgment. This independence of the virtually unconditioned judgment from the subject Lonergan calls absolute objectivity. In using the phrase "absolute objectivity," Lonergan does not intend to suggest that the subject has attained certainty. For the virtually unconditioned is absolute simply in the sense that it "stands outside of the interlocked field of conditioning and conditioned" (1958:378). The formally unconditioned has no conditions, and thus it is "intrinsically absolute" (1958:378). In contrast, the virtually unconditioned has its conditions fulfilled, and therefore it is "*de facto* absolute" (1958:378). Hence, the virtually unconditioned judgment is absolutely objective in that once the relevant questions (certainly or probably) have been raised, its occurrence has no contingency, and having no contingency, it is independent of the subject. Such judgments are "withdrawn from relativity to the subject that utters it, the place in which he utters it, and the time at which he utters it" (1958:378).

In Lonergan's cognitional theory, objectivity has three dimensions. First, there is the dimension of absolute objectivity, which, as we have seen, is attained when the subject grasps the virtually unconditioned. Because objectivity has this dimension of absolute objectivity, knowledge is objective in the sense that it is "independent not only of particular times but also of the particular mind that happens to be its subject" (1958:70). Consequently, objective knowledge is characterized by publicity (1958:378). It is a common fund that is independent of subjects and to which each subject can contribute through the grasping of the virtually unconditioned (1958:549–50, 707).

Second, there is the normative dimension of objectivity. Normative objectivity "is objectivity as opposed to the subjectivity of wishful thinking, of rash or excessively cautious judgments, of allowing joy or sadness, hope or fear, love or detestation, to interfere with the proper march of cognitional process" (1958:380). Normative objectivity is attained when the subject yields to the drive of the pure desire to know and restricts desires other than the desire to know, for desires other than the desire to know interfere with the process of understanding and with the methods and logics upon which the validity of the cognitional process depends. Therefore, "to be objective, in the normative sense of the term, is to give free reign to the pure desire, to its questions for intelligence, and to its questions for reflection" (1958:380).

Third, there is the experiential dimension of objectivity. Experiential objectivity refers to the data that are the materials for inquiry. Such data are simply given as data, and their existence can be verified simply by observing or imagining. Because data are given, all data are equally valid; accordingly, data include "not only the veridical deliverances of outer sense but also images, dreams, illusions, hallucinations, personal equations, subjective bias, and so forth" (1958:382). It is possible to select some part of the data as appropriately pertaining to the scope of a discipline according to a "reasonably affirmed principle of selection" (1958:383), and such principles are appropriately developed by the various fields of knowledge. However, such principles are developed only following understanding and reflection; selection of data cannot occur prior to understanding and judgment. Accordingly, to be objective in the experiential sense is to regard all data as equally valid and to make no a priori pronouncements that some data are valid and other data are not. For example, to affirm that only the data of sense pertain to empirical science is an appropriate definition of the scope of empirical science that can be affirmed in judgment; but it is a violation of objectivity in its experiential sense to proclaim as a dimension of a general cognitional theory that the data of imagination have no validity.

In Lonergan's cognitional theory, therefore, there are three canons of objectivity to which the subject must adhere in order to attain objective knowledge. First, the subject must not a priori assume some data to be more valid than others. Second, the subject must not allow hopes, desires, and fears to interfere with the dynamics of cognitional process. Third, yielding to the drive of the desire to know, the subject must put formulated insights to the test by raising the relevant questions. Insofar as subjects conform to these canons, they are able to develop mastery of an issue and thus to know that certainly or probably all relevant questions have been asked; when this point is reached, objective knowledge has been attained. Further, through this process a common fund of objective knowledge can be attained to which each subject contributes insofar as he or she makes correct judgments.

HORIZON AND THE DISCOVERY OF RELEVANT
QUESTIONS THROUGH ENCOUNTER

In *Method in Theology*, Lonergan discusses the concept of horizon. Horizon refers to the socially grounded frame of reference from which subjects, whether in science or common sense, perceive reality.

As our field of vision, so too the scope of our knowledge, and the range of our interests are bounded. As fields of vision vary with one's standpoint, so too the scope of one's knowledge and the range of one's interests vary with the period in which one lives, one's social background and milieu, one's education and personal development. So there has arisen a metaphorical or perhaps analogous meaning of the word, horizon. In this sense what lies beyond one's horizon is simply outside the range of one's knowledge and interests: one neither knows nor cares. (1973:236)

Hence, horizon refers to the limits to one's understanding, which are grounded in the fact that all subjects are socialized through social interaction in a number of institutions in a particular culture. Horizon refers, therefore, to the cultural boundedness of the process of knowing. Horizon defines the boundary beyond which the individual cannot see. Beyond horizon lie those relevant questions which, if known, would modify or even transform understanding. Accordingly, what lies beyond the boundary is beyond one's orientation or comprehension. What is sensible, good, or true from the viewpoint of one horizon can be nonsensical, evil, or false from the viewpoint of another horizon.

The concept of horizon points to the limitations of the process of knowing at the level of understanding. At this level, the subject formulates insights that grasp an intelligibility in the data of experience, but such insights reflect the horizon of the subject and the relevant questions contained within that particular horizon. Such insights, therefore, reflect the subject's individual viewpoint as well as the culture in which the viewpoint is grounded. Another subject, with a different viewpoint or from a different culture, may experience the data differently and may grasp a radically different intelligibility in the data. Horizon, therefore, is an obstacle to knowledge, for it functions to block relevant questions from consciousness.

Lonergan maintains that the process of "personal encounter" (1973:168) enables the subject to overcome the limitations to the attainment of objective knowledge imposed by horizon. Such personal encounter involves "meeting persons, appreciating the values they represent, criticizing their defects, and allowing one's living to be challenged at its roots by their words and their deeds" (1973:247). Such personal encounter with persons of different horizons enables the subject to discover relevant questions, particularly those relevant questions previously blocked from consciousness by horizon. Encounter, therefore, enables the subject to overcome the limitation imposed on knowledge by horizon, for encounter enables the subject to become aware of relevant questions that were initially beyond horizon. Through the process of encounter, the subject revises and reformulates the initial understanding. In some cases, a subject can gradually attain mastery of an issue, in which there is an awareness that further relevant questions are reinforcing the insight and therefore that all relevant questions either certainly or probably have been asked. In such a circumstance, the subject is compelled to make the judgment that the insight is correct. In such a case, objective knowledge is attained, for the formulation reflects relevant questions obtained through encounter with diverse horizons, and as such it is independent of the horizon of the subject.

For Lonergan, therefore, the subject need not remain at the level of understanding, a level in which insights reflecting culturally bounded viewpoints are formulated. Just as the subject is driven by the pure desire to know to formulate insights at the level of understanding, this same desire to know can push the subject beyond the level of understanding to the level of reflection and judgment. At this level of reflection and judgment, the subject discovers further relevant questions through encounter with persons of differing horizons. Such relevant questions, initially beyond the horizon and consciousness of the subject, make possible a transformation of understanding. As understandings develop through the process of encounter, the subject can experience a reaffirmation of these understandings. Such an experience brings the subject to the realization that the probability is high that all relevant questions have been asked, which compels the judgment that the understanding is correct. The understanding has become objective in that it has attained an independence from the horizon of the subject, and the subject has become aware of this fact. Through this process of bringing relevant questions to consciousness through personal encounter, a common fund of objective knowledge can be established. Such a common fund consists of judgments that can be affirmed as correct by persons possessing a variety of different horizons; such judgments transcend any particular horizon, even though judgments are formulated by a person possessing a particular horizon.

COGNITIONAL STRUCTURE IN THE REALM OF VALUE

Lonergan maintains that in judgments of value, the cognitional process is essentially the same as in judgments of fact. There are differences between judgments of fact and value, for the former are judgments concerning what is, and the latter are judgments concerning what ought to be done (1958:609). However, judgments of fact and value do not differ in structure, for in both there is the same drive of the subject through the levels of consciousness. Hence, in both judgments of fact and judgments of value, the subject experiences the data, grasps intelligibilities in the data, formulates insights, raises relevant questions through encounter, and experiences an awareness that there is a high probability that all relevant questions have been asked. Accordingly, in judgments of value, as in judgments of fact, the subject can become aware that relevant questions, emerging from different horizons, are reinforcing the insight in its present formulation. In such a case, the subject is compelled to make the judgment that the formulation is correct. Since the formulation reflects relevant questions which emerge from diverse social positions, it reflects no particular social position. The formulation, therefore, is objective in that it has attained independence from the subject and from particular social position. Objective knowledge can thus be attained in the realm of value as well as in the realm of fact (Lonergan, 1972:37; 1958:598–99).

There are, of course, differences in the cognitional process in the various fields of knowledge, in spite of the fact that knowing in all fields possesses the essential elements of the general cognitional structure. Accordingly, there are differences between natural science and social science; and there are differences among mathematics, science, and common sense. In accordance with such difference, judgments of value have their particular elements. The particular elements of judgments of value require a particular formulation of the levels of consciousness. The first level is the level of the underlying sensitive flow, which consists of what the subject feels as well as sees and imagines. The second level is the level of the practical insight. The practical insight does not grasp what is, as occurs at the level of insight in the realm of fact. Rather, the practical insight grasps possible courses of action. Third, there is the level of practical reflection, which asks if the hypothetical course of action ought to be carried out. Such reflection proceeds through the raising of relevant questions through encounter. Such relevant questions address the consequences of the proposed course of action for the individual and the society. There are two important differences between practical reflection and reflection in the realm of fact. First, whereas reflection in the realm of fact is rational consciousness, practical reflection is rational self-consciousness, for practical reflection involves an evaluation of one's own actions and possible courses of action. Second, reflection in the realm of fact culminates in knowing, at which point the drive of the subject is satisfied. In the realm of value, practical reflection culminates in knowing, but this does not satisfy the drive of the subject, for beyond knowing there is also deciding and doing. In the judgment of value, therefore, the subject arrives at a fourth level, the level of decision. In this level of decision, the subject decides to act or to refuse to act upon a course of action which, at the level of practical reflection, the subject has judged ought to be carried out. In the realm of fact, insofar as the subject can constrain other desires, the subject is driven by a desire to know. In the realm of value, the subject is driven not only by a desire to know, but also by a desire for consistency between knowing and doing (Lonergan, 1958:608–13; 1973:6–13).

COGNITIONAL STRUCTURE AND PHILOSOPHICAL ISSUES

Lonergan notes that his understanding of objectivity differs from objectivity understood as extroversion. In order to understand the meaning of objectivity as extroversion, consider the orientation of a kitten. The kitten is oriented to the satisfaction of its biological appetites by directing itself outside itself, by directing itself toward objects that are external to the kitten and confront the kitten in external situations. The kitten is oriented to encounter with the real rather than the apparent, and hence, if the kitten were to encounter a painting of a bowl of milk and were to attempt to lap it, it would find its appetite unfulfilled; in contrast, the kitten's appetites are fulfilled when it encounters a real bowl of milk (1958:251, 130, 646). Insofar as objectivity is conceived as like the extroversion of the kitten, it is viewed as an orientation to objects that are external to the subject and confront the subject in external situations; in their orientation to such objects, subjects must distinguish the real from the apparent if their purposes are to be fulfilled. Hence, to be objective in the sense of objectivity as extroversion involves looking at objects and "seeing what there is to be seen and not seeing what is not there" (1973:238).

This notion of objectivity as extroversion is intertwined with complementary notions concerning knowing and the real. According to such notions, knowing is like looking (1958:424; 1973:238); knowing "is a matter of taking a look at what is there to be seen" (1958:406). Further, knowing is knowing something, where something is an object that confronts the subject, an object that the subject encounters (1958:320). Hence, there is an interdependence between the notion of knowing as like looking and objectivity as extroversion.

The notions of objectivity as extroversion and knowing as like looking further involve the notion that knowing is taking a look at the "already out there now real" (1958:251, 412, 424; 1973:238). "Already" refers to the perception that the subject "does not create but finds its environment as already constituted" (1958:251). "Out" refers to the perception of the subject as conscious of objects that are distinct from and confront the subject. "There" and "now" refer to the space and time dimensions of the subject's encounter with the object. "Real" relates to the perception of the "already out there now" as consisting of part that is merely appearance and part that is real; accordingly, the real is a "subdivision within the field of the already out there now" (1958:251).

Lonergan maintains that these notions of objectivity as extroversion, knowing as like looking, and the real as a subdivision of the already out there now are dimensions of a view of mechanistic determinism. From the viewpoint of mechanistic determinism, the universe (like a machine) consists of elements that are systematically related and are capable of being imagined (1958:131); moreover, the relations between the elements form necessary laws, and hence the system is determined (1958:424). This world view of mechanistic determinism has its origin in philosophic assumptions that penetrated Galileo's methodology (1958:130), and it was important in science until the nineteenth century. More recent developments in the sciences (Charles Darwin, Sigmund Freud, Albert Einstein, quantum mechanics) have demonstrated the inadequacy of this world view. As a consequence, indeterminism has emerged. Indeterminism, however, is inadequate, for it does not sufficiently escape mechanistic assumptions: "The old distinction between the real and the apparent is retained, but now the real is microscopic and random, while the merely apparent is the microscopic on which classical laws seem to be verified'' (1958:135). In light of the inadequacy of indeterminism, contemporary scientists need valid concepts of objectivity, knowing, and the real. Such valid concepts are grounded in a cognitional theory that is based upon analysis of knowing as it occurs in scientific development as well as in other types of knowing. In accordance with such a cognitional theory, knowing is experiencing, understanding, and reflecting and judging (1958:425). Objectivity is the unfolding of the pure desire to know, the discovery of relevant questions through encounter, and the attainment of knowledge that is independent of horizon. The real is what is verified through this process (1958:425, 252, 257).

Confused notions concerning objectivity, knowing, and the real have occurred not only in science, for they have plagued the history of philosophy. Hence, the tradition of empiricism perceives the real as already out there now, objectivity as extroversion, and knowing as taking a look at what is there (1958:252–53, 412–13). Accordingly, the dictum of empiricism is ''observe the significant facts'' (1958:411), a dictum that fails to discern that data are observed and that facts emerge only in the act of judgment, which follows the cognitional acts of insight, formulation, and reflection. In opposition to empiricism, the idealist tradition beginning with Kant correctly perceives that knowing is not like looking, that knowing is a process of accumulating insights through raising and answering questions. However, idealism retains the notion of the real as an object out there outside the subject, and having discerned the subjective dimension of knowing, it is forced to the conclusion that the objective and the real are incapable of being discerned (1958:44; 1973:76). In contrast to empiricism and idealism, Lonergan's understanding of the real, knowing, and objectivity follow from his cognitional theory. The real and the objective are affirmed in judgment. Knowing is the process of moving through three levels of consciousness. Objectivity is attained when all the relevant questions have been asked.

Lonergan maintains that the confusion is the history of philosophy is not difficult to understand, for there are two valid types of knowing. There is an elementary type of knowing that involves looking at or in some way sensing the already-out-there-now-real. The elementary type of knowing is that in which animals as well as pre-verbal infants engage, whose world is a ''world of what is felt, touched, grasped, sucked, seen, heard. It is a world of immediate experience, of the given as given, of image and affect without an perceptible intrusion from insight or concept, reflection or judgment, deliberation or choice'' (1958:76). Moreover, this elementary type of knowing is the type of knowing engaged in by adult humans insofar as they are oriented toward experience rather than meaning, insofar as they participate in the world of immediacy rather than the world mediated by meaning. Recall, for example, Lonergan's illustration of the man who makes the concrete judgment of fact that something has happened; that man knows by mere observation that data at present differ from the data as they were. There are such basic things that adult humans do know through mere observations. Knowing in this sense refers to knowing of the elementary type. But in addition to the elementary type of knowing, there is also a fully human knowing that goes beyond experience, and adds to the experience of the data the acts of insight, formulation, reflection, and judgment. Hence, the confusion concerning the notions of real, objectivity, and knowing has its source in failing to distinguish the two types of knowing (1958:242–53; 1971:13).

Lonergan, then, understands his cognitional theory as a theory that stands in a pivotal place in the history of philosophy. Like idealism, he rejects the empiricist position that knowing is like looking, for analysis of the process of knowing brings one to the realization that knowing involves acting by the subject on the data, and accordingly, knowing occurs within a subjective perceptual context. But more than this, Lonergan has overcome the problem that has posed a major difficulty for the tradition of idealism, namely, the problem of moving from subjective perceptions to objective reality. For if knowing occurs in perceptual context, how can the knower know if perceptions are accurate? How can subjects know that they have grasped the real and not the apparently real? Lonergan's solution to this problem is to ground the definitions of knowing, objectivity, and the real in the data of consciousness. This is a solution that goes beyond idealism, for idealism grounds the definition of knowing in the data of consciousness, but accepts empiricist definitions of objectivity and the real; as a result, idealism is forced either to proclaim the real and the objective as unknowable or to introduce concepts that have no ground in the data of consciousness in order to bridge the gap between knowing and reality, such as Immanuel Kant's categorical imperatives. Lonergan, however, grounds all concepts, including the real and the objective, in the data of consciousness. Hence, beginning with the data of consciousness as in the idealist tradition, Lonergan works through not to an idealist conclusion, but to a realist conclusion: the real and the objective can be known; objective knowledge and objectivity can be attained; facts can be discerned. He accomplishes this by defining objectivity and the real in a manner different from the way they have been defined in empiricism and idealism, and different as well from the way they are used in the language of common sense.

But are Lonergan's definitions of objectivity and the real more valid than the more generally accepted definitions? The case for the greater validity of Lonergan's definitions consists in what Lonergan calls the self-affirmation of the knower. In the presentation of his cognitional theory, Lonergan asks the reader to make the concrete judgment of fact, "I am a knower." To affirm that I am a knower is to affirm that I engage in cognitional acts such as sensing, imagining, understanding, formulating, reflecting, judging. This is not to affirm that the contents of my formulations and my judgments are correct, but to affirm that I engage in the cognitional acts of formulating and judging. "For the present we are concerned simply with an account of the activity and so we have defined the knower, not by saying that he knows something, but solely by saying that he performs certain kinds of acts'' (1958:320). Lonergan believes that the evidence is overwhelming for an affirmative judgment:

When I listen to the story of Archimedes and when I read the recital of a mystical experience, there is a marked difference. What a mystic experiences, I do not know. But, though I never enjoyed so remarkable an insight as Archimedes, still I do know what it is to miss the point and to get the point, not to have a clue and then to catch on, to see things in a new light, to grasp how they hang together, to come to know why, the reason, the explanation, the cause. (1958:324)

Or again:

Do I try to understand or is the distinction between intelligence and stupidity no more applicable to me than to a stone? Have I any experience of insight, or is the story of Archimedes as strange to me as the account of Plotinus' vision of the One? Do I conceive, think, consider, suppose, define, formulate, or is my talking like the talking of a parrot? (1958:328)

Hence, the movement of the subject through the operations of experience, insight, formulation, reflection, and judgment, can be validated by each reader by virtue of his or her experiential awareness of his or her own consciousness. Once the reader accepts the validity of Lonergan's formulation of cognitional structure, the reader logically must accept Lonergan's definitions of knowing, objectivity, and the real, for these definitions logically follow Lonergan's account of cognitional process. Hence, the reader cannot reject Lonergan's formulation of the real and objective knowledge without also rejecting Lonergan's formulation of cognitional structure, which the reader has affirmed through reflection on his or her consciousness. Lonergan has demonstrated therefore the validity of his definitions of knowing, objectivity, and the real.

One could raise the objection that Lonergan, by virtue of his redefinition of objectivity and the real, does not arrive at objectivity and the real as the terms are generally defined. Although the objection would be correct, it would miss the point. It would be correct, for Lonergan maintains that if the real were already out there now and if objectivity were extroversion, then the data of consciousness clearly indicate that the real could not be grasped and objectivity could not be attained, and hence, idealism would be correct. Moreover, if the real were already out there now, the subject through insight, formulation, reflection, and judgment could not know reality (1958:499). But the objection misses the point, for to formulate the issue in terms of the real as already out there now and objectivity as extroversion is to formulate the issue in a way that is based on a confusion between elementary knowing and fully human knowing. Because the kitten knows in an elementary sense the difference between milk and a painting of it, because the infant knows in an elementary sense the difference between a pacifier and a breast, because the adult knows in an elementary sense that something has happened—because, in other words, elementary knowing is an important dimension of human experience, we have perceived the problem of knowledge in terms of such elementary knowing. Indeed, so ingrained is this procedure in our thinking that our language is full of metaphors equating knowing and looking, for example, when we say, "Do you see what I mean?" or "Do not overlook the relevant questions" or "Besides insight there is oversight." But however obvious it may appear that (1) knowing is like looking, objectivity is extroversion, and the real is the already out there now, or (2) knowing is not like looking, and hence objectivity as extroversion and the already-out-there-now-real cannot be attained, the fact remains that such perceptions are based on the erroneous method of formulating the problem of objective knowledge in terms of elementary knowing. The valid approach is to formulate the problem of knowledge in the context of a fully human knowing, which requires beginning with the observation of the data of consciousness. Using this procedure, we can see that knowing is experiencing, understanding, and judging; objectivity is the discovery of relevant questions through encounter; and the real is the verified. Defined in this way, objective knowledge and the real are capable of being attained.

LONERGAN AND SOCIAL SCIENCE

Lonergan devoted no specific part of his work principally to the social sciences. However, there are sufficient references in *Insight* and *Method in Theology* to make it possible to describe his understanding of social science, expressed primarily in the form of a comparison and contrast of social science with natural sciences.

Lonergan sees three similarities between natural and social science. First, both the natural and social sciences are empirical sciences, and, accordingly, both natural and social sciences seek an intelligibility in the data of sense rather than the data of imagination (1958:35).

Second, both natural and social sciences, as fields of knowing, must proceed in accordance with the basic structure of the knowing process. Accordingly, the empirical sciences, natural and social, cannot form scientific concepts and theories without drawing upon presuppositions. Accordingly, concepts and theories are formulated in the context of and with reference to scientific viewpoints, which are the previously accumulated understandings and formulations of a scientific discipline. Such scientific viewpoints or conceptual schemes make insight possible. Scientific viewpoints, however, can lead to oversight, for they can block relevant questions from consciousness. This problem is overcome through personal encounter with persons possessing radically different viewpoints and horizons.

Third, both natural and social sciences have as their ultimate goal the formulation of generalizations and laws that constitute explanations for a variety of cases. As such, the natural and social sciences go beyond descriptions of particular cases.

There are, however, differences between natural and social sciences as formulated by Lonergan. First, the objects of study in the social sciences are capable not only of being understood, as in the natural sciences, but are also capable of understanding. As intelligent beings capable of understanding, humans participate in a world mediated by meaning. They live in a world containing symbols that communicate what men and women understand and know (1973:76–77). This first difference between the natural and social sciences, therefore, can be expressed by saying that the social sciences study the world mediated by meaning whereas the natural sciences do not.

A second difference between natural and social science pertains to the kind of intelligibility that is anticipated. Like natural scientists, social scientists search for forms of intelligibility that are expressed by the formulation of laws, correlations, and statistical probabilities. However, in addition to these forms of intelligibilities, social scientists also seek the intelligibility of development, which refers to growth, differentiation, and change. Social scientists, then, look for and anticipate an organic, psychic, and intellectual growth, differentiation, and change in the human species (1958:451–79).

In Lonergan's view, such human development occurs in accordance with what he calls the world view of emergent probability. According to this world view, there are schemes of recurrence in the development of the world. In a scheme of recurrence, there is a series of conditioned events (*A, B,* and *C*) such that when *A* occurs, *B* will occur; when *B* occurs, *C* will occur; and when *C* occurs, *A* will recur. Not only are events conditioned in this way, but schemes of recurrence are themselves conditioned, in that schemes of recurrence have prior schemes of recurrence as conditions for their existence. Moreover, every nonexistent but possible scheme of recurrence has a probability for its actual emergence, and every actually existing scheme has a probability for its survival. Such is the nature of the development of the world as perceived by the world view of emergent probability (1958:120–22).

The world view of emergent probability is the basis for Lonergan's understanding of development in society. In society, there are social schemes of recurrence. Every social scheme of recurrence that does not exist, but has a possibility to emerge, will have a probability for its emergence given the conditions of society. Every existing social scheme of recurrence will have a probability for maintaining itself, given the conditions of society. Each event has a probability of occurring, given certain conditions. Accordingly, social schemes of recurrence are not inevitable. It is possible that a scheme will not emerge or will not survive. Accordingly, it is possible for a population to expand for a time, but with the emergence of new conditions, the population expansion can be followed by population decline. Or the emergence of new conditions can make possible an economic and technological expansion followed by an economic and technological decline. Such possibilities conform to the laws of emergent probability.

As reasoning and continually developing social beings, humans participate in the process of social development in accordance with the laws of emergent probability. For the probability of an event or scheme of recurrence occurring can be effected by the occurrence of insight (or oversight). The insight (or oversight) itself has a probability of occurring, like all conditions and events. A series of related insights (or oversights) has a probability of emerging, like all schemes of recurrence. Therefore, insights (or oversights) are themselves elements in the conditions, events, schemes, and probabilities that are elements in the dynamics of emergent probability in society. The frequency of occurrence of insights (or oversights) affects whether human social development is characterized by technical, social, and moral progress or decline.

Give the role of human understanding in human progress and decline, the proper role of the social sciences emerges: the social sciences ought to contribute to human progress. In order to do so, Lonergan maintains, they must develop a critical capacity, a capacity to distinguish between progress and decline.

Human science has to be critical. . . . It can be of inestimable value in aiding man to understand himself and in guiding him in the implementation of that understanding, if, and only if, it can learn to distinguish between progress and decline, between the liberty that generates progress and the bias that generates decline. In other words, human science cannot be merely empirical; it has to be critical; to reach a critical standpoint, it has to be normative. (Lonergan, 1958:236)

For Lonergan, although critical social science, as critical, endeavors to contribute to social progress, it confines itself, as social science, to interpretations, explanations, and generalizations in the realm of fact. It does not, as social science, enter the realm of value and endeavor to formulate what ought to be. Social scientists move to the critical and normative level when they move beyond the formal scope of their fields and enter "integrated studies" (1973:366) with theologians and ethicists. Ideally, it is in the integration of theology, ethics, and the social sciences that social policy is formulated. Thus, for Lonergan, the quest for truth drives social scientists beyond the level of reflection and judgment to the level of responsibility (1973:9–10), where the social scientists seeks to contribute to human social progress. The quest for truth therefore takes the social scientist beyond the formal boundaries of social science and to the formulation of social policy in dialogue with theologians and ethicists.

CRITIQUE

Lonergan's cognitional theory is based upon the modern insight that knowing occurs in a social context. This is seen in several aspects of Lonergan's understanding of knowing in its general form. At the level of experience, the data that are present to consciousness are relative to the spatio-temporal location and the powers of sense of the subject. The data are also relative to the orientation of the subject, depending, for example, on whether the subject is oriented to the pursuit of truth or status. At the level of understanding, the data are selected and organized in accordance with the perceptions and interests of the subject. Such perceptions and interests are grounded in the subject's occupation, culture, and historical time period. Understandings, therefore, reflect the subject's horizon. Understandings are limited, for they do not take into account relevant questions which are beyond the subject's horizon. Thus, understandings are relative to individual viewpoints and social location. Indeed, because of the connection of understanding to social position, understanding often takes the form of group bias.

This understanding of knowledge in its general form applies to science. However, at its best, science differs from common sense, because science proceeds not in the context of social position and cultural values but in the context of scientific insights and concepts. Therefore, science, at its best, involves selection and organization of data in accordance with scientific concepts that have attained a measure of autonomy from individual viewpoints, social position, culture, and historical period. However, science does not always attain this ideal, particularly in the social sciences, for since they seek to understand the world mediated by meaning, social scientific understandings and concepts commonly reflect the culturally bounded horizons of social scientists.

The idea of the social context of knowledge, of course, is widely acknowledged in social science. Lonergan's achievement is to formulate an understanding of the process through which objective knowledge can be attained in a way that does not ignore but builds upon the social context of knowledge. His cognitional theory reveals those dimensions of the knowing process that make possible the attainment of a knowledge that is independent of social position, even though social scientists continue to belong to social positions. His theory specifies the method through which such objective knowledge can be attained: seek relevant questions through encounter with persons of differing horizon.

However, in spite of Lonergan's achievement, there are shortcomings in his cognitional theory, and in this regard four observations can be made. First, Lonergan's terminology is far more traditional than his analysis. The classical terms that Lonergan employs are a barrier to the use of his cognitional theory by twentieth-century social scientists. For example, the claim that knowledge is characterized by "absolute objectivity" implies a claim that knowledge is eternal and characterized by certainty. In fact, Lonergan's cognitional theory claims that scientific knowledge is continually developing (1958:302) and that it is constituted by judgments that there is a high probability, but not a certainty, that there are no further relevant questions. Lonergan's arguments and explanations in his cognitional theory reflect his sensitivity to insights in the sociology of knowledge in the twentieth century. His classical terminology reflects his desire to reconcile those insights with classical philosophy. Lonergan's terminology makes sense in regard to that goal. However, in order to use the insights of Lonergan's cognitional theory to construct an understanding of science appropriate for twentieth-century social scientists, it will be necessary to remove Lonergan's insights from the excessively traditional language of classical philosophy.

Second, and more substantively, Lonergan's description of social science is not sufficiently comprehensive. Lonergan describes social science as formulating laws, generalizations, correlations, and probabilities; and as describing the social process of growth, differentiation, and change. This description overlooks that dimension of social science that seeks to understand the social world of actors and to formulate the cultural norms and values of particular social groups through such methods as participant observation. In contrast, Jürgen Habermas's description of sociology is much more comprehensive. Habermas, as we have seen,[1] describes sociology as using empirical-analytic procedures to formulate generalizations and as using the hermeneutic procedures of the cultural sciences to formulate an understanding of social action in the context of the meaning system of the actor. As such, sociology reflects the unfolding of both technical and practical interests. Like Habermas, however, Lonergan views social science as critical in that it endeavors to contribute to social progress.

Third, Lonergan's cognitional theory does not grasp the relation of the development of the social sciences to economic development. Lonergan maintains that further relevant questions are not grasped, "first, if there may be further, unknown facts that would raise further questions to force a revision or, secondly, if there may be further, known facts whose capacity to raise such further questions is not grasped" (1958:302). This is true enough, but unlike Marx's concept of science, it does not grasp the role of economic development and revolutionary classes in establishing the conditions that make possible awareness of previously unknown relevant questions. Hence, Lonergan's understanding of scientific development is disconnected from social relations and social movements constituted by the development of the system of production.

Related to this shortcoming, fourth, is the fact that Lonergan overlooks the role of power in the search for relevant questions. As Marx knew, in any social system, the dominant class has a vested interest in distorting social reality. It creates ideologies and endeavors to impose these distorted understandings on subjected classes. The concept of ideology, therefore, is important in understanding the common occurrence of understandings that overlook relevant questions. Moreover, subjected classes constitute revolutionary movements that formulate insights in opposition to ideologies. Therefore, in the search for relevant questions, it is not only important to seek encounter with persons of different horizons, but more precisely, to seek encounter with the revolutionary struggles of subjected groups. Through such encounter, one is able to discover relevant questions that are beyond the horizon of the dominant group. But Lonergan's cognitional theory, disconnected as it is from questions of power in society, fails to formulate the quest for relevant questions as a process of encounter with revolutionary struggles.

In spite of the limitations in Lonergan's cognitional theory, it is important for our purposes in two ways. First, it provides a perspective for understanding Marx's intellectual conversion. In his conversion, Marx experienced fully Lonergan's description of personal encounter as "meeting persons, appreciating the values they represent, criticizing their defects, and allowing one's living to be challenged at its roots by their words and their deeds'' (Lonergan, 1973:247). Marx, as we have seen,[2] encountered activists in the working-class struggle. In this encounter, Marx, first, accepted the workers as persons. Indeed, he saw a kind of heroism in them. Second, he appreciated the ideas of the working-class struggle and adopted socialist principles. Third, he criticized these ideas as he incorporated them into his own developing understanding. Fourth, Marx's life as a whole was profoundly affected by the words and deeds of the working-class struggle, for he formulated an understanding radically different from that of the established order, and this new understanding was to make him a permanent exile unable to earn a regular income. In addition, simultaneously with his encounter of the working-class struggle, Marx undertook a comprehensive study of the science of political economy.[3] Here Marx encountered a horizon different from that of both German philosophy and the working-class struggle. Marx took seriously the insights of political economy, yet he "criticized their defects," in that his work was a critique of political economy that sought to transform its concepts. Thus, the unfolding of the desire to know in Marx's intellectual development in 1843–1844 took him to an encounter with two horizons simultaneously, both of which were fundamentally different from the horizon of German philosophy. In taking seriously the insights of the working-class struggle and the science of political economy, yet transforming them in light of his developing understanding, Marx was yielding to the demands of the pure desire to know. In not dismissing the claims of the working-class struggle from the vantage point of the German middle class, and in not dismissing the claims of political economy from the vantage point of German philosophy, Marx gave priority to the unrestricted desire to understand as against the demands of group bias. He opened his heart and mind to new understandings as he experienced personal encounter.

As Marx encountered the horizons of the working-class struggle and political economy, he became aware of new insights. Through his encounter with the working-class struggle, he became aware of several insights: that capitalism leads to premature death; that workers' lives could be enhanced through shortening the working day; that capitalism mechanizes labor; that a more humane society characterized by equality could be established through abolition of private property and through collectivization and nationalization in agriculture and industry; that the interests of the working class could be attained through a working-class struggle. From political economy he learned that labor is the origin of surplus value and that there are conceptual distinctions between necessary labor and surplus labor and between productive labor and unproductive labor. His new awareness of the insights of the working-class struggle and political economy led him to the discovery of new questions. Although Marx expressed his discoveries not as questions but as formulated insights, we can nevertheless in retrospect construct questions on the basis of his formulated theory. Such questions include: How can the insights of socialism be incorporated into a theoretical system that uses the concepts of political economy and the Hegelian dialectic?

How can the concepts of political economy be transformed from a vantage point that takes as given the objective conditions of the working class? What is the origin of surplus value, the difference between productive and unproductive labor, and the difference between necessary and surplus labor from a vantage point that takes as given the objective conditions of the working class? What is the meaning of the Hegelian dialectic in light of the insights of political economy and the working-class struggle? What possibilities are established by capitalism for the development of a humane society from the point of view of the worker? What is the role of the proletariat in establishing such a society? What is the relationship between science and economic development? In addressing questions such as these, Marx could formulate his theoretical system.

Second, Lonergan's cognitional theory is important for our purposes in that we can use its insights in a reconstruction of Marx's concept of science in a manner that is appropriate for twentieth-century social science. Indeed, Marx and Lonergan complement one another. Marx's analysis addresses the relation of power and economic development to knowledge, an issue that Lonergan does not address. Lonergan, on the other hand, describes elements in the cognitional process which Marx has overlooked. Such a reconstruction of Marx's concept of science is a task to which we now turn.

NOTES

1. See Chapter 2.
2. See Chapter 5.
3. See Chapter 5.

7

A RECONSTRUCTION OF MARX'S CONCEPT OF SCIENCE

In this chapter, I formulate an understanding of social scientific method that draws upon the insights of Marx and Lonergan. This new formulation will proceed primarily in the context that Marx established, but it will revise or reconstruct Marx's concept of science in three ways. First, it will incorporate not only the insights of Marx's methodological writings, but also those insights about the process of knowing that emerged through an examination of Marx's intellectual development. Second, it will formulate a general concept of science rather than a concept tied to a particular system of production at a definite stage in its development. Marx sometimes formulated his concept of science in general terms, such as in his critique of the political economists in the *Theories of Surplus Value*. However, given that Marx was not primarily writing about methodological and epistemological questions, he often expressed his understanding in the context of nineteenth-century modern industrial capitalism and the proletarian struggle. I formulate a general understanding of the relation of science to a system of production and of the relation between science and social movements constituted by subjected social groups. Accordingly, this formulation endeavors to explain the relation between science and social movements in the twentieth-century capitalist world economy as well as in nineteenth-century industrial capitalism. To illustrate the explanatory power of this approach, I show that Marx's critique of political economy, organically connected to the working-class struggle, has all the elements of science as I have defined it. In addition, I show that Immanuel Wallerstein's world-systems perspective, a theory that is connected to Third World national liberation movements, also exhibits all elements of science. Third, the theory will incorporate the insights of Bernard Lonergan. Since Marx was not primarily interested in epistemological issues, his theory of knowledge is in some respects incomplete, even when including insights learned from an examination of his intellectual development. Accordingly, in endeavoring to formulate an understanding of these questions appropriate for social scientists today, the insights of Lonergan's cognitional theory are useful.

This attempt to formulate the basic principles of social scientific method seeks to describe a method through which social science can overcome the Western bias that has characterized its development. Appropriation of such a method is necessary if social scientists are to claim legitimately that they produce scientific knowledge as against ideas that promote the interest of the West.

THE DESIRE FOR OBJECTIVE KNOWLEDGE

Our first observation is that objective knowledge can be attained. By objective knowledge, I mean an understanding that does not promote particular interests in an economic system. As such, within any particular society, objective knowledge does not promote the interests of a particular class, race, or sex. Moreover, in the world economy as a whole, objective knowledge does not promote the interests of any region created by the international geographical division of labor, and as such it promotes neither the interests of the West nor the Third World. Rather, objective knowledge promotes the common interest of all who are bound together by the modern world economy.

Since the world economy has become global in the twentieth century, connecting virtually all people in the world, there is today a common interest that is global in scope, a common interest in maximizing human well-being to the fullest extent technically possible. This common interest is a real human interest and not an abstract principle, for a world in which goods and services are shared equitably and justly would be a world with less conflict. And a world in which there is not sustained conflict between those who seek human rights and those who fight to preserve their wealth and power would be a world in which human energies could be devoted to the development of the best human qualities. We all have an interest in living in such a world. This is the common interest which unites us all, and no amount of cynicism can entirely quench our awareness of it or our occasional yearnings for it. Such a common interest is fundamentally different from particular interests, which are interests in maximizing the power and material wealth of a particular region, class, race, or sex within the world economy. Ideologies, which are distortions of social reality, function to legitimate the claims of particular interests, and thus they are in opposition to the common interest. Science, in contrast, is grounded not in particular interests but in the common interest. Science represents the coming to the fore of that side of the human character that seeks truth, reason, and justice amidst the clamor of conflicting claims as particular interests are pursued. Science, therefore, seeks an objective knowledge that transcends particular interests in that it does not promote the interests of any particular groups. It promotes the common interest of all people connected to the world economy in maximizing human well-being.

The desire for objective knowledge is a part of the human experience. This desire is a part of all of us. We all, to some degree, want to know what is true and do what is right. Who prefers ignorance to understanding? And how many justify their actions, no matter what that action is, on the grounds that the wrong is preferable to the right? We often have difficulty discerning truth not because we have no desire for truth, but because there are desires other than the desire to know. These include the desires for prestige, power, material possessions, and material comfort. Such desires can prevent us from discerning that truth which lies behind and beyond individual and collective interest.

Although we all possess the desire to know alongside other desires, human beings differ from one another in the priorities they give to these often conflicting desires in their life-styles. Scientists are among those who orient personal priorities to the pursuit of truth. Scientists in this sense are rare, even more rare than the number of people who list their occupation as scientist on the basis of commonly accepted definitions. But such scientists do exist. Marx was an important example of a social scientist, and he is a model for all who aspire to be social scientists.

Of course, the mere possession of a desire to know as the paramount desire is not sufficient to ensure that one will eventually come to objective knowledge. Indeed, this book endeavors to formulate a method for overcoming the many obstacles to understanding that confront someone who seeks to know. But this effort is premised on the notion that there are people who desire to know, that they often succeed in placing this desire above other desires, and they orient their lives primarily to the fulfillment of this desire as against other desires. The method takes as given this scientific orientation, and it is therefore applicable only for those with such an orientation.

THE SOCIAL CONTEXT OF KNOWLEDGE

Even when objective, social scientific knowledge is historically and socially conditioned. It is not eternal. Its insights are made possible by the development of the economic system, and its insights therefore are appropriate only for that economic system at that particular stage in its development. As the economic system continues to develop, it will make possible new insights, and previous insights will be limited in applicability or transformed by these new insights. Thus, previous insights will find their appropriate use and meaning in the context of a new theoretical system. Such new theoretical systems are connected to the development of the economic system itself. Thus, social scientific knowledge is historically and socially conditioned in the sense that it is not eternal, and it develops as economic systems develop.

There is a second sense in which social scientific knowledge, even when objective, is historically and socially conditioned: it emerges in social context. As social scientists seek knowledge, they proceed in the context of a culturally bounded horizon. This horizon is shaped by social interaction. As such, it is grounded in social structure and in all that an individual experiences. One's horizon continually develops as one has new experiences and new interactions. We have seen,[1] for example, that Marx experienced a horizon shift as a result of new experiences and interactions when he was twenty-five years of age. Horizon, therefore, continues to develop throughout one's life, and it is shaped by personal experiences, social interaction, and social and technological development. Sometimes, as Marx's experience in Paris shows, this development can take the form of a transformation of fundamental ideas and assumptions, and thus it can take the form of horizon shift.

On the one hand, horizon enables us to understand, for it provides the basis for interpreting all that we see and hear. It provides us with a basis for understanding what we experience. It enables us to make sense out of and to give meaning to what we see and hear. It provides one with a standard for selecting and organizing elements in the empirical world. It provides a basis for giving meaning to all that one sees and hears.

On the other hand, horizon prevents us from understanding. In providing a basis in our individual experiences and social context to understand what we see and hear, it prevents us from imagining alternative understandings that are rooted in different individual experiences and different social contexts. Our horizon thus prevents us from seeing and hearing what others can see and hear, and it prevents us from discerning a meaning that is obvious to others. It prevents us from being aware of relevant questions which would transform our understanding. It connects our understandings so powerfully to social context that our interpretations tend to legitimate the interest of our social group, and we thus are susceptible to the errors of group bias.

Horizon, therefore, establishes a social context to knowledge. It makes possible both insight and oversight simultaneously. It establishes at one and the same time both the possibilities for and limitations to understanding.

OBJECTIVE KNOWLEDGE THROUGH PERSONAL ENCOUNTER

In some respects, the limitations imposed on understanding by horizon cannot be overcome. We can never overcome the limitations established by the time period in which we live, for economic and technological developments are continuously establishing new social contexts, which in turn make possible new insights that were previously unimaginable. Nor can we ever escape the limitations established by the system of production, for the truths that human beings formulate are never applicable to humanity as such, but to human life in the context of a particular economic system. Accordingly, objective knowledge is not knowledge that is applicable to all people in all times and places. Rather, it is applicable to all people who are connected to a system of production in a particular stage in its development.

At the same time, the limitations imposed by horizon can be overcome in degree. It is possible to develop understandings that transcend social positions created by the division of labor in a system of production. Such knowledge reflects no class, status, occupation, race, or sex within an economic system. It transcends the particular interests of such social positions. It is a truth for all in the economic system at a particular stage in its development. Moreover, in the context of the capitalist world economy of our time, the particular interests that truth transcends include the regional interests established by the geographical division of labor in the modern world economy. The truth in our time is a truth for all regions of the world, a truth for all who are connected to the modern world economy. Accordingly, while the truth in our time, as in any time, cannot escape limitations established by development of the system of production, it is a truth that represents no regional interests in the world and thus a truth that is equally valid and equally legitimate for all people in our time.

How then do social scientists who seek truth as a paramount desire move to the attainment of such knowledge which transcends particular interests and which is global in relevance? In essence, they do so through encounter with social movements constituted by subjected groups. Let us examine the elements in this process.

Social Movements and Economic Development

First, we should note that such social movements are established by economic development. The proletarian struggle of Western Europe in the nineteenth century was an example of such a social movement. This social movement could not emerge until the development of capitalism established the proletarian class, thereby laying the foundation for the emergence of a movement that seeks to identify and attain the interests of the proletarian class. In the twentieth century, a number of social movements have emerged that have focused on such issues as national liberation against imperialism, feminism, ecology, and racism. As Ronald Aronson (1985:74–76) has noted, such issues have taken center stage and have become more important than the conflict between capital and labor in the twentieth century. For purposes of illustration, let us examine one of these movements, the African nationalist movement.

Like the proletarian struggle of the nineteenth century, the African nationalist movement was established by economic development. In the nineteenth century, European colonial domination of Africa was confined to the coastal regions. With the partition of Africa in the late nineteenth century, the domination of the entire continent was made explicit as a goal, but by 1900 this remained a goal rather than an actual fact. It was not until the twentieth century that the colonial domination of Africa was established in concrete reality. With the colonial penetration of the continent in the twentieth century, the social structures of Africa were transformed. Traditional social systems were undermined or transformed to function in the new colonial structure. Of paramount importance in the colonial transformation was the development of new economic systems, for the primary reason for colonialism was use of African human and natural resources. Accordingly, land use patterns were transformed in order to produce agricultural and mining raw materials products for export to Europe. In order to support this economic transformation, new political, educational, and religious institutions were imposed. In the process of creating new religious and educational institutions, an educated elite of Africans was created. This educated elite was at first different from the mass of Africans not in an economic sense, but in a cultural sense, for the educated elite consisted of those Africans who possessed a European education and were European, to some extent, in outlook. They spoke European languages, embraced European religions, and adopted European dress and customs. This educated elite soon became a class. By virtue of their Europeanization, they were able to obtain lower-level positions in the colonial political structures as well as positions as teachers. Through income from their salaries, they were able to develop small-scale capitalist enterprises, which were similar to those of Europeans. Thus, the African educated elite was forming an emerging petty bourgeois class. This class had an interest in removing the racial barriers in the colony, which restricted its economic advance. Hence, the African nationalist movement came into being. It was a movement that endeavored to remove racial barriers to African advancement in the political, economic, educational, and religious structures that had been established by Europeans. As such, it was a movement that sought to promote the advancement of Africans within the structure of colonialism. The movement promoted fundamentally the interests of the emerging African national bourgeoisie rather than the interests of the masses of Africans. Nevertheless, the African national bourgeoisie appealed to all Africans to support this cause in the name of African solidarity, African rights, and the struggle of Africans against European rule. This appeal was successful, and the African nationalist movement emerged as a coalition of Africans of all classes which successfully wrestled control of colonial institutions from Europeans. African nationalism promoted the interests of the masses in the struggle against colonialism, in that it promoted basic African political and civil rights. However, it did so in ways that were not inconsistent with the interests of the emerging African bourgeoisie. African nationalism was a movement, therefore, with two contradictory tendencies. On the one hand, there is bourgeois African nationalism, which promotes the interests of the national bourgeoisie. On the other hand, there is revolutionary African nationalism, which promotes the interests of the African masses: the peasants, the lumpenproletariat, and the wage workers. These contradictions within the movement remained latent during the struggle against colonial rule, as the differing classes were allied in the common goal of political independence. However, once the goal of political independence was attained, the conflict of interests between the masses and the national bourgeoisie became manifest.

The African nationalist movement first began to emerge in the 1920s. By the 1950s and 1960s, it had emerged as a significant political force, with which European powers found it necessary to negotiate and compromise. Through the

1960s and 1970s, it succeeded in attaining political independence for every country in sub-Saharan Africa with the exception of South Africa.

The African nationalist movement could not emerge until economic developments had constituted its class base, for it could not emerge until colonialism developed to the point that the African petty bourgeoisie had come into existence. The African nationalist movement, therefore, like the proletarian struggle of a century earlier, was constituted by economic developments.

The Insights of Social Movements of Subjected Groups

Let us turn to a second observation in regard to the process of encounter with social movements constituted by subjected groups: social movements constituted by subjected groups possess insights that express the objective conditions of the subjected group. Such insights are possible because of the unique social position of the subjected group by virtue of its experience of subjugation. This is not to say that the subjected group understands more than other social groups. Rather, more precisely, the point is that the experience of subjugation provides the subjected group with a unique vantage point which leads to insights which cannot be attained from the vantage point of the dominant position. So the claim is not that subjected groups have a more comprehensive understanding than dominant groups. Rather, the claim is that subjected groups in social movements arrive at particular insights that are beyond the horizon of the dominant social group. We have seen these insights in the proletarian struggle of the nineteenth century: that capitalism leads to premature death due to the length of the working day; and that the workers are degraded and made dependent by the mechanization of labor in capitalism. Similarly, the African nationalist movement has insights. Since the political effectiveness of African nationalism depended upon its successful appeal to Africans of all classes to support the struggle, it sought to formulate an understanding that would strike all Africans as true in light of their experiences. Thus it sought to formulate the objective conditions that all Africans had in common. Let us examine the insights of African nationalism as articulated in the 1960s by such statesmen and writers as Julius Nyerere (1968), Kwame Nkrumah (1966), Oginga Odinga (1967), Chinua Achebe (1959), Frantz Fanon (1967; 1968), Albert Memmi (1965), and W.E.B. DuBois (1965).

Four basic insights of African nationalism can be articulated. First, pre-colonial African societies were developed societies in the sense that they were capable of providing for the basic material, emotional, psychological, and emotional needs of their members. Such formulations can be found in Odinga's description of the Luo society of his childhood prior to the arrival of the English (1967: 1–13); in Nyerere's description of traditional African society as classless and as characterized by a spirit of *ujamaa* (1968:106–10); and by Achebe's portrayal of traditional West African society (1959). Second, such developed societies were rendered underdeveloped by colonial domination. Accordingly, the present poverty and underdevelopment of Africa is a consequence of colonial domination. This is a central theme in Nyerere, Odinga, DuBois, and Achebe. Third, the colonial conquest of Africa by Europe was a multidimensional phenomenon. The most important dimension of colonialism was economic exploitation, for the basic goal was to use the land, mineral resources, and labor of Africa for the commercial and industrial development of Europe. The traditional economic institutions of Africa were undermined, and European commercial economic institutions oriented toward the production of export crops were imposed. Thus, the traditional economies of Africa, which were oriented primarily to the production of goods for use in response to human need, were replaced with economic enterprises connected to the world economy of capitalism and oriented to the production of goods for sale and profit (Nyerere, 1968; Odinga, 1967; DuBois, 1965). In order for the colonizer to facilitate such economic goals, it was necessary to establish not only economic institutions but also various social institutions that functioned to legitimate and in other ways support the newly imposed mode of production. Thus, educational institutions that taught the language, values, and history of the colonizer were established, as were religious institutions, which propagated the religion of the colonizer. Moreover, a system of government replicating political systems of the colonizer were imposed. This imposition of European social institutions was justified on the fallacious grounds that African social institutions were either non-existent or inferior (Odinga, 1967; Fanon, 1963). Colonial domination was so penetrating that, from the vantage point of the colonized, the powerlessness of the colonized was everywhere evident. As a result, colonial domination has its psychological as well as social dimension (Fanon, 1967; Memmi, 1965).

Fourth, in spite of the fact that most African nations attained political independence in the 1960s, genuine independence from colonial rule has not been attained. The newly independent nation finds that it is in a condition of economic dependency. The result is not genuine independence but neo-colonialism (Nkrumah, 1966; Odinga, 1967; Nyerere, 1968; Fanon, 1963). Thus, development, genuinely understood, requires emancipation from neo-colonial domination. Accordingly, economic development, in the sense of improving the technical capacity of the nation's economic institutions, is desired. But this development must occur in a particular way. In the first place, the development must occur in a way that preserves important aspects of the pre-colonial African culture. The importance of this can be seen in Nyerere's strategy of *ujamaa* agriculture, where the goal is to introduce modern technology in a way which preserves the traditional African characteristics of respect for one another, a strong sense of familyhood, relative equality in income and status, and common and co-operative ownership of the means of production. Second, the economic development must occur on the African nation's own terms, for if it does not, it could well mean a development that destroys all remnants of traditional African society. Nyerere's strategy of self-reliance reflects this desire to accomplish economic development through national autonomy (Nyerere, 1968; Pratt, 1976).

African nationalism, therefore, is a social movement that formulates insights into the objective conditions of Africans from the point of view of Africans. It is a formulation that focuses on colonialism, for it sees colonialism as a force that destroyed viable and humane traditional African social systems and which created underdevelopment in Africa. Moreover, it sees the legacy of colonialism, in the form of neo-colonialism, as responsible for the continuing underdevelopment of the continent. Thus, from the African nationalist point of view, colonial domination is the fundamental social reality, and Africans are, above all, colonized.

Thus, African nationalism has formulated insights into the objective conditions of the colonized, just as the proletarian movement in the twentieth century had formulated insights into the objective conditions of the worker. Both the African nationalist movement and the proletarian movement, therefore, illustrate that social movements constituted by subjected social groups formulate insights into the objective conditions of subjected social groups. These are insights into the objective conditions of the subjected group as understood from the vantage point of the subjected group. Such insights cannot be formulated from the vantage point of the dominant group.

Social Movements and Social Science

Let us now turn to our third observation in regard to the process of encounter: the social movements of subjected groups establish new possibilities for social scientific knowledge. Through encounter with such social movements, the social scientist can become aware of their insights. As the social scientist becomes aware of the insights formulated by the social movements of subjected groups, the social scientist begins to raise questions. These questions are relevant to the issue of understanding the objective conditions of the subjected group. Thus, Lonergan's formulation of this process as "discovering relevant questions" is appropriate. At the same time, these are "perverse questions" (Parekh, 1982), because, since they have their roots in the insights of the subjected class, these questions challenge the assumptions and ideologies of the established order. In this process, there is a general and fundamental question that is addressed: how can the insights of the social movement of the subjected class be reformulated within the structure of science? This general question has many particular forms, reflecting variations from one social movement to another. We have seen in the particular case of Marx's encounter with the working-class struggle that Marx was lead to the question: What is the origin of surplus value? Once such questions are asked, it becomes possible for the social scientist, first, to reformulate the objective conditions of the subjected group, and second, to formulate new insights within a scientific theoretical system. The first of these steps is illustrated by Marx's reformulation of the objective conditions of the workers as sellers of labor power. The second is illustrated by Marx's formulation of the theoretical system of historical materialism, which, as we have seen, is a creative synthesis of political economy, Hegelian philosophy, and the insights of the working-class struggle.[2] These two steps are interrelated and simultaneous, and they involve a developmental process that can consume a social scientist for years. Thus, when relevant questions are asked, the social scientist begins a process of developing a reformulation of the objective conditions of the subjected group in light of a new scientific theoretical formulation.

Thus, we have identified some basic elements in the process of encounter. Through encounter with the social movements of subjected groups, social scientists can become aware of insights of a subjected group. These insights lead to the discovery of relevant and perverse questions which, in turn, lead to a new theoretical system and to a new understanding of the objective conditions of the subjected group.

These elements in the process of encounter are illustrated in the twentieth century by the world-systems perspective of Immanuel Wallerstein. Wallerstein, a North American sociologist, was in Africa during the culmination of the African nationalist struggle in the early 1960s. During this time, Wallerstein became aware that African nationalists clearly perceive their situation as colonial. Wallerstein describes his encounter with the African nationalist struggle and the impact that it had on his understanding.

I went to Africa first during the colonial era, and I witnessed the process of "decolonization," and then of the independence of a cascade of sovereign states. White man that I was, I was bombarded by the onslaught of the colonial mentality of Europeans long resident in Africa. And sympathizer of nationalist movements that I was, I was privy to the angry analysis and optimistic passions of young militants of the African movements. It did not take long to realize that not only were these two groups at odds on political issues, but that they approached the situation with entirely different sets of conceptual frameworks.

In general, in a deep conflict, the eyes of the downtrodden are more acute about the reality of the present. For it is in their interest to perceive correctly in order to expose the hypocrisies of the rulers. They have less interest in ideological deflection. So it was in this case. The nationalists saw the reality in which they lived as a "colonial situation," that is, one in which both their social action and that of the Europeans living side by side with them as administrators, missionaries, teachers, and merchants were determined by the constraints of a single legal and social entity. (Wallerstein, 1974:4)

In our terminology, through the process of encounter with the African nationalist struggle, Wallerstein became aware of the African nationalist insight into the African condition as colonized.

Wallerstein then turned to the question, How can this insight be appropriated by social scientific knowledge? In addressing this question, Wallerstein came to believe that there is a fundamental inadequacy in conventional sociological concepts. Specifically, conventional sociological concepts endeavor to describe social systems that are assumed to have overlapping political, economic, and cultural boundaries. But in the colonial situation, economic relationships establish an economic system that incorporates several cultural and political systems.

Reflection on this phenomenon leads one to the observation that in the twentieth century there is a single global system of economic relationships that connects distinct cultural and political systems. Accordingly, conventional sociological theory, which describes the modern world as consisting of a number of distinct social systems, each assumed to be more or less autonomous political, economic, and cultural entities, is being rendered outdated by the development of the modern world economy. It is therefore necessary to reformulate sociological theoretical orientation toward an effort to describe the modern world-system, an emerging economic and political system that is global in scope (Wallerstein, 1974:4–8). Wallerstein therefore turned to a theoretical reformulation of sociology in the form of a description of the modern world-system. As he turned to this description, he addressed the question, What is the origin of the modern world economy? This is a question to which little attention had been paid in sociology. Therefore, to respond to this question, Wallerstein found it necessary to turn to extensive historical investigation. Let us examine what Wallerstein found in his investigation of this question.[3]

Wallerstein found that the modern world economy began to emerge as a response to the crisis of feudalism. During the period of 1300–1450, the feudal economy experienced a serious decline in commerce, agricultural production, and population. In response to this crisis, the landowning class sought to increase production by the transformation of feudal agricultural production into capitalist agricultural production. In this process, they turned the serf into a wage worker, consolidated farms, and converted most of the land from agriculture to pasture. Since these steps led to the increase in the production of beef and wool but to the decline of grain production, the process necessitated the importation of grains. The grain was purchased from Eastern Europe, where the landowning class used coercive techniques to facilitate production by serfs of grain for export. The funds for the purchase of the grain were available as a result of the trade between Northwestern Europe and Spain. Spain was developing an empire in the Americas and obtained gold and silver through coerced labor. Spain did not, however, develop its manufacturing and agriculture and found it necessary to purchase goods with gold and silver from Northwestern Europe. There thus emerged a system of economic relationships connecting Eastern and Western Europe and connecting Western Europe and the Americas. Northwestern Europe was the primary beneficiary of this system, for it enabled Northwestern Europe to overcome its economic decline and enter an era of economic expansion. At the same time, the system functioned to promote the underdevelopment of Eastern Europe and Spanish America, as coerced labor became predominant in these regions. Accordingly, a world economy began to emerge, an economy that connected political and cultural systems in diverse regions of the world. In this emerging world economy, the economic development of some regions became tied to the conquest of other regions, and as a result, the economic development of some regions promoted the underdevelopment of others.

This world economy has gone through four stages in its development. The first stage was the period of 1450–1640, during which the territory of the world economy included Europe and Spanish America. It was characterized by a geographical division of labor: the countries of Northwestern Europe produced a variety of products using free labor, and the regions of Eastern Europe and Latin America produced a single export crop (such as wheat and other grains, sugar, gold, silver) with coerced labor. Hence, an international economic system had emerged in which there was an economic relation between the peripheral regions and the core countries. In this economic relationship, products produced through the land, resources, and labor of the periphery were exported to the core; these imports made it possible for the economies in the core to turn to the production of a variety of products and luxury goods.[4]

The second stage in the evolution of the modern world economy was the period 1640–1815. This was a time of stagnation and consolidation in the world economy, and it was a time of competition among core countries for hegemony.

The third stage in the modern world economy was the period 1815–1917. During this period the world-system expanded into a global enterprise. This expansion was made possible by technological developments in modern industry. At the same time, these technological developments made the territorial expansion necessary, for technologically advancing industry had greater need for the world's mineral resources. Hence, there emerged a greater economic interest in Africa, and Africa and much of Asia became incorporated as peripheral regions into the modern world-system. The basic geographical division of labor between core and periphery continued intact in this third period. The periphery provided land and labor for agricultural products and mineral resources for the core. In the core, labor engaged in a variety of economic activities and earned high wages. As in the previous period, the productive capacity of the core was made possible by its economic connection to the periphery.

The fourth stage in the development of the modern world-system is the period 1917 to the present. This is a period of consolidation of the modern world economy and a time in which the geographical division of labor remains intact. It is a period in which unequal wage levels between core and periphery becomes more important than blatant political and military force in the preservation of the world economy. It is also a period of anti-systemic movements, where social movements in opposition to the world-system emerge. These anti-systemic movements include anti-colonial independence movements in the periphery and socialist movements in core countries.

Wallerstein's world-systems perspective, therefore, is an alternative theoretical formulation that transforms conventional sociology. It was formulated in response to questions that occurred to Wallerstein as a result of his awareness of the African nationalist insight into the African condition as colonized. In developing responses to these questions, Wallerstein went beyond the formulation of African nationalism itself. His theory places European colonial domination of Africa in the nineteenth and twentieth centuries into a four-century peripheralization of all regions of the world by core nations. In the process, the formulation of the objective conditions of Africans becomes transformed: whereas African nationalism defines Africans as colonized, the world-systems perspective sees Africans as peripheralized. But this transformation of the description of the objective conditions of the colonized in no sense represents an utter disregard or a dismissal of the African nationalist formulation. Indeed, Wallerstein's description of the world economy as characterized by a geographical division of labor between core and periphery is fundamentally similar to the African nationalist division of the social world between the colonizer and the colonized. Moreover, Wallerstein's insight into the connection between development and underdevelopment is basically a further extension of the African nationalist insight that European colonial domination impoverished Africa. Thus, by placing the African nationalist claims into a scientific context, Wallerstein places the phenomenon of European colonial domination of Africa into a larger historical and global context.

Marx's theory of historical materialism and Wallerstein's world-systems perspective, then, both illustrate the social scientific method. Let us reiterate the basic points of the scientific method in regard to the connection between social movements and social science.

1. In order to overcome the limitations imposed by horizon on understanding, social scientists must seek encounter with the social movements constituted by subjected groups. For example, Marx experienced encounter with the working-class struggle of nineteenth century Western Europe, and Wallerstein experienced encounter with twentieth-century African nationalism.

2. Such social movements emerge in accordance with economic development. For example, the working-class struggle emerged once the development of capitalism constituted the proletariat as a class. Similarly, the African nationalist movement emerged once colonialism had constituted the African national bourgeoisie as a class.

3. Such social movements contain insights into the objective conditions of the subjected group. For example, the working-class struggle grasped that capitalism mechanizes labor and produces the premature death of the worker. Similarly, the African nationalist struggle grasped that Africans are colonized.

4. Through encounter with the social movements of subjected groups, social scientists become aware of these insights, and this awareness leads to the discovery of relevant questions. These questions are particular versions of the basic question of how to incorporate the insights of the social movement into scientific knowledge. For example, Marx asked, What is the origin of surplus value? And Wallerstein asked, What is the origin of the modern world economy?

5. In response to relevant questions, social scientists can formulate alternative theoretical conceptions that transform social science and reformulate the social movement's understanding of the objective conditions of the subjected group. For example, Marx formulated his theory of historical materialism, according to which the fundamental objective condition of the working class is understood as a seller of labor power. Similarly, Wallerstein formulated his world-systems perspective, according to which the objective condition of Africans is understood as peripheralized.

New scientific theories, then, are rooted in the insights of social movements of subjected social groups. Accordingly, they can be said to be theories that are written from the point of view of the subjected group. But as the history of the Marxist concept of the proletarian point of view shows, such an expression is susceptible to a variety of interpretations. Therefore, to be more precise, it should be said that the new scientific theories take seriously the insights of the subjected group and formulate critiques of social science, critiques which take as given the objective conditions of the subjected group. These objective conditions are initially understood according to the formulations of the social movements of subjected social groups, but as the theory develops, these formulations are re-formulated in the process of critique of established scientific theory. Thus, the new scientific theories take seriously both past scientific insights and the insights of newly emerging social movements. As such, the new social scientific theories are simultaneously critiques of social science as well as critiques of the under-standings of social movements.

Summary

The social scientist, then, attains objective knowledge through encounter with social movements constituted by subjected social groups. Such social movements are established by economic development, and they possess insights into the objective conditions of the subjected social group. Such insights establish new possibilities for science, for they make possible the discovery of relevant and perverse questions by social scientists in encounter. Such questions lead to reformulation of the objective conditions of the subjected group in a scientific context, and they lead to the formulation of new theoretical systems.

THE DEVELOPMENT OF THEORIES OF ECONOMIC DEVELOPMENT

Let us apply this understanding of the development of social science to the development of social scientific theories of economic development. Theories of economic development emerged in the twentieth century as explanations of the different levels of development in the modern world economy, particularly the great inequality between the West and the Third World. By the 1950s and 1960s, modernization theory had emerged as the dominant theory of development. Modernization theory did not have the benefit of the insights of Third World national liberation movements. It therefore reflected a Western horizon and promoted Western interests. It represented, however, science for its time, for it was the most advanced understanding which was possible at that time, given the level of development of the modern world economy. However, in the 1960s, Third World national liberation movements attained sufficient power to penetrate Western consciousness. This political fact made possible a reformulation of the social scientific understanding of development, and the world-systems perspective emerged. The world-systems perspective is the scientific formulation that emerges from national liberation movements, and it constitutes the scientific formulation appropriate for the post–1960s. Once this reformulation occurs, modernization theory no longer represents the most advanced understanding possible, and to advocate this theory after 1970 is to engage in ideology rather than science. Let us examine these developments in the social scientific understanding of economic development in more detail.

Modernization Theory

The social sciences emerged in the nineteenth century as five distinct disciplines. In three of the new sciences (economics, political science, and sociology), the goal was to formulate generalizations applicable to all societies. This understanding of social science reflected a philosophy of positivism, the view that the method of natural science could be applied to social science. It was believed that, just as the natural sciences had discovered the laws of nature, so the social sciences could formulate lawlike generalizations for all societies. To one of the social sciences, history, was reserved the task of describing particular and historically unique developments in the history of civilization, developments that were not considered susceptible to interpretations as generalizations. To the final social science, anthropology, was reserved the task of describing those cultures considered ''uncivilized'' (Wallerstein, 1984b:177–79; 179:vii–ix).

The emergence of the social sciences coincided with British hegemony in the modern world economy, and the assumptions of social science reflected this important social fact. By the nineteenth century, Britain had mastered the world. It had used new technical knowledge to dominate nature, to conquer peoples throughout the world, and to gain a competitive edge over other Western colonial powers. It had seen the capacity of scientific knowledge to make domination possible, and it self-confidently looked to the future with optimistic forecasts of more progress in the form of ever more domination. The assumption of the validity of lawlike generalizations in the social sciences reflected this self-confident optimism of the powerful during the age of Empire, as did the assumption of the relation between knowledge and power. In addition, the assumptions that the West is civilized and only its history is worth knowing, and that the history and cultures of peoples outside the West belong to a distinct discipline, reflected the self-confident ethnocentrism of the masters of the world. The social scientific disciplines, therefore, were products of the social environment in which they were born, and their fundamental assumptions reflect this social environment (Wallerstein, 1979:viii; 1984b:179).

A basic assumption common to all social sciences is that the society is the basic unit of analysis. Each society, therefore, had an economic system, a state, and other institutions. The task of the various social sciences was to describe one or more of these institutions in each society. Moreover, given this assumption, it became possible to compare and contrast societies. One important contrast that emerged was the fact that societies have different levels of development. In particular, England was more developed than France, Western Europe (England and France) were more developed than Germany and Italy, and Europe was more developed than other regions of the world. A task of social science was to explain these different levels of development (Wallerstein, 1979:153–54; 1984b:175–77).

By the middle of the twentieth century, the predominant explanation of the different levels of development was modernization theory. With reference to the contrast between Western Europe and the rest of the world, modernization theory has three basic ideas. First, the societies of Western Europe are advanced industrial nations that have undergone a transition from traditional to modern societies. Second, the societies of the Third World are "undeveloped" in that they are still in the early stages of such a transition. Third, development requires that undeveloped societies adopt some important characteristics of modern society.

Bert Hoselitz' *Sociological Aspects of Economic Growth* (1960) illustrates modernization theory. Hoselitz uses Talcott Parsons' pattern variables to construct a typology of advanced and undeveloped economies. Advanced economies are characterized by modern economic activities, such as achievement orientation and universalism; in contrast, undeveloped economies are characterized by traditional economic activities, such as lack of achievement orientation and particularism (1960:30–41). Hoselitz' position is that economic development in the undeveloped world requires a transition from traditional to modern forms of economic organization (1960:24–27). The best way to facilitate such a transition is to create "a 'climate' for entrepreneurship" (1960:149), so that entrepreneurs can emerge as private owners of small- and medium-scale industry. This can be done if social institutions are established in which people who have the appropriate personality characteristics for entrepreneurship can emerge (1960: 149–56).

Hoselitz maintains that he is advocating the adoption of Western forms of economic activity and not the adoption of Western values and social structure. To assert the latter would be ethnocentric, he maintains, and he is critical of many Western scholars for being ethnocentric in this regard (1960:55–58). However, Hoselitz sometimes loses sight of the distinction between social structure and values, on the one hand, and economic activity, on the other (1960:76–81). As a result, his work at times has the ethnocentric bias against which he warns. But that question aside, a far more important issue in Hoselitz' analysis is that it is unaware of the role of colonial domination in the development of the advanced societies.[5] It is, of course, the case that the advanced and underdeveloped societies have different forms of economic activities. However, this cultural difference is not the only reason for the economic development of the advanced societies. Another important factor, as we now know in light of national liberation movements, is the fact that the advanced societies had access to the resources of the underdeveloped world as a result of colonial domination. That

Hoselitz overlooks the factor of colonialism is the result of the time and social location from which he wrote. National liberation movements had emerged in South Asia and Africa, but these movements had not yet impacted upon the consciousness of social scientific scholarship in the West. Thus, insight into the relation between colonial domination and Western development was beyond the horizon of Western social science in the 1950s.

In W. W. Rostow's *Stages of Economic Growth* (1971), which was originally published in 1960, we find another example of a modernization theorist who does not see the role of colonial domination in the development of the West. Rostow's thesis is that there are five stages in the modernization process, beginning with the traditional stage and culminating in a stage of high mass consumption. He maintains that the advanced industrial societies have proceeded through these stages and that the undeveloped societies are not as far along in the transition. The essential ingredient in such a transition is that an elite class of entrepreneurs must emerge. This elite class must possess modern economic values, and they must view modernization as desirable. And they must feel that they are denied traditional and conventional routes to prestige and power (1971:51–52).

Rostow's analysis does include reference to the process of colonial domination. He maintains, for example, that England's take-off to modernity was made possible by the "discovery and rediscovery of regions beyond Western Europe" (1971:31); such discovery made possible an expansion in commerce which facilitated economic development. Elsewhere he notes that, since the pre-colonial economic systems were not organized "for modern import and export activity, including production for export" (1971:110), they had to be "taken over and organized" (1971:110). However, Rostow does not view such colonial domination, which he refers to as "lateral innovation" (1971:31), as necessary for modernization. Lateral innovation facilitated the take-off in England, but it is not a necessary component, and the undeveloped world can belatedly develop without this dimension. Rostow, therefore, grasps some dimensions of the role of colonial domination in the development of the West, but he is unable to grasp the full significance of this insight. This limitation is due to the fact that he, like Hoselitz, formulated his theory before the impact of Third World nationalism on Western scholarship.

Another example of modernization theory is the work of Talcott Parsons. Parsons' views on economic development are found in *Societies* (1966) and *The System of Modern Societies* (1971).[6] Parsons sees three stages in the evolution of societies: primitive, intermediate, and modern. This development from primitive to modern is characterized by increasing differentiation. In the primitive stage, social and cultural systems are not differentiated, and kinship structures constitute the primary social organization. As a consequence of this undifferentiated social structure, technology is simple. In the intermediate stage, the development of a written language makes possible the differentiation of political and religious institutions. Examples of this intermediate stage include the ancient empires of Egypt, Mesopotamia, China, India, Islam, and Rome. The third stage of modern social systems is characterized by further differentiation beyond that of the intermediate stage. Parsons identifies the Renaissance, the Reformation, the Industrial Revolution, and the democratic revolution as factors that led to the emergence of modern social systems. As a result of these four factors, modern social systems have three characteristics. First is the differentiation of religion from society, in which there is religious pluralism, and religious belief is not imposed on societal members. Second is the differentiation of polity from society, in which the concept of citizen emerges, and leaders are chosen by an electoral process rather than by ascription. Third comes the differentiation of economy from society, in which the economic system becomes differentiated from the kinship system, and achieved status is predominant.

For Parsons, the historical development of human societies reveals the four basic components of social development. First, in order for development to occur, there must be differentiation. Differentiation involves the division of a unit or sub-system into two or more units, as when a kinship system which is a producing unit differentiates into separate economic and family systems. Second, as a result of this differentiation, adaptive upgrading occurs. That is, functions are performed more efficiently. For example, after the differentiation of the economic system from the kinship system, production is more efficient, and the family is more efficient in providing for emotional needs. Third, in order for adaptive upgrading to take hold, inclusion must emerge. That is, "the producing organization must develop an authority system which is *not* imbedded in kinship" (Parsons, 1966:22). Thus, achievement orientation must replace ascription orientation. Fourth, in order for this differentiated, efficient, and achievement-oriented system to sustain itself, value generalization must occur. Value generalization refers to the process through which values are reformulated in order to encompass the two or more distinct structures that have now emerged.

Thus, Parsons has formulated an understanding of social and economic development, according to which societies develop a greater capacity to produce and distribute goods and services insofar as their economic systems become differentiated from kinship and insofar as status is based on achievement. Moreover, Parsons makes explicit that this understanding of development was formulated through observation of the development of the United States, which Parsons takes to be the best example of a highly differentiated society. What Parsons does not make explicit, but which is clearly an implication, is that other societies can become socially and economically developed like the United States to the degree that they too become differentiated. According to this logic, Third World societies are undeveloped, meaning they lack the social and economic development of the United States. The reason for this undevelopment is their lack of differentiation. And they can become developed like the United States insofar as they differentiate their economic systems from kinship, move toward achievement as a basis for authority and status, and reformulate their values in accordance with this development.

Parsons' understanding of economic development in the modern world does not take into consideration the role of colonial domination in Western development. As a result, Parsons believes that Third World undevelopment is a consequence of the fact that the Third World lacks certain social and cultural characteristics that have been important in the development of the West. In failing to grasp the role of colonial domination in development and underdevelopment, Parsons is very much a product of his time and place, for most of his ideas were formulated before the impact of Third World nationalism on the consciousness of social scientific scholarship in the West.

World-Systems Perspective

Beginning in the 1960s, the assumptions of modernization theory and Western social science were to be challenged by the world-systems perspective. The social roots of the world-systems perspective are those social movements that Wallerstein calls "anti-systemic" (1984a:65) movements. These are movements which have human equality as a fundamental goal, and as such they stand in opposition to the modern world-system or the capitalist world economy. "Their general objective, human equality, was by definition incompatible with the functioning of the capitalist world-economy, a hierarchical system based on uneven development, unequal exchange, and the appropriation of surplus-value" (Wallerstein, 1984a:65).

The anti-systemic movements are of two forms: first, workers' movements in core and semi-peripheral regions of the world economy, and second, national liberation movements in the periphery. The first workers' anti-systemic movement occurred during the collapse of public order created by the French Revolution (Wallerstein, 1989:111). However, the movement did not succeed, and it ultimately was repressed (Wallerstein, 1989:119–22). The workers' movement took organized form in the nineteenth century. However, with the exception of the short-lived Paris Commune in 1870, the movement could not attain control of the state structure in any nation during the nineteenth century (Wallerstein, 1979:234). Beginning in the latter half of the nineteenth century, and becoming more manifest in the twentieth, the workers' movement divided between reformers and revolutionaries. The reformers, who came to be known as social democrats, "sought to achieve their objectives by a loyal participation in national parliamentary process" (Wallerstein, 1979:236). The revolutionaries, who came to be known as communists, envisioned a less piecemeal approach and a revolutionary transformation of social institutions. Both wings of the workers' movement saw significant gains in the twentieth century.[7] The social democrats in some countries of Western Europe "succeeded in becoming the government (alone or in coalition) for varying lengths of time" (Wallerstein, 1979:237). The communists attained state power in Russia through the Revolution of 1917, a political fact that "demonstrated . . . the enormous vulnerability of the world capitalist system to organized revolutionary opposition'' (Wallerstein, 1979:241).

Alongside the workers' anti-systemic movements in the core and semi-periphery, anti-systemic movements emerged in the periphery in the twentieth century. These were ''movements of national liberation against Europe's world political hegemony'' (Wallerstein, 1979:234). They first emerged in Africa and South and Southeast Asia in the 1920s, constituted by the petty bourgeoisie in the periphery, a class newly emerging as a result of colonialism. In the post–World War II era, the movements were able to take control of state structures in nearly all of their countries, particularly during the 1950s and 1960s. A parallel development has occurred in the Americas, where the formation of states under the control of European settlers in the late eighteenth and early nineteenth centuries gave rise to class conflicts overlaid with ethnic conflicts in the twentieth century, culminating in the civil rights and Black Power movement in the United States in the 1950s and 1960s, and the class conflicts of Central America and (to a lesser extent) South America in the 1970s and 1980s (Wallerstein, 1989:193–256).

An important characteristic, therefore, of the modern world-system in the twentieth century has been the emergence as a significant political force of anti-systemic movements, in the form of workers' movements in the core and semi-periphery and national liberation movements in the periphery. At the same time, in spite of the successes of these movements, what they have been able to achieve in terms of reform of the capitalist world economy has been very limited.

These antisystemic movements were, however, themselves caught in the web of the ideology of the system, and their various efforts to achieve transformation by seizure of power in individual states had ambiguous results, enmeshing them in the constraints of the interstate system and thereby leading them to act in ways that reinforced as well as undermined the operations of the capitalist world-economy. (Wallerstein, 1983:303)

Although anti-systemic movements have had ambiguous results at the political level, their impact on the world of scholarship has been more decisive. As we have seen in our discussion of the life and work of Marx,[8] the workers' movement of Western Europe gave rise to the Marxist theory of historical materialism, thereby pushing social science to a more advanced stage. The workers' movement of Western Europe therefore established new possibilities for social science. These possibilities were seized much more by social scientists in Western Europe than by social scientists in the United States, where social conditions were different and where, as a result, social scientists remained isolated from Marxism scholarship.[9] Moreover, Marxist scholarship, itself a product of a Western social movement, could not free itself from assumptions of the Western horizon. It therefore did not have the possibility of moving the social scientific understanding of economic development to a more advanced stage.[10] Marxist scholars, therefore, also adopted a modernization view of development, although the stages of development are different, and the model society is the Soviet Union rather

than Great Britain or the United States (Wallerstein, 1984b:181; Addo, 1984:
126–27).

However, national liberation movements of the twentieth century have established new possibilities for social science, and these possibilities have been seized
in the formulation of the world-systems perspective. The world-systems perspective first emerged in the 1960s (Wallerstein, 1979:52–53), and it "emerged
primarily from the intellectuals of the Third World" (Wallerstein, 1979:54). It
is a point of view that "has been expressed largely by persons from Asia, Africa,
and Latin America or by those others particularly interested in these regions"
(Wallerstein, 1979:53). It is a perspective that has emerged because of the
emergence of national liberation movements in the Third World: "The emergence
of the world-system perspective is a consequence of the dramatic challenge to
European political domination of the world which has called into question all
Europo-centric constructions of social reality" (Wallerstein, 1979:55).

The world-systems perspective rejects the fundamental assumption of social
science that the society is the unit of analysis (Wallerstein, 1974:5–7; 1979:53).
This was a useful starting point from the vantage point of hegemony in the
nineteenth-century capitalist world economy. However, if one takes as given the
objective condition of the Third World as a colonial condition, then one seeks
above all to explain the colonial phenomenon. In endeavoring to explain colonialism, one finds the assumption of the society as the unit of analysis to be a
problematic starting point, for colonialism is characterized by a relationship
between two societies and by a transformation of the institutions of one society
to serve the interests of the other. One sees that in the colonial situation the
society is part of a larger political and economic system. Taking as given the
objective condition of colonialism, the world-systems perspective proposes the
world-system as the basic unit of analysis, of which there have been two types
in human history, empires and world economies (Wallerstein, 1974:5–7, 15–
17; 1984b:147–56). Of the world economies, the capitalist world economy is
the latest, most stable, and largest in geographical scope. There is therefore a
difference in starting point between mainstream social science and the world-
systems perspective, reflecting the different social contexts in which they were
formulated. Of the two, the world-systems perspective is more advanced, for it
benefits from the insights of Third World national liberation movements of the
twentieth century, insights that were beyond the horizon of nineteenth-century
Western social scientists.

In addition to rejecting the assumption of society as the unit of analysis, the
world-systems perspective has maintained that social science is characterized by
European ethnocentrism. The European ethnocentrism of social science can be
seen in the fact that it promotes European interests. As Wallerstein has noted,
the social scientific explanation of European development alongside Third World
underdevelopment

justified, indeed glorified, monumental and growing inequalities in the world-system as
a whole. The moral implicitly preached was that the leader merited the lead because he

had somehow shown his devotion earlier and more intensely to human freedom. The laggard had but to catch up. (1984b:180)

Moreover, like Western social science, orthodox Marxism is characterized by European ethnocentrism. The European ethnocentrism of orthodox Marxism can be seen in its conception of imperialism, in which imperialism is understood as one stage in the development of capitalism. In contrast, the world-systems perspective understands imperialism to be an essential and continuous aspect of the development of the capitalist world economy (Addo, 1984:125–32).

In scientific development, whenever there is a shift from one paradigm to another, one reason for the shift is the inability of the old paradigm to answer important questions and the capacity of the new paradigm to do so (Kuhn, 1970). Consistent with this expectation, Wallerstein maintains that there were important questions that social science, modernization theory, and classical Marxism were unable to answer prior to the emergence of the world-systems perspective. These questions included the following. With the expectation of modernization theory that the inequality between the West and the Third World would decrease with increasing economic and cultural contact, why was income inequality in fact increasing? With the expectation of classical Marxism that a proletarian revolution would occur in the advanced sector of the world economy, why did it occur in Russia? With the expectation of social science and classical Marxism that nationalism would die due to increasing industrialization (for the former) or due to the emergence of an international proletarian struggle (for the latter), why has nationalism persisted as an important social and political force in the twentieth century? Why did Great Britain emerge as a dominant power in the nineteenth century? Why was Great Britain replaced by the United States in the twentieth century (Wallerstein, 1979:55–60)? Wallerstein maintains that these questions, difficult to explain given the assumptions of social science or classical Marxism, can be understood from a world-systems perspective, which takes the world-system as the unit of analysis; which understands the internal dynamics of a country in the context of its position as core, semi-periphery, or periphery in the world-system; which sees increasing inequality as a consequence of increasing peripheralization; which sees nationalism as a dimension of the competition for status within the world economy; and which sees cycles of hegemony as normal patterns in the development of the modern world economy (Wallerstein, 1979:60–65).

Summary

In spite of the limitations of Hoselitz, Rostow, and Parsons, limitations that can now be seen in light of the Third World national liberation movements, they were social scientists for their time. Their scientific formulations were grounded in the development of the economic system. They examined the economic development of the modern world from the vantage point of the colonizer, and thus took as given European domination of the world. Indeed, their theory helped to legitimate European domination, in that it presented European economic and political superiority as a consequence of qualities which Western culture defined as virtues. In taking the vantage point of the colonizer, they arrived at some insights. Their basic insight is that modern Western forms of economic activity are highly efficient. And they grasped some of the essential elements of Western economic activity that make it efficient: its differentiation from the kinship structure and its achievement orientation. However, they overlooked the role of colonial domination in the development of the West. They erroneously thought that economic development in the Third World would occur if Third World societies would adopt the social and cultural characteristics of the West. They did not see that this would only serve to reinforce colonial structures and therefore increase underdevelopment. These limitations in their analysis could be made manifest only from the vantage point of the periphery, from a vantage point that takes as given the objective conditions of the colonized. The national liberation movements of the Third World constitute such a vantage point. National liberation movements challenged, in the realm of politics as well as in the realms of ideas, European domination. These movements established new possibilities for science. Emerging in the 1960s, the world-systems perspective seized these possibilities and formulated an analysis based on the central concept of a geographical division of labor between core and periphery in the modern world economy. The world-systems perspective enables social science to move to a more advanced level of analysis and to move beyond the ethnocentrism of modernization theory. In the aftermath of the formulation of the world-systems perspective, modernization theory no longer represents science but constitutes ideology.

THE IMPACT OF BLACK NATIONALISM ON SOCIOLOGY IN THE UNITED STATES

Immanuel Wallerstein's formulation of the world-systems perspective was rapidly accepted in the late 1970s and early 1980s by those sociologists in the United States who study problems of economic development in the Third World. These sociologists have become organized in a section in the American Sociological Association known as the Political Economy of the World-System. Virtually all analyses by sociologists that address issues of Third World underdevelopment proceed in the context of the assumptions of the world-systems perspective. The relatively rapid acceptance of the new perspective was a consequence of the impact of African-American and African nationalism on sociology in the United States. Let us examine this phenomenon.

Hoselitz published *Sociological Aspects of Economic Growth* in 1960. Rostow's *The Stages of Economic Growth* was also originally published in 1960. When these publications appeared, the United States was in the midst of the upheavals centered around the challenge of the civil rights movement to segregation. From 1954 to 1965, the movement was very active and visible in the public life of the United States, and at that time, it focused on the limited goal of obtaining citizenship rights for blacks. This struggle thus concentrated on such issues as equal access to public facilities without discrimination, the right to vote, and the desegregation of public schools. The civil rights movement had many successes in this time, culminating in the Civil Rights Act of 1964 and the Voting Rights Act of 1965. As Jack Bloom (1987) has argued, these successes were made possible by an effective alliance of blacks with Southern white businessmen, the federal government, and Northern white liberals. However, the civil rights movement sought the protection of social and economic rights of blacks, above and beyond civil and political rights. Whites, however, did not have an interest in supporting these more far-reaching social and economic reforms, and the coalition that had forged the success of the civil rights movement began to fall apart. In the wake of the collapse of the civil rights coalition, black nationalism, long a tendency in the black movement (Cruse, 1967), experienced a revitalization and a resurgence. Black nationalism sought to form a new coalition with Africans and people of color throughout the world. As a dimension of this re-evaluation, an alternative understanding of racial injustice in the United States was formulated. The conventional understanding reflected the assumptions of white society. It understood the United States to be an essentially democratic society that, because of prejudice and discrimination, fails to live up to its democratic character in regard to racial and ethnic relations. The alternative understanding abandoned the description of blacks as victims of prejudice and discrimination in a society that was essentially democratic, and it abandoned the hope for democracy in the United States. Rather, it redefined the problem of racial injustice in the United States in terms of the international process of European colonial domination of the world. Accordingly, it saw blacks in the United States as colonized. In this view, the objective condition of blacks is analogous to the objective condition of Africans and other people of color. And just as Africans were seeking to control political institutions in Africa through a nationalist movement, so African-Americans should endeavor to control the political, economic, and social institutions of the black community through black nationalism.

Stokely Carmichael and Malcolm X are important examples of this resurgence of black nationalism in the late 1960s. In the widely read *Black Power*, Carmichael and Charles Hamilton argued that white domination of blacks in the United States is analogous to European colonial domination of Africa. They maintained that colonialism has three basic dimensions. First, "colonial subjects have their political decisions made for them by their colonial masters" (1967:6). Second, "the colonies were sources from which raw materials were taken and markets to which finished products were sold" (1967:17). Third, group self-hatred emerges. Carmichael and Hamilton argued that these three basic dimensions of colonialism are found in both the United States and Africa. Thus, although recognizing that the analogy is not perfect, they maintained that race relations in the United States are analogous to the colonial relationship in Africa, and that to view blacks in the United States as colonized is valid. They wrote:

Black people in this country form a colony, and it is not in the interest of the colonial power to liberate them. Black people are legal citizens of the United States with, for the most part, the same *legal* rights as other citizens. Yet they stand as colonial subjects in relation to the white society. Thus institutional racism has another name: colonialism. (Carmichael & Hamilton, 1967:5)

Malcolm X also expressed the idea that black Americans are colonized in a speech in 1964:

We have suffered colonialism for the past four hundred years. America is just as much a colonial power as England ever was. America is just as much a colonial power as France ever was. In fact, America is more so a colonial power than they, because she's a hypocritical colonial power behind it. (Malcolm X, n.d.)

Malcolm's autobiography appeared in 1965. Carmichael and Hamilton's *Black Power* was published in 1967. Harold Cruse's widely read *Crisis of the Negro Intellectual*, an insightful intellectual history of black America written from a black nationalist point of view, was published in 1967. *Rebellion or Revolution*, a collection of essays by Cruse, appeared in 1968. A collection of Malcolm's speeches was published by John Henrik Clarke in 1969. In his introduction, Clarke stressed the turn in Malcolm's last year, after his break with the Nation of Islam, toward defining the racial problem in terms of the international phenomenon of colonialism.

This resurgence of black nationalism, with its new definition of racial injustice in an international colonial context, was accompanied by a great interest in the African nationalist movement itself in the late 1960s. Accordingly, from 1965 to 1969, African nationalism was to enter the consciousness of the intellectual life of the United States. Chinua Achebe's novel, *Things Fall Apart*, had already been published in 1959. From 1965 to 1969, this important work was to be followed in quick succession by several works by African nationalists that were widely read, discussed, and debated in intellectual circles in the United States. Kwame Nkrumah's *Neo-Colonialism* was published in 1965. The American edition of Albert Memmi's *The Colonizer and the Colonized* appeared in 1967. The English translation of Frantz Fanon's *Black Skin, White Masks* appeared in 1967, to be followed by the English translation of Fanon's *The Wretched of the Earth* in 1968. Julius Nyerere's *Ujamaa: Essays in Socialism*, was published in 1968. And a new edition of W.E.B. DuBois' *The World and Africa*, originally published in 1940, was issued in 1965.

Thus, in the late 1960s, Afro-American and African nationalism became part of the intellectual landscape of the United States. This international movement promoted new understandings of the objective conditions of people of color. It rejected the notion that the Third World is undeveloped because it lacks economic and cultural traits characteristic of the Western world. It rejected the idea that the United States is fundamentally a democratic society that has customs and policies in opposition to its essential democratic nature in its discrimination against blacks, Hispanics, and Native Americans. It saw colonialism as the fundamental fact of the modern world. It defined the Western powers, including the United States, as essentially colonial powers. It saw colonial domination as the basic source of inequality in the modern world and as the cause of under-development in the Third World. It understood discrimination against people of color in the United States as dimensions of this international process of colon-ialism.

When this African and Afro-American nationalist movement entered the in-tellectual landscape of the United States, the inadequacy and ethnocentrism of modernization theory became manifest. This made possible the relatively rapid acceptance of the world-systems perspective, a perspective, as we have seen, that itself was formulated in the context of assumptions made possible by the emergence of Third World national liberation movements and that accordingly did not have the ethnocentrism of modernization theory. As a result, the world-systems perspective became an accepted theory in sociology in the United States.

MODERNIZATION THEORY, CLASSICAL MARXISM, AND THE WORLD-SYSTEMS PERSPECTIVE

The world-systems perspective transforms the insights of modernization the-ory. However, in transforming these insights, it does not nullify them. The insight of modernization theory, for example, into the essential characteristics of advanced forms of production can have applicability for an understanding of the process through which the Third World can move beyond neo-colonialism to genuine independence. Indeed, Nyerere's concept of *"ujamaa* agriculture" in the 1960s represented an effort to combine the strengths of traditional African society with the key strength of the modern West, namely, efficiency in pro-duction. But the insights of modernization theory are transformed by the world-systems perspective, in that they are placed into the social, historical, and the-oretical context of colonial domination and national liberation movements.

In the same way, the insights of classical Marxism are transformed but not nullified by the world-systems perspective. The classical Marxist insight, for example, that social processes can be understood through identifying class in-terests is an insight that has applicability in a world-systems context. Accord-ingly, Nicola Swainson (1980), Colin Leys (1974), and Michaela von Freyhold (1979) have identified the class interests of the rulers of post-colonial Kenya and Tanzania, and they have shown that the ruling elite has promoted its interests at the expense of the interests of the masses of peasants. Such analyses have made clear the foundation of the African nationalist movement in the African national bourgeoisie and the role of the African national bourgeoisie in neo-colonial Africa. Such insights of classical Marxism are transformed by the world-systems perspective and are placed in the context of the geographical division of labor between core and periphery in the modern world economy, such that class divisions are understood as dimensions of the geographical division of labor between core and the periphery. From a world-systems perspective, one cannot analyze class divisions without placing them in the context of core or periphery in the modern world economy, for class divisions function differently in the different regions of the modern world economy.

Thus, modernization theory, classical Marxism, and the world-systems perspective reflect particular vantage points. Modernization theory reflects the vantage point of the colonizer. This vantage point enabled it to grasp the essential characteristics of technological efficiency. However, from that vantage point, it overlooked the role of colonial domination in the development of the modern world economy, a limitation that now can be understood in light of national liberation movements. Classical Marxism reflects the vantage point of the proletarian struggle in the core of the modern world economy in the nineteenth century. This vantage point enabled it to grasp the role of class interests in economic and social development. Accordingly, it can grasp the different class positions in the African nationalist movement and show the manifestations of opposed class interests in neo-colonial Africa. But these insights can lead to oversight if they are inappropriately applied. This problem is illustrated by the work of Adolfo Vazquez, who argues that in spite of national liberation movements in the Third World in the twentieth century, it is the proletariat that has a "world-historical mission" (Vazquez, 1977:235) and "is the revolutionary class par excellence" (1977:235). The national liberation movements, according to Vazquez, can be revolutionary only "to the extent that they fuse their mission with that of the proletariat, even in those situations where the working class exists but has not, for historical reasons, fulfilled its role, or where that class does not yet exist at all" (1977:235–36). Such an understanding is disconnected from real historical events and social movements in the Third World in the twentieth century. In contrast, the world-systems perspective reflects the vantage point of Third World national liberation movements in the twentieth century. From that vantage point, social scientists can understand the limited applicability of classical Marxist insights and can formulate new theoretical contexts for understanding the fundamental structures of inequality in the capitalist world economy. The world-systems perspective sees inequality not fundamentally in terms of the exploitation of labor by capital but in terms of a geographical division of labor between core and periphery.

SCIENCE, SOCIAL MOVEMENTS, AND VALUES

In our reconstruction of Marx's concept of science, we have seen that science places the insights of the social movements of subjected groups into a larger historical, social, and theoretical context. Accordingly, science enables us to understand more than can be understood by the direct experience of exploitation. This can be seen with Marx, who analyzed the economic system as a whole and placed the exploitation of the working class into the larger context of the development of the contradictions of the capitalist system. This also can be seen with Wallerstein, who placed the colonial domination of Africa into a conceptual scheme which comprehends such domination as a dimension of core-peripheral relations in the world economy as a whole. Thus, science goes beyond the understandings of social movements of subjected groups. But science in no sense ignores, dismisses, or nullifies the insights of the social movements of subjected groups, for science is organically connected to the social movements of subjected groups through personal encounter, during which the social scientist learns the insights of the subjected groups. Having learned these insights, the scientist seeks to transform them by placing them into a broader theoretical context and thereby appropriating them for science.

Social scientific knowledge, therefore, represents a comprehensive understanding. It is a formulation that takes into account insights that reflect the vantage point of the established order, past social movements of subjected groups, and the social movements of subjected groups emerging in the present. In a manner of speaking, social science takes the side of the subjected groups, not in the sense of ignoring or dismissing the insights of the established order or previous social movements, not in the sense of promoting the interests of the subjected group in the context of the existing system of production and the predominant modes of understanding, and not in the sense of adopting the understandings commonly accepted by members of subjected groups. Rather, social scientists take the side of the subjected group in the sense that they seek understandings that are organically connected to the insights of social movements of subjected groups. Social scientific understandings therefore develop new understandings and transform old understandings as a consequence of taking seriously the insights of social movements of subjected groups. This transformation of the established scientific knowledge in light of the insights of emerging social movements of subjected groups constitutes the progress of social science to more comprehensive understandings.

The task of sociologists, therefore, is to seek encounter with the social movements that have been constituted by subjected groups. And the task of sociologists is to seek new scientific theories that incorporate the insights of such social movements and thus are organically connected to them. I have used throughout the example of twentieth-century national liberation movements of people of color against European domination, including the forms which this domination and this movement have taken in the United States. But the reader should understand that my intention here has been merely to illustrate, in order to show that this understanding of scientific method applies not only to nineteenth-century industrial capitalism but also to the twentieth-century capitalist world economy. I take this concept of science to be applicable to other social movements now and in the future. Indeed, the feminist movement in the twentieth century clearly is a significant social movement that has formulated insights that have challenged the conceptions of conventional science. Clearly, many sociologists, for the most part women, have formulated new scientific concepts and theories in light of the feminist movement, particularly in such areas as the sociology of the family and socialization. These developments would seem to confirm many aspects of the scientific method as here formulated. This question, however, has been beyond the scope of this investigation.

Sociologists, therefore, must avoid the naive view that sociology is value-free, that it seeks to describe what is rather than formulating what ought to be. Our discipline has been burdened throughout its history by a false dichotomy between fact and value. This dichotomy reflects questionable and problematic epistemological assumptions that are rooted in the Enlightenment and form the basis of positivism and decisionism. These include the assumptions that the only valid form of knowledge is that which is based on empirical observation; that judgments concerning correct courses of action therefore are beyond the scope of knowledge; and that such value judgments are simply matters of personal choice and decision, incapable of being demonstrated true or false in an objective sense. Such epistemological assumptions served well the dominant groups in the age of Empire, for they made possible a domination of the world unconstrained by critique. In accordance with such assumptions, technical knowledge could be used to make weapons to subdue peoples, to make tools and machines to exploit nature, and to develop systems of production and transportation to use people and nature for profit. Such technical knowledge constituted valid knowledge. On the other hand, the knowledge that such courses of action were not morally justifiable was a form of knowledge that was considered not really knowledge but merely opinion. These are epistemological assumptions which served the masters of the colonial world in the nineteenth century, just as they function to perpetuate the social status quo today.

But the fact-value dichotomy is based on a false assumption concerning how we come to know facts, namely, the assumption that descriptions of fact are based on empirical observation. In actuality, descriptions of fact reflect a horizon context, including values and aesthetic feelings. That this is so in the realm of natural science has been well documented in regard to the heliocentric formulations of Copernicus, Kepler, and Galileo (Kuhn, 1970; 1957; Ferris, 1988). In regard to the social sciences, it is illustrated by modernization theory and the world-systems perspective. Here we have contrasting descriptions of reality, each reflecting a horizon grounded in social position, a horizon that includes cultural assumptions, value judgments, philosophical ideas, and feelings. Which description is correct? The answer depends on the horizon context from which it is addressed. Moreover, once one makes a judgment concerning which description is correct, a subsequent judgment concerning which course of action is correct is in its fundamentals less problematic. If the Third World is poor because it lacks cultural characteristics of the West, then cultural diffusion is the remedy. If, on the other hand, the Third World is poor because of peripheralization, then autonomous economic development is the remedy. Thus, in opposition to the assumption of the dichotomy of facts and values, we now understand that facts and values are in reality intertwined: descriptions of reality emerge from a value context and imply particular courses of action.

In the realms of both fact and value, therefore, horizon imposes obstacles to understanding, because it blocks relevant questions from consciousness. This problem is overcome through encounter, and this process applies equally to the realm of value as to the realm of fact. The question of which course of action is correct is no more difficult than the question of which description is correct. In both cases, the answer depends on one's vantage point. But this does not mean that all vantage points are equally valid. As this analysis has tried to show, some vantage points are scientific, whereas others are not. A vantage point that takes into account the insights of social movements of subjected social groups is scientific, for it is a vantage point from which one can formulate comprehensive understandings of appropriate descriptions and courses of action for a particular stage in historical and economic development.

Thus, any effort to be detached, disengaged, neutral, or disconnected from the claims of social movements is clearly misguided, for such an effort functions to prevent a social scientist from discovering relevant questions that are connected to the insights of social movements, and understandings that overlook relevant questions become understandings that reinforce the conventional understandings and the established order. Against this pseudo-science, which unwittingly promotes the interests of dominant groups, this book has argued that the sociologist who arrives at objective knowledge will become aware of insights, discover relevant questions, and formulate new concepts and theories through personal encounter with social movements constituted by subjected social groups.

NOTES

   1. See Chapter 5.
   2. See Chapter 5.
   3. The following summary of Wallerstein's analysis is based upon Wallerstein (1974; 1979; 1980; 1984; 1989) and Shannon (1989).
   4. For Wallerstein, in addition to core and periphery in the world economy, there is also the "semi-periphery." However, in spite of this category, the modern world economy is essentially characterized by a relation between core and periphery, for the semi-periphery emerges as a dimension of the core–peripheral relation. The semi-periphery has some core-like activities and some peripheral-like activities, and it is in between core and periphery in wage level and profit margin. The semi-peripheral region emerges because it functions to the advantage of the core by promoting the political and economic stability of the world economy (Wallerstein, 1979:66–107).
   5. That Hoselitz overlooks the role of colonial domination can be seen not only by his contrast of advanced and undeveloped economies, but also in his discussion of different patterns of development (1960:85–105).

6. These two volumes were edited and combined into a single volume, *The Evolution of Societies* (1977).

7. For a discussion of the historical development of democratic socialism and communism, see Lindemann (1983).

8. See Chapter 5.

9. Throughout much of its history, the United States has occupied a position in the world economy different from that of Western Europe. The United States entered the world economy in the eighteenth century. The Southeastern United States became a part of the periphery, exporting cotton and sugar using African slave labor (Shannon, 1989:56). The Northeastern United States entered as a part of the semi-periphery on the basis of a trade relationship with the West Indies, where U.S. farmers exported agricultural goods needed in the West Indian production of sugar using African slave labor (Shannon, 1989:56; Frank, 1979:64–68). During the period 1850–1900, the Northeastern United States was able to ascend from semi-periphery to core (Shannon, 1989:63). This ascent was made possible by its capacity to develop manufacturing as a result of the capital accumulation obtained through the West Indian trade (Frank, 1989:79–82). Beginning in the 1930s, the policy of the United States government to industrialize the South (Bloom, 1986:59–68) led to its incorporation into the core. Corresponding with the position of the United States in the world economy, Native American and African American movements have had many elements characteristic of national liberation movements, including the tendency to define their condition as fundamentally a colonial situation. The workers' movement in the United States therefore developed in a social context in which (1) the United States economy was expanding rapidly as it was ascending from semi-periphery to core, and (2) settler/native and racial conflicts were a significant part of the political landscape. All this gave the workers' movement in the United States a character different from the workers' movement in Western Europe.

10. See Chapter 8 for a discussion of the limitations of Marx's analysis from a Third World point of view.

8

MARX AND THE THIRD WORLD

As Ronald Aronson has noted, contemporary Marxism is in crisis. A reason for this crisis is that

whatever its centrality, the direct conflict between capital and labour has not been dominant over the past twenty years. Imperialist war, national liberation, feminism, ecology, anti-nuclearism, student movements, domestic struggles against racism—these have occupied the centre-stage in most places, for most of the time. (Aronson, 1985:82)

These events have created a crisis for Marxism, because problems such as colonialism, patriarchy, nuclearism, ecocide, and racism are not "reducible to class oppression or derivative from the specific dynamics of capitalism" (Aronson, 1985:90). None of the problems that have come to the forefront of twentieth-century social consciousness can be understood, therefore, from the vantage point of Marxism in its classical formulation. In order to move beyond the crisis, Aronson conceives a radical pluralism, in which the movement for social change consists of a radical coalition of a variety of social movements, each with its own authenticity and integrity. Insofar as this movement has a unity, it will be a unity with diversity.

If a unitary understanding is possible, it need not be a totalizing one: it may have its distinct regions, centres of semi-autonomy, areas needing to be illuminated also by other logics and tools. The point is to widen and deepen our comprehension, to the point where it reflects and illuminates the full range or our politics. (Aronson, 1985:92)

Aronson's notion of radical pluralism is to some extent valid. In order to avoid becoming outdated, Marxism must be in theory and practice a movement that recognizes the authenticity and integrity of social movements constituted by women against feminism and by people of color against colonialism and neo-colonialism. But more than this can be said. Feminist and national liberation movements not only provide new challenges for theory and practice in social movement. They also establish new possibilities for science, in that they make possible the formulation of a scientific understanding beyond Marx and beyond Marxism in its classical formulation. In this chapter, I illustrate this through examination of Marx's understanding of the world economy in light of national liberation movements in the Third World in the twentieth century.

MARX AND COLONIALISM

Marx believed that primitive capitalist accumulation is driven by force. Marx took this fundamental fact about capitalism to be unknown, and hence referred to force as the secret of primitive accumulation. One dimension of this force which is the origin of capitalist accumulation is the forceful expropriation of the peasant from the land and the abolition of feudalism (Marx, 1967:713–34). A second dimension is the "brute force" (1967:751) of colonial domination. Marx believes that the brutality of colonial domination is unparalleled in human history.

Of the colonial system, W. Howitt, a man who makes a specialty of Christianity, says: "The barbarities and desperate outrages of the so-called Christian race, throughout every region of the world, and upon every people they have been able to subdue, are not to be paralleled by those of any other race, however fierce, however untaught, and however reckless of mercy and of shame, in any age of the earth." (1967:751–52)

For Marx, colonial domination is an important factor in primitive capitalist accumulation.

The discovery of gold and silver in America, the extirpation, enslavement and entombment in mines of the aboriginal population, the beginning of the conquest and looting of the East Indies, the turning of Africa into a warren for the commercial hunting of black-skins, signalised the rosy dawn of the era of capitalist production. These idyllic proceedings are the chief momenta of primitive accumulation. (1967:751)

This is so because colonial domination makes possible the wealth that is the origin of industrial capitalism.

The colonial system ripened, like a hot-house, trade and navigation. . . . The colonies secured a market for the budding manufactures, and, through the monopoly of the market, an increased accumulation. The treasures captured outside Europe by undisguised looting, enslavement, and murder, floated back to the mother-country and were there turned into capital. (1967:753–54)

The role of colonial domination in the genesis of industrial capitalism can be seen in the English East India Company.

The English East India Company, as is well known, obtained, besides the political rule in India, the exclusive monopoly of the tea-trade, as well as of the Chinese trade in general, and of the transport of goods to and from Europe. But the coasting trade of India and between the islands, as well as the internal trade of India, were the monopoly of the higher employés of the company. The monopolies of salt, opium, betel and other commodities, were inexhaustible mines of wealth. The employés themselves fixed the price and plundered at will the unhappy Hindus. The Governor-General took part in this private traffic. His favourites received contracts under conditions whereby they, cleverer than the alchemists, make gold out of nothing. Great fortunes sprang up like mushrooms in a day; primitive accumulation went on without the advance of a shilling. (1967:752–53)

Another illustration of the role of colonial domination in capitalist accumulation is the conquest of the indigenous peoples of the Americas.

The treatment of the aborigines was, naturally, most frightful in plantation-colonies destined for export trade only, such as the West Indies, and in rich and well-populated countries, such as Mexico and India, that were given over to plunder. But even in the colonies properly so called, the Christian character of primitive accumulation did not belie itself. Those sober virtuosi of Protestantism, the Puritans of New England, in 1703, by decrees of their assembly set a premium of £40 on every Indian scalp and every captured red-skin. (1967:753)

Another example of the importance of the colonies and colonial domination in capitalist accumulation is slavery in the United States.

Whilst the cotton industry introduced child-slavery in England, it gave in the United States a stimulus to the transformation of the earlier, more or less patriarchal slavery, into a system of commercial exploitation. In fact, the veiled slavery of the wage-workers in Europe needed, for its pedestal, slavery pure and simple in the new world. (1967: 759–60)

Because the colonial domination of the world is a dimension of capitalist development, capitalism has an inherent tendency to create a world economy. In this drive of capitalism to forge a world economy, the traditional economies of the conquered regions are destroyed, and the conquered regions function to provide raw materials that feed the industries of Europe and promote their development. Hence, capitalism creates an international division of labor, in which the conquered regions produce agricultural products for export to Europe, and Europe becomes the center of industrial production. Marx writes:

By ruining handicraft production in other countries, machinery forcibly converts them into fields for the supply of its raw material. In this way East India was compelled to produce cotton, wool, hemp, jute, and indigo for Great Britain. By constantly making a part of the hands "supernumerary," modern industry, in all countries where it has taken root, gives a spur to emigration and to the colonisation of foreign lands, which are thereby converted into settlements for growing the raw material of the mother country; just as

Australia, for example, was converted into a colony for growing wool. *A new and international division of labour, a division suited to the requirements of the chief centre of modern industry springs up, and converts one part of the globe into a chiefly agricultural field of production, for supplying the other part which remains a chiefly industrial field.* (1967:451; italics added)

With these words Marx anticipates in a rudimentary way by more than a hundred years the basic insight of the world-systems perspective: The modern world economy is characterized by a geographical division of labor between core and periphery, a division that functions to promote the development of the core as it promotes the underdevelopment of the periphery.

Nevertheless, Marx did not explore the full possibilities of this insight, and he did not grasp all its implications. This limitation was a consequence of the fact that he did not examine the capitalist world economy from the vantage point of the peripheralized. Instead, he examined the capitalist world economy from the vantage point of the industrial proletariat in the core, which reflected his social position and the historical time period in which he wrote.

The limitations of Marx's perspective, as seen from the vantage point of the peripheralized in the twentieth century, is apparent in Marx's analysis of British rule in India which appeared in the *New York Daily Tribune* in 1853. First, let us note that Marx's writing on India shows that Marx did have a penetrating understanding of the impact of colonial domination on traditional Indian society. Marx acknowledges that the British were not the first to conquer India, for India had been conquered by invaders from Central Asia, Afghanistan, and Persia (Marx & Engels, 1979:125, 652–53). However, unlike the earlier conquerors, the British were not integrated into Indian culture; rather, the British succeeded in destroying traditional Indian society (Marx & Engels, 1979:217–18). Consequently, India suffered more as a result of the British conquest in contrast to earlier conflicts: "There cannot, however, remain any doubt but that the misery inflicted by the British on Hindostan is of an essentially different and infinitely more intensive kind than all Hindostan had to suffer before" (Marx & Engels, 1979:126). And, Marx observes, in this regard the British conquest of India is similar to other European colonial conquests in Asia.

Hence, the British conquest of India, according to Marx, undermined the basic structure of Indian society.

All the civil wars, invasions, revolutions, conquests, famines, strangely complex, rapid, and destructive as the successive action in Hindostan may appear, did not go deeper than its surface. England has broken down the entire framework of Indian society, without any symptoms of reconstitution yet appearing. This loss of his old world, with no gain of a new one, imparts a particular kind of melancholy to the present misery of the Hindoo, and separates Hindostan, ruled by Britain, from all its ancient traditions, and from the whole of its past history. (Marx & Engels, 1979:126–27)

The traditional Indian society, prior to the British conquest, had for many centuries an advanced productive capacity in textile manufacturing. This Indian textile industry was the basis of a profitable trade for India with Britain.

However changing the political aspect of Indian's past must appear, its social condition has remained unaltered since its remotest antiquity, until the first decennium of the 19th century. The hand-loom and the spinning-wheel, producing their regular myriads of spinners and weavers, were the pivots of the structure of that society. From immemorial times, Europe received the admirable textures of Indian labor, sending in return for them her precious metals, and furnishing thereby his material to the goldsmith, that indispensable member of Indian society, whose love of finery is so great that even the lowest class, those who go about nearly naked, have commonly a pair of golden ear-rings and a gold ornament of some kind hung round their necks. (Marx & Engels, 1979:128)

But the British conquest of India destroyed this traditional industrial development in India: "It was the British intruder who broke up the Indian hand-loom and destroyed the spinning-wheel" (Marx & Engels, 1979:128). This destruction of traditional Indian industry was a result of trade policies which favored British manufacturing at the expense of Indian manufacturing. During the seventeenth and eighteenth centuries, the British textile manufacturers recognized that they were being ruined by the importation of Indian cotton and silk goods. In response to this problem, the British manufacturers were able to influence Parliament to enact legislation that prohibited the wearing of clothes manufactured in the East (Marx & Engels, 1979:153). At the same time, after 1813, the trading of British manufacturing in India was opened up, and there was only a nominal duty imposed on British manufactured goods in India. Thus, the policy of the British who controlled India placed Indian manufacturers at an impossible disadvantage in the competition for the British market but gave Indian manufacturers no advantage over the British in the Indian market. The result was the decline of Indian manufacturing.

Till 1813 India had been chiefly an exporting country, while it now became an importing one. . . . India, the great workshop of cotton manufacture for the world, since immemorial times, became now inundated with English twists and cotton stuffs. After its own produce had been excluded from England, or only admitted on the most cruel terms, British manufacturers were poured into it at a small and merely nominal duty, to the ruin of the native cotton fabrics once so celebrated. (Marx & Engels, 1979:154)

However, the destruction of the traditional Indian industry created some problems for British manufactures, in that the decline in Indian industry lowered the economic capacity of India to purchase British imports. Accordingly, it became necessary for Britain to develop Indian export capacity through the development of Indian capacity to produce and export raw cotton.

The more the industrial interest became dependent on the Indian market, the more it felt the necessity of creating fresh productive powers in India, after having ruined her native industry. You cannot continue to inundate a country with your manufactures, unless you enable it to give you some produce in return. (Marx & Engels, 1979:154–55).

This need was reinforced by the growing uncertainty of the cotton crop in the United States. Accordingly, as a result of Indian colonial domination, India's traditional textile industry was destroyed, and the Indian economy became oriented to the export of cotton. At the same time, India became an important market for British textile manufacturing.

Hence, Marx understood the impact of colonial domination on traditional Indian society. However, there are many aspects of Marx's analysis of British colonial rule in India that reveal that Marx had an essentially European perspective on the colonial process. In the first place, Marx evaluated traditional Indian culture from a European point of view, and accordingly, he viewed it as a barbarous culture full of superstition and cruelty. In a passage striking for its ethnocentrism, Marx writes as follows with reference to traditional Indian society:

We must not forget that these idyllic village-communities, inoffensive though they may appear, had always been the solid foundation of Oriental despotism, that they restrained the human mind within the smallest possible compass, making it the unresisting tool of superstition, enslaving it beneath traditional rules, depriving it of all grandeur and historical energies. We must not forget the barbarian egotism which, concentrating on some miserable patch of land, had quietly witnessed the ruin of empires, the perpetuation of unspeakable cruelties, the massacre of the population of large towns, with no other consideration bestowed upon them than on natural events, itself the helpless prey of any aggressor who deigned to notice it at all. We must not forget that this undignified, stagnatory, and vegetative life, that this passive sort of existence evoked on the other part, in contradistinction, wild, aimless, unbounded forces of destruction and rendered murder itself a religious rite in Hindostan. We must not forget that these little communities were contaminated by distinctions of caste and by slavery, that they subjugated man to external circumstances instead of elevating man the sovereign of circumstances, that they transformed a self-developing social state into never changing natural destiny, and thus brought about a brutalizing worship of nature, exhibiting its degradation in the fact that man, the sovereign of nature, fell down on his knees in adoration of Kanuman, the monkey, and Sabbala, the cow. (Marx & Engels, 1979:132)

Given this fundamentally ethnocentric view of traditional Indian society, it is not surprising that Marx maintains that the destruction of this society by colonialism in the final analysis was desirable. He argues that however vile the motives of the British may have been, British colonialism and its destruction of traditional Indian society is necessary for the fulfillment of human destiny. He writes:

England, it is true, in causing a social revolution in Hindostan, was actuated only the vilest interest, and was stupid in her manner of enforcing them. But that is not the question. The question is, can mankind fulfill its destiny without a fundamental revolution in the social state of Asia? If not, whatever many have been the crimes of England she was the unconscious tool of history in bringing about that revolution.

Then, whatever bitterness the spectacle of the crumbling of an ancient world may have for our personal feelings, we have the right, in point of history, to exclaim with Goethe:

"Should this torture then torment us
Since it brings us greater pleasure?"

(Marx & Engels, 1979:132–33)

For Marx, this fulfillment of human destiny occurs through colonial domination, because during British colonial domination of India, the British bourgeoisie lays the material foundation for the emancipation of Indian society. Marx identifies several elements in this material foundation. First was the political unity of India, established first through military conquest and subsequently through the electric telegraph. Second was the free press, introduced for the first time into India through British rule. Third was the formation of an educated class "endowed with the requirements for government and imbued with European science" (Marx & Engels, 1979:218). Fourth was irrigation, which increases agricultural capacity. Fifth was improved communication and transportation, made possible by railroads and steamships. The railroads, Marx argues, are especially important, because they make possible further industrial development.

I know that the English millocracy intend to endow India with railways with the exclusive view of extracting at diminished expenses the cotton and other raw materials for their manufactures. But . . . you cannot maintain a net of railways over an immense country without introducing all those industrial processes necessary to meet the immediate and current wants of railway locomotion, and out of which there must grow the application of machinery to those branches of industry not immediately connected with railways. The railway-system will therefore become, in India, truly the forerunner of modern industry. (Marx & Engels, 1979:220)

Colonialism, therefore, lays the material foundation for the emancipation of India. However, the benefits of colonialism will not be realized until Great Britain becomes socialist or until India becomes independent.

The Indians will not reap the fruits of the new elements of society scattered among them by the British bourgeoisie, till in Great Britain itself the now ruling class shall have been supplanted by the industrial proletariat, or till the Hindoos themselves shall have grown strong enough to throw off the English yoke altogether. (Marx & Engels, 1979:221)

From the point of view of the periphery in the twentieth century, there are limitations to Marx's analysis of British rule in India. In the first place, given that pre-colonial traditional societies were autonomous from foreign rule and functioned to provide for basic human needs, and given that colonialism promoted underdevelopment, the traditional society becomes an evaluative standard, an ideal society that defines the collective soul of the nation. Accordingly, although the future must be constructed, as a matter of technical necessity, on the material foundation laid by colonialism, the ideal for the future involves incorporating as much of the traditional values and way of life as is technically possible. According to this view, Marx's devaluation of traditional society and his assumption that future development requires an industrial foundation are examples of Western ethnocentrism. They fail to appreciate the humane qualities of the cultures of people of color, and they implicitly seek to remake all humanity in the image of Europe. In opposition to this Western ethnocentric view, a Third World view envisions the possibility of a future socialist development that is based upon an agricultural foundation and self-consciously incorporates the best qualities of traditional society.

Julius Nyerere's vision of *ujamaa* socialism and *ujamaa* agriculture (Nyerere,1968) is an example of this Third World view. *Ujamaa* socialism is a socialism built upon the basic principles of traditional African society. These principles include socialism, in which there are no class divisions created by private property and in which there is relative equality in the distribution of goods. And these traditional principles include *ujamaa* or familyhood, in which there is a spirit of living and working together based on extended family ties. But *ujamaa* socialism does not endeavor to recreate the traditional society, for there are weaknesses in the traditional society, including low levels of production. Accordingly, *ujamaa* agriculture incorporates elements of Western technical efficiency, which were brought to Africa during colonial domination, including large-scale farms and the use of machinery. Thus, *ujamaa* socialism is a socialism based on an agricultural foundation, and it is characterized by democratic cooperation and collective ownership of large-scale farms. As such, it develops from the economic and social foundation of colonialism, but it also incorporates traditional African values, values that colonialism endeavored to destroy.Marx's view of India, however, fails to envision the possibility of socialism on an agricultural foundation or a socialism that incorporates traditional values. Writing from the vantage point of nineteenth-century Europe, Marx did not see the strengths of traditional societies, and he equated progress with industry. He did not consider the possibility of agricultural socialism until late in his life with his study of the Russian peasant commune, and even here, as we shall see, he endorsed the notion of agrarian socialism in a very limited context.

Moreover, Marx, in his analysis of British rule in India, does not grasp the dynamics of what we today call neo-colonialism. As is now clear in the wake of independence movements in the Third World, the political unity, the Western systems of government, and the educated class schooled in Western knowledge, all created by colonialism, all function to perpetuate European economic domination of the Third World in the post-colonial period. Accordingly, although the material foundation laid by colonialism establishes the possibility for a modern emancipation, this foundation also establishes possibility of a subtle form of domination, a form of domination that has a more legitimate appearance and hence is easier to perpetuate. This latter possibility, which has become the dominant pattern, was not foreseen by Marx.

But these limitations in Marx's analysis reflect Marx's historical time period and social position. Writing before the full development of colonialism and the development of independence movements in opposition to colonialism, he could not have grasped the contradictions of national liberation movements against colonial rule. Once these national liberation movements played out their role in history, their contradictions became manifest. And at that time it became possible to grasp the domination of the national liberation movements by the national bourgeoisie and the interest of the national bourgeoisie in preserving the essential economic features of the colonial relationship. And it also became possible to see the ethnocentric character of Western social scientific analysis, including its most progressive elements. But social scientists, including Marx, could not arrive at such insights prior to the emergence of national liberation movements in the Third World in the twentieth century.

MARX'S STUDIES OF RUSSIA

Since, for Marx, the industrial proletariat is the revolutionary force in capitalism, Marx expected that the most advanced sectors of the world economy, where the industrial proletariat is more developed as a class, would be the centers of revolutionary activity. In opposition to this expectation, Marx discovered in the late 1860s that there was much revolutionary activity in economically backward Russia, a country about which he had written disparagingly. As Teodor Shanin writes:

As the 1860s drew to a close, Marx became increasingly aware that alongside the retrograde official Russia, which he so often attacked as the focus of European reaction, a different Russia of revolutionary allies and radical scholars had grown up, increasingly attracted by his own theoretical work. (Shanin, 1983a:11)

As a result, Marx threw himself into a study of Russia.

In 1870–71 Marx taught himself Russian in order to immerse himself in the research and debates in that language. Marx's wife, in a letter to Engels, complained that he had begun to study Russian 'as if it was a matter of life and death.' Marx proceeded with equal vigor to study Russian sources, accumulating a massive annotated library in the process. (Shanin, 1983a:11)

Isaiah Berlin, in his biography of Marx, describes the personal impact of Russian revolutionary activity on Marx.

To his own surprise, Marx found that the nation against which he had written and spoken for thirty years provided him with the most fearless and intelligent of his disciples. He welcomed them in his home in London, and entered into a regular correspondence with Danielson, his translator, and Sieber, one of the ablest of Russian academic economists. . . . Letters reached him from Danielson, in Russia, and from the exiles Lavrov and Vera Zasulich, begging him to apply himself to the specific problems presented by the peculiar organization of the Russian peasants into primitive communes, holding land in common, and in particular to state his view on propositions derived from Herzen and Bakunin and widely accepted by Russian radicals, which asserted that a direct transition was possible from such primitive communes to developed communism, without the necessity of passing through the intermediate stage of industrialism and urbanization, as had happened in the West. Marx who had previously treated this hypothesis with contempt as emanating from sentimental Slavophile idealization of the peasants disguised as radicalism . . . was by now sufficiently impressed by the intelligence, seriousness, and, above all, the fanatical and devoted socialism of the new generation of Russian revolutionaries to re-examine the issue. In order to do this he began to learn Russian; at the end of six months he had mastered it sufficiently to read sociological works and government reports which his friends succeeded in smuggling to London. (Berlin, 1963:273–74)

The Russian revolutionaries who influenced Marx belonged to the school of thought known as revolutionary populism (Shanin, 1983b:8–11). Especially important here was Chernyshevskii, whose paper on the peasants, which Marx read in the latter half of 1870, apparently stimulated a turn in Marx's thinking (Shanin, 1983b:45). Central to the philosophy of Russian revolutionary populism was the Russian peasant commune. As Shanin explains, the peasant commune was a communal agricultural system that was important in the Russian economy and society of the nineteenth century.

About three-fifths of the arable land of European Russia was in the hands of the peasant and cossack communes. Within them, each household held unconditionally only a small plot of land, i.e. house and garden plus its livestock and equipment. The use of arable land was assigned to a family on a long-term basis by its commune, the meadows were reassigned annually and often worked collectively, the pastures and forest were in common use. The diversity of wealth within the commune was expressed mainly in differential ownership of livestock, of non-agricultural property, and in some private land bought from non-communal sources. The use of wage-labour inside the commune was limited. Many vital services were run collectively by the commune: a village shepherd, the local guards, the welfare of the orphans, and often a school, a church, a mill. (Shanin, 1983b:11)

Russian revolutionary populism saw the commune as the foundation of socialism in Russia. As Shanin observes:

To the revolutionary populist the peasant commune was the proof of the collectivist tradition of the majority of Russian people. . . . It was seen as a possible tool for the mobilisation of the peasants for the anti-tsardom struggle. It was to be a basic form for the future organisation of local power which would eventually rule Russia together with a democratically elected national government. For Chernyshevskii, it was also an effective framework for collective agricultural production in post-revolutionary Russia. (Shanin, 1983b:12)

Given this agricultural foundation of Russian socialism, the populists believed that the Russian road to socialism would bypass the capitalist stage and that

Russian development would not mirror that of Western capitalism. Further, the populists believed that the peasants were to be an important force in the revolutionary movement.

The revolutionary populists put their trust in a class war of the Russian laboring class seen by Chernyshevskii as "peasants, part-time workers . . . and wage workers" (this trinity became peasants, workers and working intelligentsia in later populist writings). (Shanin, 1983b:9)

Some of the Russian revolutionaries with whom Marx was in contact did not share this populist enthusiasm for the peasant commune. This group, known as the Black Repartition, believed in the necessity of a capitalist stage and a proletarian revolution. They viewed the peasant commune as a backward social organization which had to be removed in order to clear the way for a proletarian revolution.They interpreted Marx's work as supporting their position. However, starting in 1870, Marx, under the influence of revolutionary populism, was to take a position that differed to some extent from his earlier formulation. Let us examine Marx's writings after 1870 in order to see exactly what it was that Marx came to believe during this period.

One indication of the new direction Marx's thought was taking in this period is the revision he made in *Capital* for its publication in French in January 1875. In Chapter 26, "The Secret of Primitive Accumulation," there was in the first two German editions the following passage.

The expropriation of the agricultural producers, of the peasant, from the soil, is the basis of the whole process. The history of this expropriation, in different countries, assumes different aspects, and runs through its various phases in different orders of succession, and at different periods. In England alone, which we take as our example, does it have the classic form. (quoted in Shanin, 1983b:49)

In the French edition this passage was replaced with the following:

At the bottom of the capitalist system is, therefore, the radical separation of the producer from the means of production. . . . The basis of this whole evolution is the expropriation of the peasants. . . . It has been accomplished in a final form only in England . . . but all the other countries of Western Europe are going through the same movement. (quoted in Shanin, 1983b:49)

There is a significant difference between these passages relevant to the revolutionary populist belief that Russian socialism will be constructed on the material foundation of the peasant commune. The first passage implies that all countries will experience the expropriation of peasants that is the genesis of capitalist accumulation. In contrast, the second passage explicitly confines this expropriation to the countries of Western Europe. This, of course, leaves open the possibility that Russia will not experience this appropriation and that socialism in Russia can be constituted on the foundation of the peasant commune.

The evolution of Marx's thought in regard to this issue is also revealed in his correspondence with Russian revolutionaries from 1878 to 1881. In 1878, Marx wrote a letter to the editor of *Otechestvennye Zapiski*. The letter was in response to an article by Mikhailovskii, who had argued that Marx's theory was not applicable to the Russian situation. With reference to Chapter 26 of *Capital*, Mikhailovskii criticizes Marx's belief that all countries would have to go through the process of the expropriation of the peasant as had been the case in England. Mikhailovskii believes in the possibility of an alternative development in Russia. In response to Mikhailovskii, Marx argues that the chapter on primitive accumulation does not imply that all countries must go through the same process of accumulation. Marx maintains that his account of capitalist development is simply a historical sketch of how capitalism developed in Western Europe. He writes, "The chapter on primitive accumulation claims no more than to trace the path by which, in Western Europe, the capitalist economic order emerged from the womb of the feudal economic order" (Shanin, 1983b:135). It is simply a "historical sketch of the genesis of capitalism in Western Europe" (Shanin, 1983b:136). It is not "a historico-philosophical theory of the general course fatally imposed on all people, whatever the historical circumstances in which they find themselves placed" (Shanin, 1983b:136). In his argument, Marx quotes the French edition of *Capital* for which Marx had recently made changes reflecting the position he was now taking. Curiously, Marx did not mention the changes he had made for the French edition. This was somewhat unfair, for Mikhailovskii had access to the German edition, where the language supports Mikhailovksii's interpretation. Possibly, Marx for some reason, perhaps egoism, was reluctant to acknowledge that he had changed a position that he had held for many years. Or perhaps Marx did not consider the changes he made in the French edition of *Capital* to be a change in his understanding, but merely a change in formulation in order to make his understanding clearer. In any event, it is clear from the available evidence that Marx's study of Russia in the 1870s at the very least prompted him to revise his formulation of the process of primitive accumulation in *Capital* and to make clear in the letter to the editor of *Otechestvennye Zapiski* that his view is that alternative development is possible for regions outside of Western Europe.

On February 16, 1881, Vera Zasulich, one of the leaders of the Black Repartition group, wrote a letter to Marx. She notes that although Marx is aware of the great popularity of *Capital*, he is probably not aware of "the role in which . . . *Capital* plays in our discussions on the agrarian question in Russia and our rural commune" (Shanin, 1983b:98). In her view, there are two possibilities. On the one hand, the rural commune "is capable of developing in a socialist direction." On the other hand, "the commune is destined to perish." In the former case, "the revolutionary socialist must devote all his strength to the liberation and development of the commune." In the latter case, socialists must "conduct propaganda solely among the urban workers" (Shanin, 1983b:98). Therefore, this is an urgent question facing the revolutionary movement in Russia. And, Zasulich informs Marx, those who argue that the commune is destined to perish maintain this is Marx's position. She writes:

Nowadays, we often hear it said that the rural commune is an archaic form condemned to perish by history, scientific socialism and, in short, everything above debate. Those who preach such a view call themselves your disciples *par excellence*: "Marksists." Their strongest argument is often: "Marx said so." (Shanin, 1983b:99)

She asks Marx to address this question.

So you will understand, Citizen, how interested we are in Your opinion. You would be doing us a very great favour if you were to set forth Your ideas on the possible fate of our rural commune, and on the theory that it is historically necessary for every country in the world to pass through all the phases of capitalist production.

In the name of my friends, I take the liberty to ask You, Citizen, to do us this favour.

If time does not allow you to set forth Your ideas in a fairly detailed manner, then at least be so kind as to do this in the form of a letter that you would allow us to translate and publish in Russia. (Shanin, 1983b:99)

In response to Zasulich's letter, Marx wrote four drafts of a letter before finally sending a fifth draft. The first two drafts, written in 1881, were reflective statements on the issue raised by Zasulich, and these two drafts are important documents for the literature on the "late Marx."

In the first two drafts, there are four basic points that Marx makes. First, he reiterates what he had stated in the letter to the editor of *Otechestvennye Zapiski*, namely, that the description of primitive accumulation in the West in *Capital* is not intended as applicable to countries outside the West. After quoting the French edition of *Capital*, Marx writes, "I expressly restricted this 'historical inevitability' to '*the countries of Western Europe*' " (Shanin, 1983b:100).

Second, Marx maintains that there is a basic difference between Russia and the West, in that in Western Europe, feudalism centuries ago destroyed communal property; whereas in Russia, communal property has not been destroyed, and "the land is not and never has been the private property of the agricultural producer" (Shanin, 1983b:100). Given that feudalism in the West was a system of private property, capitalist appropriation in the West involved "the substitution of one form of private property for another form of private property" (Shanin, 1983b:101). Accordingly, "if capitalist production is to be established in Russia, the first step must be to abolish communal property and expropriate the peasants" (Shanin, 1983b:100). In other words,

if capitalist production is to establish its sway in Russia, then the great majority of peasants—that is, of the Russian people—will have to be transformed into wage-labourers, and hence be expropriated through the prior abolition of their communist property. (Shanin, 1983b:101)

But such a transformation is not inevitable. The Russian liberals hope that it will occur, "but does their *wish* prove more than Catherine II's wish to implant the Western medieval craft system in Russian soil"? Moreover, "the Western precedent would prove nothing at all [about the 'historical inevitability' of the process]" (Shanin, ed., 1983b:100–101).[1]

Third, Marx maintains that the possibilities for the development of the Russian peasant commune are influenced by the fact that the West has reached the capitalist stage, for Russia does not "live in isolation from the modern world" (Shanin, 1983b:110). "Russia exists in a modern historical context: it is contemporaneous with a higher culture, and it is linked to a world market in which capitalist production is predominant" (Shanin, 1983b:102). Because the rural commune is linked to capitalist production by the world market, in its future development it would be able to take advantage of the technological advancement made possible by capitalist production.

Its historical context—the contemporaneity of capitalist production—provides it with the ready-made material conditions for huge-scale common labour. It is therefore able to incorporate the positive achievements of the capitalist system, without having to pass under its harsh tribute. The commune may gradually replace fragmented agriculture with large-scale, machine-assisted agriculture particularly suited to the physical configuration of Russia. (Shanin, 1983b:111–12)

Thus, for Marx, the development of socialism in Russia on the foundation of the rural commune is possible because the capitalist world economy has become advanced. In the world economy as a whole, the stage of advanced capitalism, a necessary prerequisite for socialism, has been reached. But not every country or every region need go through this stage. Alternative developments are possible in different regions. The expropriation of the peasants by capitalist production was necessary somewhere, but not everywhere. Now that capitalist accumulation has occurred through expropriation of the peasants in the West, other regions can reap the benefits of this accumulation without going directly through the process of peasant expropriation. Now that one region has reached the stage of large-scale capitalism, other regions can take advantage of the technological achievements made possible by this stage. Accordingly, development in alternative directions, not involving expropriation of the peasants, is a possibility for other regions.

However, in order for the rural commune to appropriate in this way the technological achievements of the West, the West cannot have an exploitative relation with other regions, for an exploitative relation nullifies the possibility of the appropriation of Western technology for the development of rural communes in the peripheral regions. There must be a cooperative relation between the different regions in order for this complementary development to be attained, and this would require that the West become socialist. Thus, the appropriation of the material advantages of advanced capitalism for the socialist development of the Russian rural commune can occur only on the condition that the socialist revolutions in the West succeed. As Marx wrote in the Preface to the Russian edition of *The Communist Manifesto* in 1882, "If the Russian revolution becomes a signal for a proletarian revolution in the West, so that the two can supplement each other, the present Russian communal land ownership can serve as a point of departure for communist development" (Shanin, 1983b:70–71). In the drafts of the letter to Zasulich, Marx is optimistic that this condition of socialism in the West will be met, and thus prospects are good for the development of socialism on the foundation of the rural commune in Russia. Marx writes:

Historically favourable to the preservation of the "agricultural commune" through its further development is the fact not only that it is contemporaneous with Western capitalist production and therefore able to acquire its fruits without bowing to its *modus operandi*, but also that it has survived the epoch when the capitalist system stood intact. Today it finds that system, both in Western Europe and the United States, in conflict with the working masses, with science, and with the very productive forces which it generates— in short, in a crisis that will end through its own elimination, through the return of modern societies to a higher form of an "archaic" type of collective ownership and production. (Shanin, 1983b:111)

Fourth, Marx maintains that Russia is unlike South Asia, which has suffered colonial domination. He writes that Russia has not "fallen prey, like the East Indies, to a conquering fallen power" (Shanin, 1983b:106). Thus, the conditions in Russia differ from other regions of the world. Unlike the West, communal forms of production have not been abolished by feudal private property. And unlike the peripheral regions of the world economy, communal forms have not been undermined by colonial domination.

But even in Russia, the communal forms are threatened. In fact, the Russian commune has a dual character. On the one hand, there is common landownership. But on the other hand, there is small plot cultivation, where "each peasant cultivates and works . . . his field on his own account, like the small Western peasant" (Shanin, 1983b:104). This latter element can lead to the disintegration of the commune. Marx writes:

It is easy to see that the dualism inherent in the "agricultural commune" may give it sturdy life: for communal property and all the resulting social relations provide it with a solid foundation, while the privately owned houses, fragmented tillage of the arable land and private appropriation of its fruits all permit a development of individuality incompatible with conditions in the more primitive communities. It is just as evident, however, that the very same dualism may eventually become a source of disintegration. Apart from the influence of a hostile environment, the mere accumulation over time of movable property, beginning with wealth in livestock and even extending to wealth in serfs, combines with the ever prominent role played by movables in agriculture itself and with a host of other circumstances, inseparable from such accumulation. . . . All these factors, then, serve, to dissolve economic and social equality, generating within the commune itself a conflict of interests which leads, first, to the conversion of arable land into private property, and ultimately to the private appropriation of forests, pastures, waste ground, etc., already no more than communal appendages of private property. (Shanin, 1983b:109)

Moreover, the capitalist class has an interest in supporting these tendencies toward private property and in abolishing communal property. Therefore, "to save the Russian commune, there must be a Russian Revolution" (Shanin, 1983b:116).

As a result, then, of Marx's study of Russia in the 1870s, Marx's understanding of the modern world economy developed further. In contrast to his earlier writing, his writing in the 1870s makes clear that the movement of all regions and countries through the capitalist stage is not inevitable, and that in the case of Russia, the construction of an agrarian socialism on the foundation of the peasant commune is a possibility. He thus developed in the 1870s a notion of multilinear development, discarding his earlier unilinear view. Moreover, in opposition to his earlier sentiments on the question, Marx in the 1870s hopes that the communal tendencies of the peasant commune will be sufficiently intact at the time of the socialist revolution to enable the construction of agrarian socialism in Russia. However, Marx qualified his endorsement of agrarian socialism for Russia in two ways. First, he maintained that agrarian socialism in Russia was possible because of capitalist accumulation in Western Europe, and in order for the Russian commune to appropriate the material benefits of capitalist accumulation, a socialist revolution in Western Europe was a necessary prerequisite. Thus, Marx maintained that socialism in Western Europe was a necessary condition for the development of agrarian socialism in Russia. Second, Marx did not view the social conditions of Russia as typical of other regions of the world. Russia differed from the West, where feudalism had destroyed communal property. And it differed from the colonized regions of the world, where European colonial domination had destroyed traditional structures. Even in Russia, which had not experienced colonial domination, the disintegration of communal property by tendencies within the commune, tendencies encouraged by the state and the capitalist class, was a possibility. Marx's endorsement of agrarian socialism for Russia, therefore, was not a blanket endorsement of agrarian socialism in the agricultural regions in the periphery of the world economy.

These qualifications that Marx placed on his endorsement of agrarian socialism for Russia are important in addressing twentieth-century questions. For example, would the late Marx have supported the notion of agrarian socialism for the Third World in the twentieth century? Clearly, it would misrepresent Marx's position to quote his support of agrarian socialism in Russia in the 1870s as evidence that he would support agrarian socialism in the Third World today, for in the Third World in the twentieth century, there exist two conditions, both of which Marx specifically wrote would eliminate the possibility of agrarian socialism. First, the world economy today remains a capitalist world economy. The West has not become socialist. Therefore, there is a colonial relationship (in a neo-colonial form) between the West and the Third World. Second, the Third World regions virtually all have been victimized by colonialism, during which their traditional economic and social systems were undermined and transformed. Like the peasant commune, many pre-colonial Third World cultures had elements of private and communal property. Typically, in pre-colonial Third World societies, some of the land was held in common, and some of the land was worked individually but allotted by political authority. Alongside these land use patterns, there typically were social constraints on inequality. In some areas of the Third World, this traditional social system was totally obliterated by colonialism. This occurred where there was the development of a plantation economy or where European settlers arrived in large numbers. But even in those areas where peasants continue to cultivate small plots of land, a significant transformation of the traditional economies occurred. Especially important here was the replacement of traditional political authority with Western political institutions and the coercive introduction of cash crop production connected to the world economy. These transformations greatly accentuated the elements of private property. Therefore, the conditions of the Third World would not likely be the conditions for which Marx would endorse agrarian socialism. Indeed, as we have seen, he explicitly rejected the possibility for India, because of its legacy of colonialism.

In the end, Marx decided not to send to Zasulich the elaboration of his views that are found in the first two drafts of the latter. He apparently decided that an important statement should not be sent to the Black Repartition group, with which he did not agree on the question of agrarian socialism in Russia. He thus sent to Zasulich a succinct although clear statement of his views. In the letter, he quotes the statement in the French edition of *Capital* that the historical inevitability of capitalist production applies only to Western Europe. For the Western case involves the transformation of one type of private property to another, whereas Russia still has viable communal forms of property. Therefore, he writes, *Capital* "provides not reasons for or against the Russian commune" (Shanin, 1983b:124). But, he writes, his own study of Russia has convinced him that "the commune is the fulcrum for social regeneration in Russia" (Shanin, 1983b:124).

THE SIGNIFICANCE OF THE "LATE MARX"

In recent years, some scholars have turned to an analyses of the views of the "Late Marx" and their implications in regard to issues of Third World underdevelopment. Shanin, for example, maintains that the new direction in Marx's thinking in the 1870s has important implications for issues in regard to Third World underdevelopment in the twentieth century. Shanin maintains that prior to 1870, Marx wrote in the context of the socialist challenge to industrial capitalism in Western Europe. Marx took from this social and intellectual context a belief in progress, evolution, and development. As a dimension of this, Marx saw colonialism as a necessary stage, and he saw the capitalist world economy "as a global unifier which drags the a-historical societies of Oriental Despotism on the road to progress" (Shanin, 1983b:5–6). However, according to Shanin, Marx in the 1870s revised his understanding on this issue as a result of (1) the Paris Commune, (2) greater scientific knowledge of pre-history and rural non-capitalist societies, and (3) developments in Russia. This last element was especially important, because Marx had personal contact with Russian revolutionaries. Accordingly, in the 1870s, Marx developed "a more complex and more realistic conceptualization of the global heterogeneity of societal forms, dynamics, and interdependence" (Shanin, 1983b:6). He rejected his earlier understanding of development as unilinear and arrived at an understanding of global development as multilinear. "Marx comes not to assume . . . for the future a multiplicity of roads of social transformation, within the global framework of mutual and differential impact" (Shanin, 1983b:18).

Shanin maintains that Marx's movement toward a notion of multilinear global development took Marx to the issue of what we would today call the problem of underdevelopment in the periphery of the world economy.

The issue of the peasant commune was used by Marx . . . as a major way to approach a set of fundamental problems, new to his generation, but which would be nowadays easily recognized as those of "developing societies," be it "modernisation," "dependency" or the "combined and uneven" spread of global capitalism and its specifically "peripheral" expression. (Shanin, 1983b:17)

Moreover, Shanin maintains that Marx's reflection on these issues led him to "a re-evaluation of the place of peasantry and its social organisation in the revolutionary processes to come"(Shanin, 1983b:29). Shanin's own view is that the peasants have become a significant revolutionary force in the twentieth century:

Revolutions were spreading by the turn of the century through the backward "developing" societies: Russia in 1905 and 1917, Turkey 1906, Mexico 1910, China 1910 and 1927. Peasant insurrection was central to most of them. None of them were "bourgeois revolutions" in the West European sense and some of them proved eventually socialist in leadership and results. At the same time, no socialist revolution came in the West nor did a socialist "world revolution" materialize. (Shanin, 1983b:25)

Thus, Shanin belongs to that strain of Marxism that seeks to reconstruct Marxism in light of revolutionary struggles in the periphery of the world economy in the twentieth century and accordingly sees the peasants in the periphery, rather than the industrial proletariat, as the decisive revolutionary force. And Shanin maintains that the work of Marx in the 1870s provides the foundation for this re-interpretation of Marxism, in that Marx was beginning such a re-interpretation himself in light of the revolutionary movement in Russia.[2] Shanin writes:

The Marx of those days was beginning to recognise for what they really are the nature, problems and debate concerning "developing" and post-revolutionary societies of the twentieth century. The expression "neo-marxist," often used for those who stepped on from *Capital*, Volume I in their interpretations concerning "developing societies," is clearly misconceived. Most of the so-called neo-marxism, often treated as original or scandalous, is Marx's Marxism. . . . It was Marx who laid the foundations for the global analysis of "unevenness" of "development," for the socialist treatment of peasantry not only as the object or the fodder of history, for the consideration of socialism which is more than proletarian, and so on. Indeed, Marx's approach to the Russian peasantry, whom he never saw, proved on balance more realistic than that of the Russian marxists in 1920. (Shanin, 1983b:29–30)

Although I support the idea that national liberation movements in the Third World mandate a redefinition of Marxism, I would argue for caution in our interpretations of the significance of Marx's later writings for the Third World, for there was a limit to what Marx could have understood on this issue, given that he wrote before the emergence of national liberation movements in the Third World. Through a careful examination of his later writings, it becomes clear that, although Marx supported the idea of an agricultural socialism for Russia, his support was conditioned on the technically advanced regions of the world becoming socialist and on the continued viability of traditional communal structures. He specifically noted in the drafts to Zasulich that India, unlike Russia, had experienced the destruction of its traditional communal structures through colonialism. In contrast to Marx's view on India, Peter Hudis believes that communal structures are still viable in India and the Third World, and that this makes possible a different form of socialism for the Third World. Hudis writes:

Many indigenous elements exist within Third World societies (large disenfranchised peasantry, communal relations of tilling the land, reliance on non-capital intensive technologies in rural areas) which *can*, if articulated and grappled with anew, become building blocks for socialism.Despite a century of unmitigated imperialist intrusion and "independent" capitalist development in India and Pakistan, the majority of the peoples of both lands continue to live within the rural sector. While the indigenous "communal relations" of possession of land of the type Marx encountered are very different today (and in large measure do not exist) the persistence of communal forms of human association in the countryside can be taken up as a potential foundation for by-passing either a private capitalist or state-capitalist form of human relations. (Hudis, 1983:33)

This is perhaps true, and the fact that Hudis entertains these possibilities is a consequence of the impact of Third World national liberation movements on Western consciousness. Marx, however, writing before the emergence of national liberation movements, did not reflect on these possibilities. Before 1870, Marx wrote that the traditional cultures of the colonized regions world were destroyed, and the world was better off for it. After 1870, Marx, as a result of the influence of the revolutionary movement in Russia, abandons his pejorative view of traditional agricultural communities, and he advocates an alternative development for Russia. However, he did not at this time investigate the question of the survival of communal forms in the colonized regions, and there is no evidence that he re-evaluated his earlier position on this issue. Some scholars today, influenced by the insights of national liberation movements, may want to investigate the possibility of an alternative development in the Third World, a development based on an agricultural foundation and on the surviving communal elements of traditional societies. However, Marx wrote before the emergence of national liberation movements in the Third World, and such questions were beyond his horizon.

We should not expect too much of Marx. He was a great scholar whose work possesses profound insight and whose devotion to scholarship ought to be a model for social scientists. Nevertheless, he was a product of his time and place, and he could not be expected to understand what can be understood only in the wake of social movements which came after his time. To be sure, he did live long enough to see the emergence of revolutionary populism in Russia, and he did modify his views as a result of his encounter with this movement. However, as he himself understood, Russia, although economically backward, had not been colonized, and thus it was unlike the colonized regions of the periphery of the world economy. Therefore, the Russian Revolution was in important respects different from the national liberation movements which were to emerge in the Third World in the twentieth century.[3] Given that Marx wrote before the emergence of national liberation movements, he could not arrive at insights that are possible today. We should face squarely the limited social context and the limited meaning of his words, and we should not attribute to him understandings which are possible only in our own time.

For those of us who see the need for a reconstruction of Marxism in light of twentieth-century social movements, in order to appropriate Marx's insights, we should turn primarily not to Marx's necessarily dated reflections on India and on agrarian socialism in Russia. Rather, we should turn to Marx's concept of science, to his understanding of how social scientists come to a scientific understanding. In doing so, we see that Marx's profound insights were a consequence of his encounter with the social movements of the subjected social groups of his time. And just as Marx's understanding was a critique of scientific concepts and theories in light of the social movements of his time, so our own scholarship must involve a critique of social science in the wake of national liberation movements and other social movements of the twentieth century. In this context, the significance of Marx's development in the 1870s can be seen. It was not that he began to understand what we can only understand today. Rather, he began to revise his understanding in light of the Revolutionary Populist movement in Russia. In doing so, he demonstrated his continuing commitment through his later years to the search for truth and to science as he had come to understand it in practice. This commitment to science embodied his life to the end.

NOTES

1. The bracketed phrase was crossed out by Marx in the manuscript.
2. Hudis (1983:29–34) shares this view that Marx in the 1870s was moving toward a notion of the peasants in the periphery as the decisive revolutionary force.
3. For more on this point, see Arrighi et al. (1987).

BIBLIOGRAPHY

Achebe, Chinua. 1959. *Things Fall Apart*. Greenwich, Conn.: Fawcett Publications.
Addo, Herb. 1984. "On the Crisis in the Marxist Theory of Imperialism." *Contemporary Marxism* 9:123–47.
Althusser, Louis. 1971. *Lenin and Philosophy and Other Essays*. New York: Monthly Review Press.
Althusser, Louis. 1976. *Essays in Self-Criticism*. London: New Left Books.
Aron, Raymond. 1968. *Main Currents in Sociological Thought*, Vol. I. Translated by Richard Howard and Helen Weaver. Garden City, N.Y.: Doubleday, Anchor Books.
Aron, Raymond. 1970. *Main Currents in Sociological Thought*, Vol. II. Translated by Richard Howard and Helen Weaver. Garden City, N.Y.: Doubleday, Anchor Books.
Aronson, Ronald. 1985. "Historical Materialism, Answer to Marxism's Crisis." *New Left Review*, No. 152, pp. 74–94.
Arrighi, Giovanni, Terence K. Hopkins, and Immanuel Wallerstein. 1987. "The Liberation of Class Struggle?" *Review* 10:403–24.
Ball, Terence, and James Farr, eds. 1984. *After Marx*. New York: Cambridge University Press.
Barbalet, J. M. 1983. *Marx's Construction of Social Theory*. Boston: Routledge and Kegan Paul.
Barth, Hans. 1976. *Truth and Ideology*. Berkeley: University of California Press.
Becker, Howard. 1966. "Whose Side Are We On?" *Social Problems* 14:239–47.
Benton, T. 1981. " 'Objective' Interests and the Sociology of Power." *Sociology* 15:161–84.
Berger, Peter L., and Thomas Luchman. 1967. *The Social Construction of Reality: Treatise in the Sociology of Knowledge*. Garden City, N.Y.: Doubleday, Anchor Books.
Berlin, Isaiah. 1963. *Karl Marx: His Life & Environment*. New York: Oxford University Press.

Bernstein, Richard J. 1971. *Praxis and Action*. Philadelphia: University of Pennsylvania Press.

Blauner, Robert. 1972. *Racial Oppression in America*. New York: Harper & Row.

Bloch, Ernst. 1971. *On Karl Marx*. New York: Herder and Herder.

Bloom, Jack M. 1987. *Class, Race, and the Civil Rights Movement*. Bloomington: Indiana University Press.

Bober, M. M. 1950. *Karl Marx's Interpretation of History*. 2nd ed. Cambridge, Mass.: Harvard University Press.

Bottomore, T. B., ed. 1964. *Karl Marx: Early Writings*. New York: McGraw-Hill.

Burtt, Edwin Arthur. 1954. *The Metaphysical Foundations of Modern Science*. Garden City, N.Y.: Doubleday, Anchor Books.

Butterfield, H. 1957. *The Origins of Modern Science*. New York: Macmillan.

Callinicos, Alex. 1983. *Marxism and Philosophy*. Oxford: Clarendon Press.

Cameron, Kenneth Neill. 1985. *Marxism: The Science of Society*. Amherst, Mass.: Bergin and Garvey.

Carlsnaes, Walter. 1981. *The Concept of Ideology and Political Analysis*. Westport, Conn.: Greenwood Press.

Carmichael, Stokely, and Charles V. Hamilton. 1967. *Black Power*. New York: Vintage Books.

Carver, Terrel, ed. 1975. *Karl Marx: Texts on Method*. New York: Barnes and Noble.

Chirot, Daniel, and Thomas D. Hall. 1982. "World-Systems Theory." *Annual Review of Sociology* 8:81–106.

Clarke, John Henrik, ed. 1969. *Malcolm X*. Toronto: Collier Books.

Cocks, Joan. 1983. "Hegel's Logic, Marx's Science, Rationalism's Perils." *Political Studies* 31:584–603.

Cohen, G. A. 1978. *Karl Marx's Theory of History*. Princeton, N.J.: Princeton University Press.

Cohen, Jean L. 1982. *Class and Civil Society*. Amherst: University of Massachusetts Press.

Colletti, Lucio. 1972. "Marxism: Science or Revolution?" in Robin Blackburn, ed., *Ideology in Social Science*. Fontana: Collins.

Coser, Lewis A. 1971. *Masters of Sociological Thought: Ideas in Historical and Social Context*. New York: Harcourt Brace Jovanovich.

Cruse, Harold. 1967. *The Crisis of the Negro Intellectual*. New York: William Morrow.

Cruse, Harold. 1968. *Rebellion or Revolution*? New York: William Morrow.

DuBois, W.E.B. 1965. *The World and Africa*. New York: International Publishers.

Durkheim, Emile. 1951. *Suicide*. Translated by John A. Spauding and George Simpson. Edited with an Introduction by George Simpson. New York: The Free Press.

Durkheim, Emile. 1964a. *The Division of Labor in Society*. Translated by George Simpson. New York: The Free Press.

Durkheim, Emile. 1964b. *The Rules of Sociological Method*. 8th ed. New York: Macmillan Publishing Co., Free Press.

Durkheim, Emile. 1965. *The Elementary Forms of the Religious Life*. Translated by Joseph Ward Swain. New York: The Free Press.

Durkheim, Emile. 1974. *Sociology and Philosophy*. Translated by F. Pocock. Introduction by J. G. Peristiany. New York: Macmillan.

Fanon, Frantz. 1967. *Black Skin, White Masks*. New York: Grove Press.

Fanon, Frantz. 1968. *The Wretched of the Earth*. New York: Grove Press.

Farganis, James. 1974. "An Exposition of Weber's Approach to *Verstehende Sociologie.*" *Sociological Focus* 7:66–88.

Ferguson, Kathy E. 1980. "Class Consciousness and the Marxist Dialectic: The Elusive Synthesis." *The Review of Politics* 42:504–32.

Ferris, Timothy. 1988. *Coming of Age in the Milky Way.* New York: Doubleday, Anchor Books.

Fleischer, Helmut. 1973. *Marxism and History.* London: Allen Lane, Penguin Press.

Frank, André Gunder. 1967. *Capitalism and Underdevelopment in Latin America.* New York: Monthly Review Press.

Frank, André Gunder. 1969. *Latin America: Underdevelopment or Revolution.* New York: Monthly Review Press.

Frank, André Gunder. 1979. *Dependent Accumulation and Underdevelopment.* New York: Monthly Review Press.

Friedrichs, Robert W. 1970. *A Sociology of Sociology.* New York: Macmillan.

Furfey, Paul Hanly. 1965. *The Scope and Method of Sociology.* New York: Cooper Square Publishers.

Gans, Herbert. 1965. *The Urban Villagers: Group and Class in the Life of Italian-Americans.* New York: The Free Press, First Free Press Paperback Edition.

Garaudy, Roger. 1976. *Karl Marx: The Evolution of His Thought.* Westport, Conn.: Greenwood Press.

Gellner, Ernest. 1986. "Soviets Against Wittfogel: or, the Anthropological Preconditions of Mature Marxism." In John A. Hall, ed., *States in History.* New York: Basil Blackwell.

Geras, Norman. 1972. "Althusser's Marxism: An Account and Assessment." *New Left Review* 78:57–86.

Geras, Norman. 1983. *Marx and Human Nature.* London: NLB.

Giddens, Anthony. 1971. *Capitalism and Modern Social Theory: An Analysis of Marx, Durkheim, and Max Weber.* Cambridge: Cambridge University Press.

Giddens, Anthony. 1976. *New Rules of Sociological Method.* New York: Basic Books.

Goldman, Lucien. 1969. *The Human Sciences and Philosophy.* Translated by Hayden White and Robert Anchor. London: Jonathon Cayre.

Goldstick, Danny. 1983. "Objectivity and Moral Commitment in the World-View of Marx and Engels." *Science and Society* 47:84–91.

Goran, Therborn. 1973. "The Working Class and the Birth of Marxism." *New Left Review* 79:3–15.

Gouldner, Alvin. 1962. "Anti-Minotaur: The Myth of a Value Sociology." *Social Problems* 9:199–213.

Gouldner, Alvin. 1965. *Enter Plato.* New York: Basic Books.

Gouldner, Alvin. 1968. "The Sociologist as Partisan: Sociology and the Welfare State." *The American Sociologist* 3:103–16.

Gouldner, Alvin. 1970. *The Coming Crisis of Western Sociology.* New York: Avon Books.

Gouldner, Alvin. 1974. "Marxism and Social Theory." *Theory and Society* 1:17–35.

Gouldner, Alvin. 1979. *The Future of Intellectuals and the Rise of the New Class.* New York: Seabury Press.

Gouldner, Alvin. 1985. *Against Fragmentation: The Origins of Marxism and the Sociology of Intellectuals.* New York: Oxford University Press.

Gramsci, Antonio. 1971. *Selections from the Prison Notebooks*. New York: International Publishers.

Gross, Llewellyn, ed. 1959. *Symposium on Sociological Theory*. Evanston, Ill.: Row, Peterson.

Gutiérrez, Gustavo. 1973. *A Theology of Liberation*. Maryknoll, N.Y.: Orbis Books.

Gutiérrez, Gustavo. 1983. *The Power of the Poor in History*. Maryknoll, N.Y.: Orbis Books.

Habermas, Jürgen. 1970. *Toward a Rational Society*. Boston: Beacon Press.

Habermas, Jürgen. 1971. *Knowledge and Human Interests*. Boston: Beacon Press.

Habermas, Jürgen. 1973. *Theory and Practice*. Boston: Beacon Press.

Haberman, Jürgen. 1975. *Legitimation Crisis*. Boston: Beacon Press.

Haldane, J.B.S. 1939. *The Marxist Philosophy and the Sciences*. New York: Random House.

Heilbroner, Robert L. 1984. "Economics and Political Economy: Marx, Keynes, and Schumpeter." *Journal of Economic Issues* 18:681–95.

Heller, Agnes. 1976. *The Theory of Need in Marx*. London: Allison and Busby.

Hogan, Lloyd. 1984. *Principles of a Black Political Economy*. Boston: Routledge & Kegan Paul.

Hook, Sidney. 1958. *From Hegel to Marx*. New York: Humanities Press.

Horkheimer, Max. 1972. *Critical Theory*. Translated by Matthew J. O'Connell and others. New York: Herder and Herder.

Horkheimer, Max. 1974. *Eclipse of Reason*. New York: Seabury Press.

Horkheimer, Max, and Theodor W. Adorno. 1972. *Dialectic of Enlightenment*. Translated by John Cumming. New York: The Seabury Press, A Continuum Book.

Hoselitz, B. F. 1960. *Sociological Aspects of Economic Growth*. Glencoe, Ill.: Free Press.

Hudis, Peter. 1983. *Marx and the Third World: New Perspectives on Writings from His Last Decade*. Chicago: News and Letters Publication.

Hughes, H. Stuart. 1958. *Consciousness and Society: The Reorientation of European Social Thought 1890–1930*. New York: Random House, Vintage Books.

Jay, Martin. 1973. *The Dialectical Imagination: A History of the Frankfurt School and the Institute for Social Research, 1923–1950*. Boston: Little, Brown, and Co.

Johnson, Carlos. 1983. "Ideologies in Theories of Imperialism and Dependency." Pp. 75–104 in Ronald H. Chilcote and Dale L. Johnson, *Theories of Development*. Beverly Hills, Calif.: Sage.

Johnson, Carol. 1983. "Philosophy and Revolution in the Young Marx." *Science and Society* 47:66–83.

Kaplan, Abraham. 1964. *The Conduct of Inquiry: Methodology for Behavioral Science*. Scranton, Pa.: Holt, Rinehart, and Winston.

Kieve, Ronald A. 1983. "The Hegelian Inversion: On the Possibility of a Marxist Dialectic." *Science and Society* 47:37–65.

Kolakowski, Leszek. 1962. "Karl Marx and the Classical Definition of Truth." In Leopold Labedz, ed., *Revisionism: Essays in the History of Marxist Ideas*. New York: Frederick A. Praeger.

Kolakowski, Leszek. 1971. *Marxism and Beyond*. London: Paladin.

Kolakowski, Leszek. 1978. *Main Currents of Marxism*, Vol. 3. Translated by P. S. Falda. New York: Oxford University Press.

Kolb, William L. 1957. "The Changing Dominance of Values in Modern Sociological

Theory." Pp. 93–132 in Howard Baker and Alvin Boshoff, eds., *Modern Sociological Theory in Continuity and Change*. New York: Holt, Rinehart, and Winston.

Korsch, Karl. 1970. *Marxism and Philosophy*. London: New Left Books.

Kuhn, Thomas S. 1957. *The Copernican Revolution*. Cambridge, Mass.: Harvard University Press.

Kuhn, Thomas. S. 1970. *The Structure of Scientific Revolutions*, 2nd ed., enlarged. Chicago: University of Chicago Press.

Larrain, Jorge. 1979. *The Concept of Ideology*. Athens: University of Georgia Press.

Larrain, Jorge. 1983. *Marxism and Ideology*. Atlantic Highlands, N.J.: Humanities Press.

Lenin, V. I. 1960. *Collected Works*, Vol. I. Moscow: Progress Publishers.

Lenin, V. I. 1962. *Collected Works*, Vol. XIV. Moscow: Progress Publishers.

LeoGrande, William M. 1977. "An Investigation into the 'Young Marx' Controversy." *Science and Society* 41:129–51.

Levy-Bruhl, L. 1973. *The Philosophy of Auguste Comte*. Clifton, N.J.: Augustus M. Kelley.

Leys, Colin. 1974. *Underdevelopment in Kenya: The Political Economy of Neo-Colonialism 1964–1971*. Berkeley: University of California Press.

Lindemann, Albert S. 1983. *A History of European Socialism*. New Haven, Conn.: Yale University Press.

Little, Daniel. 1986. *The Scientific Marx*. Minneapolis: University of Minnesota Press.

Lonergan, Bernard. 1958. *Insight*. New York: Philosophical Library.

Lonergan, Bernard. 1967. *Collection*. F. E. Crowe, S. J., ed. Montreal: Palm Publishers.

Lonergan, Bernard. 1971. *Doctrinal Pluralism*. Milwaukee, Wisc.: Marquette University Press.

Lonergan, Bernard. 1973. *Method in Theology*, 2nd ed. New York: Herder and Herder.

Lonergan, Bernard. 1974. *A Second Collection*. Williams, F., J. Ryan, S. J., and Bernard J. Tyrrell, S. J., eds. Philadelphia: The Westminster Press.

Lukács, Georg. 1971. *History and Class Consciousness*. Cambridge, Mass.: MIT Press.

Lukes, Steven. 1975. *Emile Durkheim: His Life and Work*. New York: Penguin Books, Peregrine Books.

Lynd, Robert. 1939. *Knowledge for What?* Princeton, N.J.: Princeton University Press.

Maier, Joseph. 1976. "Vico and Critical Theory." *Social Research* 43:845–56.

Malcolm X. 1965. *The Autobiography of Malcolm X*. New York: Grove Press.

Mannheim, Karl. 1936. *Ideology and Utopia*. New York: Harcourt, Brace & World.

Marable, Manning. 1983. *How Capitalism Underdeveloped Black America*. Boston: South End Press.

Marcuse, Herbert. 1960. *Reason and Revolution*. Boston: Beacon Press.

Marcuse, Herbert. 1964. *One-Dimensional Man*. Boston: Beacon Press.

Marcuse, Herbert. 1968. *Negations*. Boston: Beacon Press.

Marquit, Ervin. 1978. "Nicolaus and Marx's Method of Scientific Theory in the Grundrisse." *Science and Society* 41:465–76.

Marx, Karl. 1909. *Capital*, Vol. III. Chicago: Charles H. Kerr.

Marx, Karl. 1933. *Capital*, Vol. II. Edited by Frederick Engels. Chicago: Charles H. Kerr.

Marx, Karl. 1963. *The Poverty of Philosophy*. New York: International Publishers.

Marx, Karl. 1967. *Capital*, Vol. I. New York: International Publishers.

Marx, Karl. 1969a. *Theories of Surplus Value*, Vol. I. London: Lawrence & Wishart.
Marx, Karl. 1969b. *Theories of Surplus Value*, Vol. II. London: Lawrence & Wishart.
Marx, Karl. 1970. *A Contribution to the Critique of Political Economy*. New York: International Publishers.
Marx, Karl. 1972. *Theories of Surplus Value*, Vol. III. London: Lawrence & Wishart.
Marx, Karl. 1973. *Grundrisse: Foundations of the Critique of Political Economy*. New York: Random House, Vintage Books.
Marx, K., and F. Engels. 1932. *Gesamtausgabe*, Band 5. Berlin: Marx-Engels-Verlag G.M.B.H.
Marx, K., and F. Engels. 1948. *The Communist Manifesto*. New York: International Publishers.
Marx, K., and F. Engels. 1965. *The German Ideology*. London: Lawrence & Wishart.
Marx, K., and F. Engels. 1970. *The German Ideology*, Part One. New York: International Publishers.
Marx, K., and F. Engels. 1975a. *Collected Works*, Vol. I. New York: International Publishers.
Marx, K., and F. Engels. 1975b. *Collected Works*, Vol. II. New York: International Publishers.
Marx, K., and F. Engels. 1975c. *Collected Works*, Vol. III. New York: International Publishers.
Marx, K., and F. Engels. 1975d. *Collected Works*, Vol. IV. New York: International Publishers.
Marx, K., and F. Engels. 1979. *Collected Works*, Vol. XII. New York: International Publishers.
Mayer, Carl. 1975. "Max Weber's Interpretation of Karl Marx." *Social Research* 42:701–19.
McBride, William Leon. 1977. *The Philosophy of Marx*. New York: St. Martin's Press.
McKelvey, Charles. 1984a. "Christian Epistemology and Social Scientific Method: Bernard Lonergan's Achievement." *Thought* 59:334–47.
McKelvey, Charles. 1984b. "Sociological Knowing in a Humanist Sociology." *Humanity and Society* 8:283–303.
McKelvey, Charles. 1988. "Nationalism, Class Conflict, and Neo-Colonialism in East Africa: The Vantage Point of the Peasant." *Humanity & Society* 12:51–66.
McLellan, David. 1969. *The Young Hegelians and Karl Marx*. New York: Frederick A. Praeger.
McLellan, David. 1970. *Marx Before Marxism*. London: Macmillan.
McLellan, David. 1973. *Karl Marx: His Life and Thought*. New York: Harper & Row.
McLellan, David, ed. 1977. *Karl Marx: Selected Writings*. Oxford: Oxford University Press.
McMurtry, John. 1978. *The Structure of Marx's World View*. Princeton, N.J.: Princeton University Press.
McNall, Scott. 1984. "The Marxian Project." *The Sociological Quarterly* 25:473–95.
McQuarie, Donald. 1978a. "A Further Comment on Karl Popper and Marxian Laws." *Science and Society* 16:477–84.
McQuarie, Donald. 1978b. "Marx and the Method of Successive Approximations." *Sociological Quarterly* 19:218–33.
Meldolesi, Luca. 1984. "Braudel and Lenin: Capitalism Is a Superlative." *Contemporary Marxism* 9:99–122.

Memmi, Albert. 1965. *The Colonizer and the Colonized*. Boston: Beacon Press.

Merton, Robert K. 1967. *On Theoretical Sociology*. New York: Macmillan, Free Press.

Merton, Robert K. 1972. "Insiders and Outsiders: A Chapter in the Sociology of Knowledge." *American Journal of Sociology* 78:9–47.

Mills, C. Wright. 1959. *The Sociological Imagination*. New York: Oxford University Press.

Mills, Charles W. 1986. "Marxism and Naturalistic Mystification." *Science and Society* 49:472–83.

Mouzilis, Nicos. 1984. "On the Crisis of Marxist Theory." *The British Journal of Sociology* 35:112–25.

Myrdal, Gunnar. 1944. *An American Dilemma: The Negro Problem and Modern Democracy*, 2 vols. With the assistance of Richard Sterner and Arnold Rose. New York: Harper & Row.

Myrdal, Gunnar. 1959. *Value in Social Theory*. Edited by Paul Streeten. New York: Harper & Row.

Myrdal, Gunnar. 1969. *Objectivity in Social Research*. New York: Random House, Pantheon Books.

Natanson, Maurice, ed. 1963. *Philosophy of the Social Sciences*. New York: Random House.

Nisbet, Robert A. 1966. *The Sociological Tradition*. New York: Basic Books.

Nisbet, Robert A. 1976. *Sociology as an Art Form*. New York: Oxford University Press.

Nkrumah, Kwame. 1966. *Neo-Colonialism: The Last Stage of Imperialism*. New York: International Publishers.

Nordahl, Richard. 1982. "Marx on the Use of History in the Analysis of Capitalism." *History of Political Economy* 14:342–65.

Nyerere, Julius. 1968. *Ujamaa: Essays on Socialism*. Dar es Salaam, Tanzania: Oxford University Press.

Oakley, Allen. 1984. *Marx's Critique of Political Economy*. Vol. I. Boston: Routledge and Kegan Paul.

Odinga, Oginga. 1967. *Not Yet Uhuru*. New York: Hill and Wang.

Ollman, Bertell. 1982. *What Is Marxism?* New York: Red Hot Publications.

Padover, Saul K. 1978. *Karl Marx: An Intimate Biography*. New York: McGraw-Hill.

Padover, Saul K., ed. 1979. *The Letters of Karl Marx*. Englewood Cliffs, N.J.: Prentice-Hall.

Parekh, Bhikhu. 1982. *Marx's Theory of Ideology*. Baltimore: Johns Hopkins University Press.

Parsons, Talcott. 1951. *The Social System*. New York: The Free Press of Glencoe.

Parsons, Talcott. 1961. "An Outline of the Social System." In Talcott Parsons et al., eds., *Theories of Society*. New York: The Free Press of Glencoe.

Parsons, Talcott. 1966. *Societies: Evolutionary and Comparative Perspectives*. Englewood Cliffs, N.J.: Prentice-Hall.

Parsons, Talcott. 1967. "Evaluation and Objectivity in Social Science." In Talcott Parsons, *Sociological Theory and Modern Society*. New York: Free Press.

Parsons, Talcott. 1968. *The Structure of Social Action*, 2 vols. New York: Macmillan, Free Press.

Parsons, Talcott. 1971. *The System of Modern Societies*. Englewood Cliffs, N.J.: Prentice-Hall.

Parsons, Talcott. 1977. *The Evolution of Societies*. Englewood Cliffs, N.J.: Prentice-Hall.

Piccone, Paul. 1975. "Reading the Grundrisse: Beyond 'Orthodox' Marxism." *Theory and Society* 2:235–55.

Plamenatz, John. 1970. *Ideology*. New York: Macmillan.

Postone, Moishe, and Helmut Reinicke. 1975. "On Nicolaus 'Introduction' to the *Grundrisse.*" *Telos*, pp. 130–48.

Pratt, Cranford. 1976. *The Critical Phase in Tanzania 1945–1968*. Cambridge: Cambridge University Press.

Prokopczyk, Czeslaw. 1980. *Truth and Reality in Marx and Hegel*. Amherst: University of Massachusetts Press.

Rader, Melvin. 1979. *Marx's Interpretation of History*. New York: Oxford University Press.

Ritzer, George. 1975. *Sociology: A Multiple Paradigm Science*. Boston: Allyn and Bacon.

Ritzer, George. 1988. *Sociological Theory*, 2nd ed. New York: Alfred A.Knopf.

Rostow, W. W. 1971. *The Stages of Economic Growth*, 2nd ed. Cambridge: Cambridge University Press.

Runciman, W. G. 1972. *A Critique of Max Weber's Philosophy of Social Science*. London: Cambridge University Press.

Ryan, Alan. 1970. *Philosophy of the Social Sciences*. New York: Random House, Pantheon Books.

Ryan, Cheyney C. 1981. "The Friends of Commerce: Romantic and Marxist Criticisms of Classical Political Economy." *History of Political Economy* 13:80–94.

Salamini, Leonardo. 1974. "Gramsci and Marxist Sociology of Knowledge: An Analysis of Hegemony-Ideology-Knowledge." *Sociological Quarterly* 15:359–80.

Sallack, David L. 1974. "Class Domination and Ideological Hegemony." *Sociological Quarterly* 15:38–50.

Sayer, Derek.1979. *Marx's Method*. Atlantic Highlands, N.J.: Humanities Press.

Schaff, Adam. 1976. *History and Truth*. New York: Pergamon Press.

Schmidt, Alfred. 1981. *History and Structure*. Cambridge, Mass.: MIT Press.

Shanin, Teodor. 1983a. "Late Marx and the Russian Periphery of Capitalism." *Monthly Review* 35, No. 2:10–24.

Shanin, Teodor, ed. 1983b. *Late Marx and the Russian Road*. New York: Monthly Review Press.

Shannon, Thomas Richard. 1989. *An Introduction to the World-System Perspective*. Boulder, Colo.: Westview Press.

Shaw, William H. 1978. *Marx's Theory of History*. Stanford, Calif.: Stanford University Press.

Sherman, Howard. 1981. "Marx and Determinism." *Journal of Economic Issues* 15:61–71.

Simmel, Georg. 1977. *The Problems of the Philosophy of History: An Epistemological Essay*. Translated and edited, with an introduction, by G. Oakes. New York: Macmillan Publishing Co., Free Press.

Simonds, A. P. 1982. "How Many Marxisms?" *Social Theory and Practice* 8:113–26.

Spencer, Herbert. 1961. *The Study of Sociology*. Ann Arbor: University of Michigan Press, Ann Arbor Paperbacks.

Sprinzak, Ehud. 1975. "Marx's Historical Conception of Ideology and Science." *Politics and Society* 5:395–416.

Suchting, W. 1983. "Knowledge and Practice: Towards a Marxist Critique of Traditional Epistemology." *Science and Society* 47:2–36.

Suppe, Frederick, ed. 1974. *The Structure of Scientific Theories*. Urbana: University of Illinois Press.

Swainson, Nicola. 1980. *The Development of Corporate Capitalism in Kenya 1918–1977*. Berkeley: University of California Press.

Therborn, Goran. 1973. "The Working Class and the Birth of Marxism." *New Left Review* 79:3–15.

Therborn, Goran. 1976. *Science, Class, and Society*. London: NLB.

Tracy, David. 1970. *The Achievement of Bernard Lonergan*. New York: Herder and Herder.

Truzzi, Marcello, ed. 1974. *Verstehen: Subjective Understanding in the Social Sciences*. Reading, Mass.: Addison-Wesley.

Vazquez, Adolfo Sanchez. 1977. *The Philosophy of Praxis*. Atlantic Highlands, N.J.: Humanities Press.

Veltmeyer, Henry. 1975. "Toward an Assessment of the Structuralist Interrogation of Marx: Claude Levi-Straus and Louis Althusser." *Science and Society* 38:385–421.

von Freyhold, Michaela. 1979. *Ujamaa Villages in Tanzania*. New York: Monthly Review Press.

Wallerstein, Immanuel. 1974. *The Modern World-System*, Vol. I. New York: Academic Press.

Wallerstein, Immanuel. 1979. *The Capitalist World Economy*. New York: Cambridge University Press.

Wallerstein, Immanuel. 1980. *The Modern World-System*, Vol. II. New York: Academic Press.

Wallerstein, Immanuel. 1982. "World-Systems Analysis: Theoretical and Interpretative Issues." Pp. 91–103 in Terence K. Hopkins, I. Wallerstein, R. Bach, C. Chase-Dunn, and R. Mukherjee, *World-System Analysis: Theory and Methodology*. Beverly Hills, Calif.: Sage.

Wallerstein, Immanuel. 1983. "An Agenda for World Systems Analysis." Pp. 299–308 in W. Thompson, ed., *Contending Approaches to World-System Analysis*. Beverly Hills, Calif.: Sage.

Wallerstein, Immanuel. 1984a. "Patterns and Perspectives of the Capitalist World Economy." *Contemporary Marxism* 9:59–70.

Wallerstein, Immanuel. 1984b. *The Politics of the World Economy*. New York: Cambridge University Press.

Wallerstein, Immanuel. 1989. *The Modern World-System*, Vol. III. San Diego: Academic Press.

Wardell, Mark L. 1979. "Marx and His Method: A Commentary." *Sociological Quarterly* 20:425–36.

Weber, Max. 1947. *The Theory of Social and Economic Organization*. With an Introduction by Talcott Parsons. New York: Free Press.

Weber, Max. 1949. *The Methodology of the Social Sciences*. New York: Free Press of Glencoe.

Whyte, William Foote. 1955. *Street Corner Society: The Social Structure of an Italian Slum*, 2nd ed. Chicago: The University of Chicago Press.

Winch, Peter. 1958. *The Idea of a Social Science and Its Relation to Philosophy*. New
    York: Humanities Press.
Zeitlin, Irving M. 1968. *Ideology and the Development of Sociological Theory*. Engle-
    wood Cliffs, N.J.: Prentice-Hall.
Zelený, Jindřich. 1980. *The Logic of Marx*. Totowa, N.J.: Rowman and Littlefield.

INDEX

About the Author

CHARLES McKELVEY is Associate Professor of Sociology at Presbyterian College in Clinton, South Carolina. He is also writing a forthcoming book entitled *The Jackson Campaign: The Civil Rights Movement is Born Again*. Dr. McKelvey has contributed articles to *Humanity and Society*, *Thought*, and the Indiana Consortium of International Programs.